The Holocaust

The Holocaust

Jeremy Black

THE
SOCIAL
AFFAIRS
UNIT

British Library Cataloguing in Publication Data
A catalogue record of this book is available from the British Library

Printed and bound in the United Kingdom

ISBN-13: 978-1-904863-27-4

Social Affairs Unit
314–322 Regent Street
London W1B 5SA
www.socialaffairsunit.org.uk

CONTENTS

For
David Mushin

ABOUT THE AUTHOR

Jeremy Black is Professor of History at the University of Exeter. Graduating from Cambridge with a Starred First, he did postgraduate work at Oxford and then taught at Durham, eventually as Professor, before moving to Exeter in 1996. He has lectured extensively in Australia, Canada, Denmark, France, Germany, Italy, New Zealand and the USA, where he has held visiting chairs at West Point, Texas Christian University and Stillman College. A past council member of the Royal Historical Society, Black is a fellow of the Royal Society for the Encouragement of Arts, Manufactures and Commerce, and a senior fellow of the Foreign Policy Research Institute. He was appointed to the Order of Membership of the British Empire for services to stamp design.

He is, or has been, on a number of editorial boards, including the *Journal of Military History*, the journal of the Royal United Services Institute and *History Today*, and was Editor of *Archives*.

His books include *War and World, 1450–2000* (Yale), *The British Seaborne Empire* (Yale), *Maps and History* (Yale) and *European Warfare in a Global Context, 1600–1815* (Routledge).

PREFACE

The history of the Holocaust needs underlining in the face of continuing attempts to deny its veracity or scope. The arrest of David Irving in Austria in November 2005, on the charge of Holocaust denial, served as a pointed reminder of its contentious character, and, the following month, Mahmoud Ahmadinejah, the new President of Iran, publicly joined the sordid ranks of the deniers. In fact, Adolf Hitler's determination to rid Europe, if not the world, of Jews and Jewish ideas in all their manifestations was central to his ultimate goal of establishing a thousand-year Reich. The opportunity was provided by the extensive German conquests in the early stages of the Second World War, and, therefore, the history of the Holocaust in part properly belongs to the Second World War. Indeed, I deliberately included a volume on the Holocaust in the seven-volume collection of articles and essays by scholars that I edited in 2007.[1] This brief history is written in part in response to the continuation of Holocaust denial and also because of the need for a short introductory study.

The complex roots of the slaughter are discussed in the first two chapters. The German extermination policies which led to the Holocaust that consumed much of European Jewry were the culmination of powerful currents in nineteenth-century thought, as refracted through the prism of Nazi ideology and Hitler's messianic fantasies. There is an emphasis in the book on the extent to which Hitler's war strategy and the war against Jews cannot be detached from one another. Indeed, the mass murder of Jews should be part of the analysis of the German conduct of the war. This study underlines the importance of the killings by *Einsatzgruppen*, especially mass shootings, alongside the more usual emphasis on the slaughter in the extermination camps.

The Holocaust is also of separate significance, not only as the most brutal episode of anti-Semitism, and a warning of whither that most stupid of attitudes can lead, as well as a formative background to the creation and ethos of the state of Israel, but also as an indication of where ethnic and organic notions of the state can proceed. It is both appropriate to be emotive when writing about the Holocaust – how else to treat genocide, an abstraction that means smashing living babies' skulls against walls – and yet that also is both less and more than the story.

The treatment of the Holocaust in these pages requires explanation because so much space is devoted to post-war discussion and memorialisation (Chapter 5) and to consideration of the Holocaust today (Chapter 6). This is not in pursuit of some absurd postmodernist relativism, but rather because the subject of the Holocaust is, at once, the brutal mass murder of the Jews perpetrated by the Germans and their allies and, yet, also the post-war consideration of this slaughter. Discussion of the latter does not lessen, in any way, the murder but simply notes that, as personal recollection fades with the passing generation, it is through this consideration that the Holocaust is grasped. It is, for example, through post-war films, such as *Schindler's List*, as much as, if not far more than, through wartime photography that the Holocaust is understood visually, and that is of increasing importance for a society for which the visual is supplanting the literary as both means and medium of thought. Given the dominance of German documentation for the surviving written sources of the Holocaust, this visual account is of even greater consequence.

Moreover, memorialisation of the Holocaust throws light on post-war societies, on the contentious nature of the Second World War and on the persistence of anti-Semitism. As such, however ahistorically, it also offers gleams of understanding about the policies and attitudes that made the Holocaust not only possible but also a terrible fact. Moreover, the post-war recognition of the Holocaust was often suppressed or minimised, which represented a continuation of the wartime German attempt to hide their crimes or their connivance in, or acceptance of, the treatment of Jews.

The book is footnoted more generously than a work of this type might ordinarily merit, but that reflects the need, in the face of Holocaust deniers and diminishers, to draw attention to detailed scholarship that makes the scale and nature of the slaughter readily apparent. In light of the likely readership, references are restricted to English-language literature. There is also extensive and important scholarship in German, and the quality of much of this literature in recent years is one of the few heartening signs to emerge from this mentally difficult subject. Readers who wish to pursue this literature can consult the footnotes and bibliographies of the English-language literature.

I appreciate the opportunity to outline some of the ideas in this book, provided by an invitation to speak to the History Forum of the Department of History at the University of Hawaii, Manoa, in 2005. Being asked to lecture by *History Today* enabled me to visit Holocaust sites in eastern Europe, although personally the site that holds my mind is Natzweiler, a concentration camp in Alsace which I visited in 1971: the contrast between the beauty of the setting and the events that unfolded there was potent.

I have benefited from the comments of Ian Bickerton, Harald Kleinschmidt, Jeremy Noakes and Thomas Otte on an earlier draft, and David Cesarani, Peter Hoffenberg, Eric Mark, Bill Purdue, Harvey Sicherman and Dietmar Seuss on an earlier draft of a section of this work, and from discussing the subject with, or information from, Pippa Black, Michael Bregnsbo, Roger Burt, James Chapman, Jim Davies, Olavi Fält, John Gascoigne, Michael Gehler, Charles Ingrao, Stewart Lone, Malcolm McKinnon, Stephen Morillo, Peter Stachura, Mark Stevens and Gareth Stansfield. None is responsible for any errors that remain.

In dedicating this book, I look back on four decades of friendship, not least to formative years together at school. Spending $11^1/_3$ years at the same school, and an excellent one at that, was probably far more influential in my development than I appreciate. There is no doubt that one of the key legacies is a number of strong friendships. I have always been impressed by David's acute grasp of events, his unwillingness to accept cant and the warmth of his strong personality.

CHAPTER 1

UNTIL BARBAROSSA

ANTI-SEMITIC BACKGROUND

In a horrific form, the Holocaust, particularly the extermination and concentration camps, testified to a persistent and widespread use of concepts of race in order to rank peoples and to develop and express national cohesion. This was more common in the political thought and practice of the twentieth century than is generally appreciated, and was particularly important in state-building and also in the creation of new political allegiances. Thus, in Egypt in the 1950s, the republican revolution of 1952 was followed by pan-Arab nationalism.

In Europe, towards the close of the nineteenth century, the proponents of the increasingly insistent organic notions of the nation became readier to draw on, if not create, an often mystical sense of identity between people and place or, as it generally was expressed, race and country. Organic notions of the nation drew on, and sustained, a range of political and cultural notions and ideas, including the legacies of romanticism and social Darwinism, and, in turn, they fed into early fascism. The corresponding claim that people's thoughts and actions did not follow universal and timeless patterns, but, instead, were shaped by time and place, lent itself to the idea of distinctive cultures, as part of an anti-humanistic ideology. This stress on distinctive cultures undermined universalism and, thus, the idea of tolerance and rights for others. The organising narrative, instead, was the nation, and the function of history became that of providing the vision of a single people with a national destiny.

Those who could be excluded from the narrative sometimes faced persecution, if not violence, and Jews, who were frequently presented as different, were a major category for exclusion. In the late nineteenth century, some nationalist bodies, such as the Union of the Russian People, provided the context for pogroms: large-scale anti-Semitic violence. In Germany, however, where Jews were comparatively well integrated, there were no comparable pogroms.

Racism drew on essentialist notions of identity. It also appeared to be endorsed by science, including the concept of natural selection and also the development of ethnography, and thus appeared to be progressive, while yet also appealing to the anti-scientific anti-modernism that was a powerful feature of the period. As such, racism, moreover, offered a vehicle for older identities and prejudices, not least a religious aversion on the part of Christians that was important to long-standing anti-Semitism.[1] This element led, for example, to the frequent pogroms in Easter Week in Russia.

The major emphasis in the scholarship on the Holocaust is on racism, which is correct as far as the Nazis were concerned, as the harsh fate of Jewish converts to Christianity indicated. However, a strand of Christian anti-Semitism was also important to the Holocaust. This was the case not only in helping explain the background of the Holocaust, both in terms of the isolation of Jews and of the antipathy of some elements in Germany and Austria, but also in terms of the response to the Holocaust within occupied and pro-Axis Europe. Thus, in 1941, in the face of the Ustasha terror by the Croat fascist movement, Jews in Croatia who converted to Catholicism were not killed, but this was not an option offered to Jews by the Germans.

Alongside that religious theme, there were other strands of anti-Semitism. These included hostility to Jewish efforts to assimilate, as well as the biological-racist competitiveness associated with social Darwinism; the nationalist hostility to the cosmopolitanism and, thus, alien influences associated, by critics, with Judaism; and a sense that Jews were central to an unwelcome, indeed threatening, modernism.[2] Thus, the Holocaust has been seen as part of Hitler's 'revolt against the modern world',[3] although, in rhetoric and practice, he was only in revolt against certain aspects of the modern world.

Ironically, there was also a habit of viewing Jews as opposed to progress. Thus, the Emperor Joseph II, ruler of the Habsburg lands in the 1780s (including what became Austria, Hungary, Czechoslovakia and southern Poland), who saw himself as a supporter of religious toleration, left little scope for Jews whose wish to maintain a separate identity led them to seek more than freedom to worship. Jewish emancipation then was felt to entail not only the cessation of legal restrictions on the part of government but also the end of Jewish customary practices, such as the wearing of traditional clothes, as well as the end to autonomous Jewish institutions which were seen as barriers to integration. A sense of Jews as opposed to their concept of progress affected liberal German commentators, especially from the 1870s, in particular when they looked at Jewish communities of eastern Europe, which, indeed, tended to be more conservative and less assimilated than Jews in Germany and Austria.

German nationalism led in the nineteenth century to a powerful state, the German Empire proclaimed in 1871, which controlled the strongest economy in Continental Europe, but the idea that this state should be based on the supposed community of the *das Deutsches Volk* (the German people) was abhorrent to Otto von Bismarck, who created the German Empire and effectively ran it for twenty years, resigning the Chancellorship in 1890. Instead, the idea of the *das Deutsches Volk* was advanced by the Pan-German League, which emerged in the 1890s. Such views were increasingly influential among the educated middle class and, by 1914, they were becoming more important among conservatives. Anti-Semitism, meanwhile, was more potent from the 1880s, as it became central to a language of social commentary and criticism that increasingly was an automatic reflex for many of those unhappy with social, economic and cultural change.[4] Jews were decried as cosmopolitan and plutocrats.

The German Empire or Second Reich (the first was the medieval Holy Roman Empire that ended in 1806) collapsed as a result of its total failure in the First World War

(1914–18). This collapse was accompanied by the fall of the other ruling families, such as the Wittelsbachs of Bavaria, and ensured that loyalty and identity shifted from the dynasties, particularly the Hohenzollerns of Prussia who had ruled the Empire.

HITLER

Defeat led, instead, to a largely grim emphasis on the history of the *Volk* and the hardship and dispossession it suffered as a consequence of this defeat. The defeat was presented by right-wing populists as undeserved and as due to betrayal from within, particularly by Jews and Communists.[5] The two were linked by critics as several prominent Communists were indeed Jews, although most Jews were not Communists. It was only in 1919 that Adolf Hitler (1889–1945), an Austrian-born veteran of the trenches, defined his views on Jews, although he had displayed hostility to them in pre-war Vienna.

The Austrian background to Hitler's ideas is important. In part, he drew on Austrian anti-Semitism. His assumptions also represented the refraction of pre-1914 right-wing nationalist and racist views, through the prism of German defeat and of the disintegration of Habsburg (Austrian) hegemony over part of Slavic Europe. The year 1918 saw the collapse of the Habsburg Empire and the creation of new states in eastern Europe: Yugoslavia, Czechoslovakia and Poland.

In response, Hitler aspired to reverse Germany's defeat in the First World War and to recreate an acceptable (i.e., German-dominated) Europe, specifically by controlling eastern Europe, where *Lebensraum* (living space) was to be pursued for Germans. Although there was a tension between Nazi views and conservative geopolitics,[6] Hitler's views drew on a long-standing nationalist belief that Germany's destiny included domination of eastern Europe. The racial inflections of this belief focused on a supposed struggle between Germans and non-Germans, one in which there was no uncertainty where virtue, progress and destiny lay. Nor, to Hitler, was there any doubt about the villain. He saw Jews as the active force behind opposition to Germany, whereas other peoples, such as Slavs and Gypsies, were, in his eyes, far more passive, in so far as they were not stirred up by Jews.

The belief in German destiny had a mythic dimension and dynamic that helped mould more particular and pragmatic nationalist expressions of German interest. The mythic component was to appeal to Nazi destiny-makers. Thus, eastern Europe offered the prospect for a conflation of nationalism and racist imperialism, and German conquest of the region was to make it operative. The quest for an Aryan geography had some surprising aspects. In *Die Entdeckung des Paradieses* (*The Discovery of Paradise*),[7] Franz von Wendrin argued that the Garden of Eden had been in Germany but that Jews had falsely claimed it for Asia. His cartographic claims were accompanied by statements on the need to liberate Germany from the inferior races. Atlases presented Germany as under threat from Jews and Communists. Archaeologists were among those also expected to demonstrate Aryan cultural and economic superiority over others.[8]

These themes were strongly present in the 1920s as an aspect of a determination to overturn the Versailles Peace Settlement that had followed the First World War and, instead, to ensure German domination of east central Europe. Hitler did not invent the racial prospectus of reordering the East, a prospectus that included expelling the allegedly undesirable from Germany, but he benefited from the extent to which these ideas were already widely in circulation. This was to make the implementation of his aspirations far easier, not least by discouraging opposition to them. For example, the opening page of maps in the 1931 edition of *F.W. Putzgers Historischer Schul-Atlas* included one of Germany as the bulwark of European culture against the Asiatic hordes, the latter depicted in terms of Huns, Avars, Arabs, Magyars, Turks, Mongols, Jews, tsarist Russia and Communism.

Germany also provided a vehicle for the central European nationalism that Hitler, an Austrian, expressed and, in many respects, encapsulated, because his was a German nationalism of a particular type. This was a consequence of the advent of Western-style nation-states in multi-ethnic central Europe, a process from which Jews were to be the prime victims. This was not least because, despite discrimination, Jews had earlier benefited considerably from the opportunities provided by the multi-ethnic Habsburg Empire. The implications of central European nationalism links anti-Semitic German policy in the Second World War with that of allies such as Croatia and Slovakia, which became independent (as German client states) in 1941 and 1939 respectively as a result of Hitler's destruction of Czechoslovakia and Yugoslavia. These and other allies, such as Hungary and Romania, also benefited from Hitler's support, not only for ethnically coherent territories for his allies,[9] but also for gains by them at the expense of other peoples. Austria provided a central link because it helped bring a 'more extreme Central-European nationalism' to Germany, as well as providing key personnel for the pursuance of the Holocaust.[10]

Racism and the Holocaust were a central drive for both Nazi Germany, one that sat alongside other elements that have attracted attention such as theories of fascist politics or analyses of the Nazi state as a political system. The aggressive racial nationalism at issue was also actively anti-liberal, not least because it opposed the liberal protection for freedoms and liberal toleration that gave space to individualism and minorities. As a result, the fate of Jews was an aspect of the crisis of European liberalism, a liberalism Hitler presented as the cause and product of weakness, in Germany and more generally.

Although Hitler himself made several statements explicitly rejecting the personality cult, National Socialism, in practice, rested on such a cult, not to say political religion, based on the pivotal figure of the Führer (leader), as well as on a confused mixture of racialism, nationalism and a belief in modernisation through force. Force certainly characterised Hitler's regime, with, from the outset, a brutal attitude towards those judged unacceptable that culminated as a genocidal attack on Jews. His was an anti-Semitism that would not be satisfied with discrimination. For Hitler, there had to be persecution, and it had to be not an ongoing aspect of Nazi rule but, instead, a decisive and total step that would end what he saw as the Jewish challenge. To Hitler, this was a meta-historical issue, not an add-on designed to fulfil other policies, such as the redistribution of territory, the raising of funds or the rallying of popular support. Jew-hatred, rather than the ideology of anti-Semitism, was the basis of Hitler's decision-making, and helped give purpose to his foreign policy and, indeed, his territorial expansionism.

Prior to his gaining power on 30 January 1933, Hitler's policies were not clearly worked out, but he certainly wanted Jews to emigrate. Their challenge, in his eyes, underpinned Marxism, which, indeed, he saw as a cover for Jewish goals. In his book *Mein Kampf* (*My Struggle*), which he had dictated in 1924 while imprisoned after the failure of his 1923 attempt to overthrow the Bavarian Government, the dual nature of the struggle was clearly outlined. Jews were blamed for German defeat in 1918 and for problems thereafter. Jews were seen by him as universally malign and as responsible for radical, political, economic, financial and cultural threats.

Indeed, to Hitler, the ubiquity of Jews was readily apparent because they were seen as responsible both for trade-union activism and for plutocratic oppression. If Jews were allegedly powerful in the Soviet Union, indeed central to Communism, Hitler also claimed they were so elsewhere, for example in France. Thus, the widespread nature of Jews and the degree of assimilation they showed were, to Hitler, aspects of their threat, as they could be held responsible for whatever international forces he saw as a challenge. This adaptability was to be useful when Hitler came to explain the problems eventually posed in the Second World War by conflict with what was a very dissimilar coalition. Jewry to him provided the link that bound together Britain, the Soviet Union and the USA in enmity to Germany.

The Nazis gained power in Germany in January 1933 and in Austria, which they joined to Germany, in March 1938. They presented German nationalism very much in terms of the *Volk* (people) and concentrated on ethnic rivalry with non-Aryans, especially Jews. They were treated as a threat to the organic, ethnic concept of Germanness, and as automatically antithetical to the *Volksgemeinschaft* (people's or national community) that was the Nazi goal. The *Atlas zur Deutschen Geschichte der Jahre 1914 bis 1933* (1934), by Konrad Frenzel and the Nazi intellectual Johann von Leers, opened with a passage from *Mein Kampf* and included pages headed *Versklavung* (The Enslaving of Germans as a Result of the Post-War Peace Conferences), *Die Ausbreitung der Juden* (The Spread of the Jews) and *Chaos*, the last dealing with reparations and inflation. Leers fled to Egypt after the war and became Nasser's Goebbels, under an Arab name.

In the *Neuer deutscher Geschichts-und Kulturatlas* (1937), edited by Fritz Eberhardt, conflict between 'Indogermanic' peoples and Semites in the ancient world was stressed, while Jews, described as an excrescence, were presented as a threat to modern Germany. The spread of Jews was also presented as a challenge in Bernhard Kumsteller's *Werden und Wachsen, Ein Geschichtsatlas auf völkischer Grundlage* (1938), a work that saw the Germans as upholders of civilisation.

The cosmopolitanism of Jews was presented as an antithesis to nationalism and, thus, as making necessary the assault on their prominent cultural role in German values or, indeed, any role or employment, in order, allegedly, to protect the true values of German art, music, etc. 'Degenerate' art and music were castigated, not least for Jewishness, with prominent critical exhibitions in 1937 and 1938 respectively.[11] An emphasis on race led to the criticism, indeed dehumanisation, of the racial outsider, with Aryans and non-Aryans ('the blood enemy') treated as clear-cut and antagonistic categories, indeed as super-humans and sub-humans. The association of Jews with modernity as well was treated as a challenge, although, conversely, some Nazis regarded them as a primitive constraint on Nazi modernity. The two approaches combined in the idea that Jews were preventing Germans from achieving their potential and fulfilling their mission.

In focusing on an Aryan *Volk*, the Nazis downplayed the earlier tradition of studying classical (i.e., non-German) influences in German history, while a stress on the *Volk* challenged individualism and notions of progress and liberty in terms of the celebration and protection of the self which were associated with a now-damned liberalism. The focus on the Aryans ensured that serious regional, political, religious, social and economic differences and divisions within Germany were deliberately downplayed, and this was an extreme accentuation of the process by which the state created in 1871 overlaid earlier identities and loyalties. A focus on apparent external threats was thus linked to the goal of depoliticisation within a united and assertive Germany, but this was an involuntary depoliticisation as a product of a dictatorial drive.

Furthermore, there was a pronounced cult of personality that was linked to a sense of historical mission. History, to Hitler, was a lived process that he embodied, so that his personal drama became an aspect of the historic, and, thus, at once, historical and timeless, mission of the German people. To Hitler, racial purity was a key aspect of this mission, at once both means and goal. He was not interested in the light that scientific advances threw, and subsequently were to throw, on the complexities of racial identity: namely, that no race possesses a discrete package of characteristics, that there are more genetic variations within, than between, races and that the genes responsible for morphological features, such as skin colour, are atypical.

Races, indeed, are constructed as much as described, and this was the case with the Nazi construction of both Aryans and Jews, but the Nazis were convinced of the elemental characteristics of race and overlooked the extent to which their definitions were an aspect of construction. With his organic concept of the people, Hitler was opposed to the bi-racial marriages and unions that help to underline the very fluidity of ethnic identity and that challenge classification in terms of race.

Jew-hatred was integral, indeed necessary, to Hitler's thought, while anti-Semitism was an explanatory factor in his thought. Although Hitler's ideology and vocabulary were often vague, he did not display vagueness in the case of Jews, while he argued that there was no room for ambiguity or equivocation in German thought and society. Instead, to him, both were obfuscations of the existential nature of the struggle between the national mission and its opponents. They were also aspects of the individualism he deplored as a threat to necessary conformism. It was scarcely surprising that irony was as unwelcome to him as ambiguity.

SUPPORTING IDEAS

Hitler alone, nevertheless, is not the issue. Of late, there has been a focus on widespread support for the extermination of all Jews among those termed 'racial warriors', a support which paralleled that of many enthusiastic circles for the Nazi regime, not least because it provided them with the opportunity to fulfil their aspirations. Alongside Hitler's frequent interventions comes an emphasis on the large cohort of enthusiastic followers.[12]

The basis of support for genocidal policies, however, was varied, as, indeed, was the genesis of the latter. Adolf Eichmann, a key figure in the Holocaust, in the 1950s described himself in the third person: 'this cautious bureaucrat was joined by the fanatical warrior for the freedom of the blood from which I descend.'[13] Much recent work focuses on how aspects of self-consciously modernising beliefs, such as demographics[14] and eugenics, led, or were used, to these ends. For example, ideas about how best to deal with epidemics and to destroy parasites, which played a role in medical thinking, were focused on Jews.[15]

Echoes continued to resonate after the Second World War. For example, Wilhelm Schier's *Atlas zur Allgemeinen und Österreichischen Geschichte* (1982) used the same map to show the movement of Jews in the Middle Ages and the spread of plague – the Black Death. There was, in fact, no connection between the two, but a link between Jews and disease was central to Nazi ideas and focused their pronounced notions of racial purification. The attempt by Heinrich Himmler – the head of the SS (*Schutzstaffel*, protective force), which he turned into the key Nazi coercive force – to make the SS an ethnically 'pure' corps of Aryans rested on ideas of Aryan triumphalism. These involved much pseudo-science, as well as a quest to discover the roots of Aryanism in the mountains of Central Asia,[16] particularly the Pamirs and Tibet; a quest I noted some legacies of when visiting Afghanistan in 1976.

NAZI ANTI-SEMITISM, 1933–9

In the short term, prior to the outbreak of the Second World War in 1939, propaganda, legislation and action against the just-over half a million German Jews (about 0.75 per cent of the population) provided opportunities to radicalise German society towards Nazi goals, as well as to divert attention from the strains created by rearmament. Hitler's linkage of Jews with Communism drew on, and stimulated, a widespread tendency to link the two and to see each as a greater threat as a result.

Most German Jews, in fact, were politically liberal and on the left, and also saw themselves as patriots and as assimilated into German society. Many were veterans of the First World War. Jewish organisations emphasised this patriotism when seeking to persuade the Nazi regime of their good intentions. Zionism (interest in Israel and support for the idea of it as a Jewish homeland and state) was very weak among German Jews, and intermarriage was high: about a quarter of Jewish men and a sixth of Jewish women.

Nazi legislation and the practice of power, however, turned German Jews into persecuted people, and far more rapidly than Jewish leaders had anticipated. The extent and objectives of Nazi anti-Semitism were not initially widely understood. There were acts of violence – indeed numerous violent physical attacks on individual Jews – from the outset. These were an aspect of the violent nature of Nazi government even in the years of peace. Nevertheless, the process of discrimination and exclusion, as the 'national community' was created, essentially rested on legislation and administrative acts and on institutional and popular acceptance, if not enthusiasm. In 1933, Jews were removed from much of professional life, the number of Jewish pupils in schools and universities was limited, and Jews were banned from owning land or being journalists.

The pace of legislative action varied, with little new legislative discrimination occurring in 1934 or in the run-up to the 1936 Berlin Olympics, and this encouraged discontented radical Nazis to press for more anti-Semitic measures. Amongst the legislation, the Nuremberg Laws of 15 September 1935 were particularly important. They defined a Jew as anyone with at least three Jewish grandparents or with two Jewish grandparents, who was also a member of the Jewish faith. Marriages between Jews and non-Jews were banned, and full citizenship was restricted to the latter. This was seen as a clear signal to Jews to emigrate. Also, in 1935, Jews were banned from military service. The process of legal discrimination continued, as in May 1939 when the abrogation of leases with Jews was permitted. This inequality before the law was a crucial feature of the treatment of Jews.

Initially, in response to the so-called 'Jewish Question', there was pressure to make much of Germany 'Jew-free'. This entailed driving Jews out from much of Germany, particularly rural small-town Germany. The Jews moved to larger towns or emigrated. The latter was permitted by the Government until October 1941, although not for men of military age after the outbreak of the war in 1939. Emigration was, indeed, encouraged as a means to achieve racial purity and to create opportunities for non-Jewish Germans.

By 1938, over half the Jewish population of Germany had emigrated. Many fortunately reached the New World, including 102,200 to the USA and 63,500 to Argentina, or destinations that were not to be overrun by the Germans during the Second World War: 52,000 to Britain; 33,400 to Palestine, then a British-ruled territory; 26,000 to South Africa; and 8,600 to Australia. Unfortunately, others had to take refuge in lands that were to be overrun, particularly 30,000 (including Anne Frank) in the Netherlands, 30,000 in France and 25,000 in Poland. This scarcely fulfilled Hitler's hope that all Jews would leave Europe. Opportunities for emigration were limited: the cost and the possibilities of finding employment and shelter (which, in part, arose from existing contacts, especially family links) were important in determining the rate and destinations of emigration.

In many states, there were also restrictions on immigration – restrictions that reflected the seriousness of the world depression, not least high unemployment. Immigration (and thus emigration from Germany) at a time of worldwide economic depression was very difficult. Anti-Semitism also played a role as an aspect of a broader xenophobia. Thus, in France, in 1933 and 1938, there were major drives against immigration.[17] American anti-Semitism was echoed in the State Department, while, from 1930, there was a standing instruction to American consuls not to issue visas to those 'likely to become a public charge', i.e., to require financial support, a category the size of which was expanded by expropriatory German policies directed at Jews. The State Department pressed American consuls to be cautious in granting visas, and those who ignored this pressure suffered in career terms.[18]

Partly as a result of restrictions overseas, there were worries among German Jews about the possibility of a successful new start elsewhere, and these anxieties exacerbated an unwillingness to abandon the assets that were owned in Germany. The German Government did not allow Jews to take their monetary and other possessions with them. More generally, the rate of emigration was higher among younger Jews and, conversely, lower among older Jews, particularly those who hoped to see out the crisis, believing that the Nazis would change policy or be replaced, or who had less confidence in a new start. Indeed, in the early years of the Nazi regime, in response to the apparent balance of problems, there was some re-emigration back to Germany.

Jewish emigration provided the German Government and German civilians with opportunities to seize assets or to acquire them at greatly reduced prices. At a larger scale, what the regime termed its Aryanisation and Dejewification policy drove out Jewish businessmen through discrimination (in taxation and much else) and expulsion. This policy provided opportunities for banks and for industrialists such as Friedrich Flick. The policy also offered much to ordinary small-scale businessmen who acquired vacant Jewish real estate throughout the country. Some were opportunists, others anti-Semites.[19] This was a combination also seen in the informing on Jews to the authorities, in order to gain the benefit of being allocated houses owned or occupied by Jews.[20] As an aspect of Aryanisation, new economic and financial activities were profitably established: for example, the brokering of takeovers by banks,[21] and their role in managing Jewish bank accounts. These accounts were blocked on the orders of the Government, and high fees were charged by the banks for access to the accounts for approved purposes such as emigration.

Anti-Semitic legislation and Jewish emigration also widened the pool of those who benefited from discrimination against Jews by opening up jobs. For example, the Nazis were obsessed with the idea that education provided Jews with an opportunity to pollute the young with liberal ideas. Jews were, therefore, purged from educational institutions which, in turn, provided opportunities for many of the second-rate 'intellectuals' who congregated round Nazism, and further encouraged them to publish their views and to present them as normative.

At this stage, mass murder was not a policy aimed at German Jews, but the brutality of the Government was already apparent. Violence was also directed against individual Jews, with the *Anschluss*, the takeover of Austria in March 1938, encouraging more action in Germany. Thuggery became normative and increasingly organised, most prominently in the *Kristallnacht* – 'Night of the Broken Glass' pogroms in Germany on 9–10 November 1938. This violence, which had drawn, in part, on the anti-Semitic persecution in Austria after the *Anschluss*, served, in turn, to lower barriers against fresh violence, as well as to draw participants and bystanders into a web of complicity.[22] On the *Kristallnacht*, synagogues and Jewish businesses and homes across Germany were attacked and destroyed and damaged, without the police intervening. This was a deliberate attempt not only to cow

Jews, so as to speed up their emigration, but also to destroy their presence in society.

Attacking the community through its synagogues was a crucial precursor, as it was an attempt to wreck Jewish cohesion as much as to destroy a presence that was at once different and yet also integrated physically into the centre of the German society. This had already been seen in June 1938 when the Nazi leader in Upper Bavaria, Adolf Wagner, ordered the destruction of the main synagogue in Munich. Located on Herzog-Max-Strasse, close to the Marienplatz, the main square in the old town, this was a major building, to Hitler an 'eyesore', that Wagner wanted totally destroyed and replaced by a car park. Other centres of German Jewish culture and activity were also destroyed (e.g. the main synagogue in Dresden). This was an organised process.

After the *Kristallnacht*, in which ninety-one Jews were killed, the number of Jews held in concentration camps shot up. So, also, did the killing of Jews in the camps. Whereas fewer than 100 had been murdered there prior to *Kristallnacht*, possibly 1,000 were killed in the next six months. Furthermore, after *Kristallnacht*, economic measures against Jews were stepped up, not least with the expropriation of businesses in December 1938. Measures to encourage emigration were also pushed forward, but Hitler, at this stage, turned down Reinhard Heydrich's idea for Jews to be made to wear an identifying badge, as well as Joseph Goebbels' suggestion for the establishment of ghettos. It was not until 1 September 1941 that a decree was issued insisting that Jews wear a yellow star.

Concentration camps serve as central sites for discussion of the Holocaust, but when they were established after Hitler gained power in January 1933, they were intended as detention centres for those the Nazis wished to incarcerate rather than as central places for a war against Jewry, let alone for genocide. The focus for those in 'protective custody', which meant detained without trial, was initially on political opponents of the Nazis, and, by the summer of 1935, there were only about 3,500 prisoners, with Dachau, opened near

Munich in March 1933, the most prominent camp. The system expanded from 1935, not least in order to use the forced labour of the larger numbers detained. Prominent camps included Sachsenhausen, opened in 1936, Buchenwald in 1937 and Mauthausen in Austria, which was established after the *Anschluss*. The development of the camps was to provide an important element in the institutional genesis of the Final Solution.

Hitler's long-term views about the fate of Jews interacted with the short-term opportunities, problems and anxieties presented by developments. Thus, prior to the outbreak of the Second World War, international relations were a key issue, particularly for Hitler. In seeking to further his goals, Hitler sought to minimise international hostility and, thus, downplayed aspects of anti-Semitism as put forward by radical Nazis. In 1936, for example, during the Berlin Olympics, there was an attempt to avoid giving cause for international criticism. Moreover, as an instance of the role of opportunities and problems, events, specifically the numbers of Jews brought under German control by successive advances in 1939–41, were to be important to the chronology and contours of the Holocaust.

Opportunities, problems and anxieties, however, do not exist in the abstract but are sensed and created, and Hitler's views largely conditioned the process. Although it is difficult to establish a consistently coherent account of Hitler's views, he came, as a long-term goal, to feel it his mission to extirpate what he (inaccurately) regarded as the Jewish-dominated Communist Soviet Union, which he felt would secure his notions of racial superiority and living space. This was to be accompanied by the removal of Jews, the two acts creating a Europe that would be dominated by the Germans, who were to be a master race over the Slavs and others. The Slavs were identified as a sub-human race. German dominance in eastern Europe was, thus, to have a linked political and racial complexion, a view that brought together Nazi views with pre-existing German ideas on eastern Europe from a variety of perspectives.

Pre-war discrimination against, and brutality towards, German Jews had led many to flee, giving effect to the policy of expulsion, with the SD (the security service of the SS) developing the concept of forced emigration as, by 1938, the solution to what was termed the 'Jewish Question'.[23] The policy of deportation was then followed when Austria was occupied in March 1938; after which, with the two states united, German anti-Semitic legislation was applied, with considerable success, in a society that, anyway, was strongly anti-Semitic. Under the ruthless pressure of Adolf Eichmann, the SD official responsible, over 100,000 Austrian Jews emigrated in 1938–9, and, in turn, this served as a model for policy within Germany. In December 1938, Göring announced that Hitler had decided that forced emigration was to be pressed forward rapidly.[24]

Emigration, however, became more difficult as concerns over refugee numbers led to restrictions elsewhere or encouraged their enforcement. Restrictions were an issue, for example, in Britain and the USA, a point that was subsequently minimised in post-war discussion in both countries. Jewish refugees also faced difficult conditions where they could flee; for example, in France and Poland.

Arab pressure, not least violent opposition to British policies and control, both in the Wailing Wall riots of 1929 and, more seriously, in the Arab Rising of 1936–9,[25] helped limit emigration to Palestine, which was then a League of Nations mandate administered by Britain. This emigration was actively sponsored by Jewish agencies and, indeed, approved by Nazis who wanted Jews to leave Europe. The British were also concerned about Arab views elsewhere in the Middle East, not least because their position in both Egypt and Iraq was fragile but also in Saudi Arabia and Transjordan. Moreover, the heavy commitment of troops in Palestine to contain the Arab Rising was disproportionate to Britain's general military requirements. The White Paper of May 1939 about the future of Palestine reflected British concerns about Arab views on and in Palestine.

Forced emigration, nevertheless, was the policy pushed by the Germans. The deportation of Jews from occupied areas was the policy envisaged for Bohemia and Moravia (modern Czech Republic), which were seized by the Germans on 15 March 1939. Adolf Eichmann was sent to Prague in July 1939 to encourage emigration, through the Central Office for Jewish Emigration, as he had done in Vienna in 1938. 'Encourage' is a misnomer for the harassment involved, in what was really forced migration.

POLAND INVADED

Hitler was keen on conflict and determined not to be thwarted of it, as he had been with the Munich Agreement of 1938. In turn, the Poles were determined not to respond to German pressure by making concessions. The German attack on Poland on 1 September 1939 led Britain and France to declare war two days later. As far as Jews were concerned, Poland had a population of about 3.3 million Jews, and they were a larger percentage of the population than their German counterparts had been. As with Germany, Austria, Bohemia and Moravia, the German conquerors wanted Jewish emigration from Poland. That policy, however, proved unrealistic there and for the vast majority of Jews in areas that the Germans conquered from 1939. The murderous, but not yet genocidal, intent of German policy became readily apparent that year. Having rapidly overrun Poland in September, the Germans and the Soviets, with whom they cooperated in the conquest, at once began to kill Poland's leaders and intelligentsia in order to further their ends of creating a docile slave population. In addition, several thousand Jews were killed by the Germans during, or soon after, the conquest, a key episode in eroding inhibitions and encouraging slaughter as a means of policy and, therefore, a wider option.[26] Indeed, on 8 September, Reinhard Heydrich, an SS *Gruppenführer* who was Head of the Security Police and SD, and who now became Head, as well, of the Reich Security Main Office established that month, noted of Poland: 'We want to leave the little people alone. The nobility, the priests and the Jews have to be done away with.'[27]

For brutality, there was also the example of the Soviet Union. Following on from the earlier mistreatment and slaughter of those judged opponents of Communism, in 1939–40, 1.17 million people were deported from Soviet-occupied eastern Poland to Soviet labour camps,[28] and, in 1940, about 127,000 more were deported from the Baltic states – Estonia, Latvia and Lithuania – which were occupied that year. Many others who were not deported were slaughtered.

The Nazis had been happy to see Polish Jews flee into exile as they overran the country, but, once Poland was conquered, Nazi policy from September 1939 called for a comprehensive movement of Poland's Jews in what was one of the biggest moves of civilians hitherto in Europe. Jews were to be moved from the areas annexed to Germany – Austria, Czechoslovakia and western Poland – and to be sent, instead, to the General Government, the part of Poland – central Poland – that was occupied by the Germans but not annexed, and to a Jewish reservation in Poland's eastern borderlands.

In the General Government, Jews were to be controlled and exploited by being made to live in urban ghettos. The first was established in Piotrków in October 1939. Among other cities, Łódź followed in April 1940, and Warsaw that November: it contained a third of the city's people, 380,000, in slightly over 2 per cent of the area. Deportation to these small, crowded ghettos also entailed the movement of large numbers of Jews (including those who had converted to Christianity) from other parts of the same cities. It was a serious undertaking for the German administration, although one lessened by the use of Jewish elders' councils or *Judenräte* for the internal control of the ghettos and as their intermediary with the German authorities.[29] From 1 December 1939, Jews themselves were to be distinguished by wearing armbands with the Star of David.

The ghetto inhabitants were subject to harsh conditions, especially limited food and forced labour in cruel conditions. All Jewish men between twelve and sixty were now under an obligation for forced labour, and forced-labour camps were established from October 1939. Those who tried to leave the 300 ghettos or 437 labour camps were killed, and others were tortured. In addition, some German Jews were deported to

Polish ghettos. These ghettos and labour camps, like the later concentration camps, proved to be incubators of death through epidemics, particularly typhus, as the inhabitants were exposed to serious levels of malnutrition, overcrowding, totally inadequate heating, problems with water supplies and sanitation and a shortage of medical supplies.[30]

These living conditions confirmed the anti-Semitic prejudices of German leaders. The German doctors supposedly responsible for overseeing 'public health' in occupied areas saw Jews as natural carriers of disease, and their attitudes and actions reflected the extent to which the professions were, in large part enthusiastically, open to Nazi penetration. The destitution of the harshly treated Jews was then used to justify mistreatment.

In some respects, this was a halfway stage to the more deliberative slaughter of the 'Final Solution'. Starvation certainly was accomplishing this end, although, at the level of ghetto managers, most of the responsible Germans sought to provide Jews with sufficient food, primarily in order to ensure that the ghetto population could work.[31] This was an instance of the cross-currents in German policy. By June 1941, 2,000 Jews were dying monthly from starvation in the Warsaw ghetto, and by August the monthly death rate was 5,500. This was a slow death that, in the meanwhile, left a large supply of forced labour. Thus, the Łódź ghetto specialised in uniforms for the German army (in June 1941, Himmler visited a factory there doing so), as well as other military supplies. In the labour camps, large numbers also died.

The ghettos, however, were initially intended as a stage in the path to the expulsion of Jews; in effect, a storage stage. Indeed, in September 1939, the Germans expelled thousands of Jews from their part of Poland to the Soviet occupation zone. Heinrich Himmler, not only Head of the SS but also, from October 1939, Reich Commissar for the Strengthening of German Nationality, was opposed, at this stage, to the large-scale slaughter of Jews. Instead, the emphasis was on the creation of a Jewish reservation in Poland's eastern borderlands, a policy Hitler advocated from late September, and the new German–Soviet border in Poland was revised accordingly on 28 September 1939. On 6 October, Hitler told the Reichstag that the new racial order in Europe would include the resettlement of peoples and the regulation of the Jewish problem. This provided the opportunity for Adolf Eichmann, the SS officer in charge of the Central Office for Jewish Emigration, to implement his plans to deport Jews to Poland's eastern borderlands.

Nisko, on the River San, was the first area designated. It was seen as a Jewish reservation, where Jews could be deported prior to further movement to the east, but the plan failed, in part due to competing pressures on land (for settlement) and rail transport, and in part because of opposition by Hans Frank, the Governor of the General Government, who wished to control developments.[32] Moreover, Jews, many from Vienna, sent to this infertile area were maltreated and lacked the necessary farming tools. Some were shot or sent into Soviet territory. The Nisko experiment was followed, in 1940, by the Lublin Plan. The Jews sent there were housed in labour camps and used as slave labour, a policy instituted by Odilo Globocnik, an SS protégé of Himmler who was later prominent as an organiser of mass slaughter (see p. 66).

As an aspect of Hitler's bureaucratic Darwinism – namely, giving far-reaching and clashing powers to rival satraps – the poorly organised and brutally administered deportation plans fell foul of competing schemes to settle occupied territories with German settlers. These settlers were to be drawn from refugees from Soviet rule and those whose repatriation from Soviet territories was arranged by the German Government in cooperation with the Soviet Union. These schemes drew on a long-standing agrarian romanticism that had been directed by right-wingers, and then the Nazis, to focus on strengthening Germany's borders and the German race. Farming was seen as a healthier way to build up the German master race. Himmler, who, as Reich Commissioner for the Strengthening of German Nationality, was also in charge of German settlement outside Germany, sought an SS-based population of farmers and warriors as a way to incorporate the new territories. In practice, few Germans wished to settle in Poland, but Himmler saw it as an opportunity to provide land for those of German descent who were to be repatriated from communities further east. Jews were not welcome in this prospectus, and this limited the options for them, as many were moved from areas designated for German settlers, especially in the Warthegau, which had been part of Poland but was now annexed to Germany.

The option of expelling Europe's Jews to the French colony of Madagascar in the Indian Ocean was discussed in 1940 and approved by Hitler in June, the month in which France surrendered to the successful German invaders. A pro-German government based in Vichy took over the part of France not occupied by the Germans, and it initially controlled most of the French colonies, including Madagascar. The option of expelling the Jews to Madagascar drew on a long-standing idea that European colonial expansion should provide the solution to the question of a separate Jewish homeland, possibly Uganda within the British Empire. In part, this was a philo-Semitic concept, with the emphasis being on providing a safe haven from the anti-Semitic pogroms in the Russian Empire in the late nineteenth and early twentieth century.

In part, however, the emphasis was anti-Semitic and designed to facilitate the movement of Jews from Europe and, indeed, had been employed in that sense by Hitler in a conversation with Göring in November 1938 and with the Polish Foreign Minister, Beck, in January 1939. Reinhard Heydrich wrote to the Foreign Minister, Joachim von Ribbentrop, about the idea in June 1940. It was hoped to persuade Vichy to cede Madagascar to Germany, which could then use it to deport Jews.

Such deportation was not intended to provide a pleasant exile, not least because Madagascar was noted as an unhealthy environment, with yellow fever being particularly deadly there, as it had been for the French when they conquered the island in the mid-1890s. Furthermore, the infrastructure and economy would not be able to support the millions of Jews who were to be sent there. Similarly, later plans to complete an invasion of the Soviet Union by marching Jews to Siberia was intended to lead to their death.

The Madagascar option, however, was rendered impossible by British naval power, which was also to be the basis for the British conquest of the island from Vichy forces in May–November 1942. As a result, the Germans, instead, came to think of Madagascar as an eventual post-war destination for Jews. It was mentioned under this head, alongside Siberia, by Hitler when he met Marshal Slavko Kvaternik of Croatia on 21 July 1941. Other parts of Africa were sometimes considered, Hitler telling Goebbels on 29 May 1942 that central Africa would be a sensible destination, not least as the climate would weaken Jews.

For the present, however, the deportation of Jews from the Axis sphere, the policy apparently sought by Hitler in February 1941,[33] was not feasible. Meanwhile, the conquest of Denmark (1940), Norway (1940), Luxembourg (1940), the Netherlands (1940), Belgium (1940), France (1940), Yugoslavia (1941) and Greece (1941) brought large numbers of Jews under German control – or, at least, direction, via allies and client states. At the same time, preparations escalated for the attack, by Germany and its allies, on the Soviet Union, which was to be launched in June 1941.

While this was being prepared, all arrangements for Jews seemed transitional, as this attack would alter the international situation, as well as provide more land that could be seen as a solution for the 'Jewish question', if land was indeed to offer a solution. In the event, alongside the mass slaughter of Jews in Soviet territory as the Germans advanced, the problems or failure of deportation plans, combined with the fact that the attack on the Soviet Union was not to provide the Germans with a solution for the Jews elsewhere in Europe, encouraged a stress on schemes for immediate mass murder.

The plans already mentioned reflect the extent to which there was no clear-cut path towards genocide. Instead, the treatment of Jews was an aspect of a wider characteristic of German policy. It was, at once, confused, haphazard, brutal and a mismatch between broad anti-Semitic aspirations that lacked clear formulation, and, indeed, coherence and an absence of clarity over prioritisation and execution. At the same time, changes within the German state, society and culture had removed the barriers, first, to active and violent discrimination against and, finally, to the mass murder of fellow Germans and other Jews. Thus, the judiciary and press had been brought under Nazi control, while the police had been militarised, and legal restraints on killing had been removed. In early 1941, under Operation 14f13, SS killing squads were dispatched into the concentration camps to kill those judged most unacceptable – a category that included Jews.

Moreover, these changes interacted with ideological pressures and international developments that made the Holocaust seem not only possible and acceptable but also necessary – indeed, essential. Hitler told the Reichstag on 30 January 1939: 'If the international Jewish money power in Europe and beyond again succeeds in enmeshing the peoples in a world war, the result will not be the Bolshevisation of the world and a victory for Jewry, but the annihilation of the Jewish race in Europe.' This was a speech he was to refer to in 1941. Global war brought forward the millenarian strain in Nazism and encouraged Hitler to give deadly effect to his aspirations and fears, bringing the areas where Europe's Jews had settled under his control, with an urgency that reflected his sense of challenge for Germany and his forebodings of an early death. The slaughter of Jews became a war aim, in a war that was seen as an existential struggle for racial and cultural identity as well as superiority. Indeed, this identity was presented as a guarantee of superiority, one that could only be achieved by the removal of Jews from a German-dominated Europe.

CHAPTER 2

TOWARDS GENOCIDE

The German invasion of the Soviet Union in 1941 – Operation Barbarossa, launched on 22 June – brought far more people judged unsuitable by Hitler, both Jews and Slavs, under his control, providing both a problem and also opportunities for the implementation of Nazi plans. The war against the Soviet Union was conceived as a genocidal war, and the *Wehrmacht* (German armed forces), in conjunction with German civilian authorities, such as the Ministries of the Eastern Territories and Agriculture, planned for 30 million Soviet deaths, in part in order to ensure food for the army. At the same time that plans were entertained for detaining and deporting Jews to Siberia, which the Germans did not intend to occupy, four SS action groups (*Einsatzgruppen*), advancing close behind the troops from the opening day of the invasion, killed Jews, political commissars and others deemed 'undesirable'.[1] Other SS units also played a major role, particularly the *Kommandostab* brigades. German police battalions, moreover, took a prominent role in the killing, as they also did with mass shootings in Polish Galica. Both the SS and the police received special anti-Semitic indoctrination to this end.

THE GERMAN ARMY

In general, the killing was with the cooperation of the army, which in Ukraine was willing to complain about brutal German treatment of Ukrainians, but also to support the slaughter of Jews and to see them as the key source of resistance, which they were not.[2] The harsh content and tone of orders for the day by many army commanders to their units scarcely encouraged a reasonable treatment of Jews, Communists and prisoners. Instead, many called on their troops to annihilate Hitler's targets.[3] SS task forces were particularly murderous, but the Army were also killers, as in both the Soviet Union and, in particular, in Serbia, where Jews were killed in mass shootings in late 1941 and early 1942. They were the prime group shot in response to Serbian partisan activity, with the army officers accepting the Nazi identification of Communists and Jews, and willingly having the latter shot because they could not catch the former or other partisans.[4] In Greece and France, the Army played a role in the deportation and murder of Jews.

Violence by the German military against civilians looked back to a recent tradition of such action by German forces in both Europe and overseas. Crucially, the Franco-Prussian War (1870–1) had not proved the swift and cheap victory the Germans had anticipated and that they had gained at the expense of Austria in 1866. Problems in 1870–1 included supply difficulties, continuing French resistance and opposition from a hostile population. The Germans responded harshly to the *francs-tireurs*, deserters or civilians who fought back, and treated them as criminals, not soldiers. Summary executions helped dampen opposition, but they were also part of a pattern of German brutality in this war, which included the taking of hostages, the shooting of suspects (as well as of those actually captured in arms), the mutilation of prisoners and the destruction of towns and villages, such as Châteaudun. In part, this practice reflected the problems posed for the Germans by hostile French citizen volunteers, who did not wear uniforms and were impossible to identify once they had discarded their rifles. In response, the Germans adopted a social typology that prefigured those of the following century, treating every 'blue smock', the customary clothes of the French worker, as a potential guerrilla.[5]

German atrocities in Belgium and France in 1914, the opening campaign of the First World War, in part appear to have reflected fury that Belgium unexpectedly resisted German attack and, therefore, affected the German advance.

German losses at the hands of Belgian regular units led to reprisals against civilians as well as the killing of military prisoners, while a high degree of drunkenness, confusion and 'friendly fire' among German units contributed directly to their belief that they were under civilian attack, which encouraged their attitude that it was acceptable and, indeed, sensible, to inflict reprisals on the innocent. This was then defended by strategies of deception and propaganda, organised by the German Army and Government in 1914.[6]

While indicative, these instances were very different to the overlap between operational and genocidal warfare seen in the Second World War.[7] Earlier, violence against civilians was not the German goal but, rather, a response to an uncertainty and fear that they could not accept psychologically. The use by regulars of violence against civilians suspected of opposition was deadly when it was seen as necessary and became an automatic response, but, prior to 1941, this was very much a secondary aspect of German military conduct.

A far more pertinent background was that of German campaigning in Africa, particularly in the 1900s when antisocietal practices with genocidal consequences, such as driving people into a waterless desert, were followed.[8] The Herero prisoners sent to prison and labour camps were treated with great cruelty, such that large numbers, about 45 per cent of those in military custody by 1908, died.[9] The German army had, in responding to the Herero rebellion in German South-West Africa (now Namibia) in 1904–5, the Nama rebellions there in 1890 and 1905–9, and the Maji-Maji rebellion in German East Africa (now Tanzania) in 1905, become used to seeing entire ethnic groups as race enemies and had developed the practice of racial conflict.

In part, these assumptions and practices were transferred to Europe in the twentieth century, first with the massacres in Belgium during the First World War and, far more clearly, consistently and violently, in eastern Europe during the Second World War. A key prelude to German policy in eastern Europe during the Second World War was possibly set by the extensive German campaigning on the Eastern Front in the First World

War. A disparaging sense of the people overrun, not least seeing them as weak, dirty and diseased, became commonplace, in part in response not only to those who were conquered but also to the vast areas that now had to be psychologically understood and overcome.[10] Jews were prominent in the Russian borderlands that were overrun. The Russian Empire had then included central and eastern Poland, Lithuania and Ukraine, all of which were overrun by the Germans in 1915–18.

This episode has been seen as important to the development of a hostile and violent response to conquered peoples as a central aspect of German war policies, although it is possible that, in part, this represents a retrospective perspective, owing something to knowledge of what was to happen in the Second World War. Indeed, a less critical view of the German army in the First World War has been advanced,[11] and the Nazi dimension was, of course, absent then.

Furthermore, rather than emphasising racism, Isabel Hull has argued that against the Herero, there was 'a typical European war in which genocide developed out of standard military practices and assumptions', and that 'genocide in South West Africa was in any event not the product of ideology, but of institutional action'.[12] This is a conclusion that casts an instructive light on the German army's quest for a crushing victory in a battle of annihilation. Civilians were dispensable in this view, while there was also an emphasis on the punitive treatment of Germany's enemies that was unconstrained by international law.

In the Second World War, racial violence was displayed by the Germans in Poland in 1939, while the massacres of about 3,000 French African soldiers by both the regular army and the SS in France in 1940 showed that the German military was also willing in western Europe to embrace the Nazi notion of racialised warfare and its murderous applications. These massacres were not a response to official policy, but, instead, were sporadic and a product of racial violence from below, albeit a violence that reflected Nazi ideology and also propaganda from 1910 onwards against the French use of African soldiers.[13]

On the Eastern Front from 1941, the institutionalised ruth-
lessness of the Army was accentuated by Nazi ideology, and
there was a far greater willingness to ignore international laws
and to respond almost instinctively in a brutal fashion that
reflected a belief that the population were sub-human, and that,
therefore, German violence was appropriate. Many members of
the Army appear to have accepted the identification and conflation of Jews with Communism, a conflation interpreted to mean
that the slaughter of the first would ensure the weakening of the
second and, thus, stabilise German conquest. German generals
also personally benefited, as Hitler felt it necessary to bribe
them. This was an aspect of the close relationship between
Hitler and the military elite, and one the latter played down
after the war. The Navy also provided eager support for the
regime,[14] while the major role of the SS in creating military units
– the Waffen-SS – indicated the eventually close relationship
between ideology and the German war effort. Over 800,000
men served in the Waffen-SS, and it became an important part
of Germany's fighting forces, serving under the operational
command of the Army, although it was a separate structure.

German propaganda, for example the popular film *Ohm
Krüger* (1941), was to refer to the British establishment of
concentration camps during the Second Boer War of 1899–
1902, between the British and the Boers of Transvaal and
Orange Free State in modern South Africa. This was a totally
misleading comparison, as the intention of the camps was
very different. To deprive the Boer guerrillas of civilian support, the British Army moved their families into detention
camps. A total of 27,927 Boer civilians died there from disease, but there was no active mistreatment of the civilians, the
British forces themselves suffered heavily from disease, and
the camps were criticised in Britain, not least on the head of
the deaths, with a freedom that scarcely bears comparison
with Nazi Germany. Nor, indeed, did the public opposition to
the Boer War in Britain and the Government's willingness to
face a general election. The German film presented it as unacceptable to put Boers in the camps; the latter themselves were
not the object of criticism.

THE *EINSATZGRUPPEN*

In stark contrast to the Boer War, and, thus, as a dramatic illustration of the point about the misuse of comparisons discussed in Chapter 6, close to 1 million Jews were killed within six months of the start of Operation Barbarossa in the territories conquered by the Germans; in other words, before the Wannsee conference that receives so much attention in the literature. This was also the period of most killing of Jews in the occupied Soviet Union during the war.[15] Most were killed by Germans, although Romanians did their malign part in the area they overran, slaughtering tens of thousands in Odessa. This was one of the cosmopolitan cities the Germans found so abhorrent, because they encapsulated the cosmopolitanism deplored by them. Vienna and Salonika were other examples, and Alexandria would have been one had it been captured in 1942.

In Lithuania, Belarus, Ukraine and Latvia, the Germans had much local support.[16] While most anti-Semitic violence in these areas took place under German supervision or with active encouragement or toleration, the Germans did not always need to intervene. They were able to draw on widespread anti-Semitism, as in Lvóv where the Ukrainians did much of the killing. A German eyewitness in Złoczów, in the Tarnopol province of south-east Poland, reported on 3 July 1941:

I saw that in the ditches, about 5 meters deep and 20 meters wide, stood and lay about 60–80 men, women, and children, predominantly Jewish. I heard the wailing and screaming of the children and women, hand grenades bursting in their midst. Beyond the ditches waited many hundreds of people for execution. In front of the ditches stood 10–20 men in civilian clothes [Ukrainian nationalists] who were throwing grenades into the ditch.[17]

The Waffen-SS were also active in this massacre.

The large-scale slaughter developed as the Germans advanced, particularly from mid-August 1941, suggesting that successive orders had been issued to that end. The slaughter was not a product of the slowing-down, still less failure, of Barbarossa in November–December 1941 later in the year (which left the Germans with an apparently intractable struggle with the Soviet Union), as is sometimes suggested, but, instead, began in the optimistic days of advancing panzers and apparently imminent victory. Written instructions came from Heydrich, backed by Himmler, that local pogroms were to be encouraged. Hitler certainly sought and received the *Einsatzgruppen* reports. From August, the killing escalated to include large numbers of women and children, again in response to instructions from Himmler and Heydrich, which were conveyed with the assurance that they had Hitler's support. At the start of the month, Himmler ordered the killing of all Jews in the town of Pinsk. Mass slaughter now appeared a realistic option to those who wanted it.[18] Unlike in Poland in 1939, this was genocide.

Similarly, although there was little real partisan threat, the Germans used indiscriminate brutality against those they alleged to be partisans or their supporters. Jews were routinely slaughtered in what were presented as anti-partisan operations, an aspect of the anti-Semitic convictions and assumptions that were widespread among 'ordinary' Germans.[19]

At the same time, from the outset, Barbarossa proved more difficult, and German casualties higher, than had been anticipated. Motivated by ideological and ethnic contempt, overconfident after earlier successes and certain that their armed forces were better in every respect, the Germans had underestimated Soviet capability, effectiveness and determination. To the surprise of Hitler, some Soviet forces fought well and effectively from the outset.[20] Soviet resistance also accentuated the consequences of a prior German failure to settle strategic choices, while, as Filippo Anfuso noted when he accompanied Mussolini to Hitler's headquarters – the Wolf's Lair in East Prussia, on 25 August 1941 – the space of the Soviet Union had not been conceptually overcome.[21] Hitler told Mussolini that day that Franklin Delano Roosevelt, the American President, was controlled by a Jewish group.

In Lithuania, mass killings of all Jews by the Germans, as opposed to simply adult males, began in August 1941. Food and security issues interacted with racist assumptions about the desirability of such a slaughter,[22] but the latter were foremost. The killings there were in open country, not in extermination camps, and Lithuanians played a major role in them. On 1 December 1941, Karl Jäger, Commander of the 150 men in *Einsatzkommando* 3 of *Einsatzgruppe* A, produced a list of Jews killed daily from 2 July to the end of November: 133,346, including large numbers of children from the middle of August. He claimed to have 'solved the Jewish problem in Lithuania. In Lithuania there are no more Jews except for work-Jews.'[23] The Jews of the city of Vilnius were taken the 6 miles to Ponary, a former holiday resort, where they were shot by both Germans and Lithuanians at the edge of the deep fuel pits, dug by the Soviet forces in nearby woods. Some were stabbed or bludgeoned. Infants were frequently flung into the pits. Between 50,000 and 60,000 Jews were killed there. Also in Lithuania, 10,000 Jews from the city of Kovno were marched to nearby Fort IX, where they were shot at the edge of pits.

Similarly, at the ravine of Babi Yar, outside Kiev, the major city in Ukraine, the Germans – *Einsatzkommandos* (helped by the Army and by Ukrainians) – recorded slaughtering 33,771 Jews in three days at the close of September: they were machine-gunned. A standard German technique as they advanced was to make the victims dig a ditch or pit, shoot them on the edge of it, so that they fell in, and then shoot other victims so that they fell in on top, suffocating any survivors. Such killings were designed to ensure that the outcome in the former Soviet Union would not be a large number of ghettos, as in Poland, although some ghettos were created as Jews were confined.[24] The determination to kill extended to the murder of the ill and the old in their beds.

Those who carried out killings were sufficiently without shame to take photographs of their murders, photographs that were displayed in barracks and of which copies could be ordered. Soldiers not directly involved were often aware of what was going on, not least because the killing was public.

The mass shootings led to the destruction of many existing ghettos. Thus, in Belarus, 7,000 Jews were slaughtered on 20 October, as the Borisov ghetto was destroyed with the active complicity of Belarus auxiliary police. On 15 November, many members of the Minsk ghetto were slaughtered with the active participation of Lithuanian militia. On 30 November and 7–8 December, all bar 2,500 of the 30,000 Jews from the ghetto in the Latvian capital Riga were killed: with 1,000 Jews from Berlin, who arrived by train on 30 November, they were marched to the Rumbula forest, made to undress, forced into pits and shot in the back of the head. Latvian auxiliaries assisted the Germans in this operation. *Einsatzgruppe* D slaughtered the Crimean Jews: there were large-scale massacres at Bakchiserai and Simferopol.

After Babi Yar, Field Marshal Walter von Reichenau, on 10 October, issued an order urging soldiers to support the systematic killing of Jews as 'a hard but just punishment for the Jewish sub-humans', an instruction at total variance with international law. He presented this as a way to pre-empt resistance in the rear of the German advance. Reichenau's instruction was praised by Hitler, and his superior officer, Field Marshal Gerd von Rundstedt, the Commander of Army Group South, signed a directive to his other subordinate commanders suggesting they issue comparable instructions, although he favoured leaving the killing to the *Einsatzgruppen*. At the Nuremberg trial, Rundstedt denied any knowledge of the episode.[25]

It is typical of conventional military history that his role is not mentioned in standard guides. For example, the entry in Trevor Dupuy's *Encyclopedia of Military Biography* (1992) refers to Rundstedt as 'an example of the best of the old Prussian officer corps'.[26] Similarly, in his biography of Josef 'Sepp' Dietrich, one-time Commander of Hitler's bodyguard, who commanded an SS division on the Eastern Front in 1941–3 and then an SS corps, and who was later imprisoned for war crimes, Charles Messenger displayed what can be seen as the worrying failure of critical judgement seen in too much work on the Waffen-SS.[27] From personal experience in work on compendia like that of Dupuy, publishers do not like reference to the complicity of German commanders in atrocities.

In 1941, this complicity was true both of Nazi sympathisers, such as Reichenau, who ordered the killing of Jewish children under five when a staff officer had tried to postpone it, and of others, for example Field Marshal Wilhelm von Leeb, the Commander of Army Group North until January 1942. General Erich Hoepner, the Commander of Fourth Panzer Group, referred, in May 1941, to the forthcoming war as the 'warding off of Jewish Bolshevism'. The order he issued to his units emphasised the need for the 'total annihilation of the enemy' and the supporters of the 'Russo-Bolshevik system'.[28] Hoepner, who had been given the task of disarming the SS in the military plot to overthrow Hitler in 1938, was to be tortured and hanged for his role in the July 1944 Bomb Plot against Hitler. More generally on the part of the generals, there was not only a lack of interest in the fate of civilians and prisoners of war but also a wish to see them removed so as to make military operations easier.

In some circumstances, German generals were willing to defy orders. When, in December 1941, Hitler ordered Rundstedt, at the furthest point of his advance, to stand fast at Rostov, rather than to retreat to a better defensive position further west, he resigned. More generally, in the face of the Soviet winter counter-offensive, commanders who responded to Hitler's 'stand or die' order by advocating withdrawal were ignored, even dismissed. In total, thirty-five generals were removed, including Guderian and Hoepner. However, Hitler did not face comparable opposition over his treatment of the Jews.

This, indeed, casts a light on post-war justification of German generals, such as support in Britain for Field Marshal Erich von Manstein when he was tried and convicted for war crimes.[29] Manstein served as a general on the Eastern Front from 1941 to 1944. As Commander of the Eleventh Army in the Crimea, he had known about the slaughter of local Jews, providing support for the *Einsatzgruppen*, including supplies. His army order of 20 November 1941 declared 'The Jewish-Bolshevist system must now once and for ever be exterminated. Never again must it be allowed to interfere in our European *Lebensraum*.' He added that Jewry was the progenitor of Bolshevik terror.

Basil Liddell Hart, an influential British ex-military supporter of German generals,[30] who wrote a foreword to the 1952 translation of Guderian's memoirs, stressed the need to obey orders as an aspect of 'the essential requirements of military discipline', in response to a complaint by Sir James Butler, the editor of the British official history of the war:

> It doesn't seem to me that there is any comparison, for instance, between reprehensible acts which British and American commanders may have been instructed to carry out in the nineteenth century and the sort of things which Guderian and his fellows put up with on the part of the Nazi government without protest or without effective protest.[31]

As far as the bulk of the German Army was concerned, it was not until 1943 that it was felt necessary to introduce the National Socialist Leadership Officers, who were designed to act like Nazi commissars. In 1941, soldiers' letters suggest that anti-Semitic propaganda had been widely internalised.

On 1 September 1941, Ulas Samchuk, the leader of the pro-German Ukrainian movement OUN (Organisation of Ukrainian Nationals), declared in the newspaper *Volyn*: 'The Jewish problem is already in the process of being solved.'[32] This killing by the *Einsatzgruppen* and allied killers is of great significance not only for the numbers killed, but also for the general understanding of the Holocaust. It is all too easy to treat the killing in the field as a prequel to the 'Final Solution' of the extermination camps and then to focus on the latter. Indeed, that is the general tendency of public attention. Understandably so, in part because the sources for the camps, however limited, are better than for the killing in the field, particularly in so far as Auschwitz remains as a central site to mark all the extermination camps.

Other source factors are also pertinent. The testimony of survivors is particularly crucial. By the nature of things, the extermination camps left very few indeed; but, in the public mind, there was an elision between them and the concentration camps. Very brutal as the latter were, and, particularly prone as the Germans were to kill Jews, there were survivors from the concentration camps, and their testimony then misleadingly served for all Jews sent to the camps. In contrast, there were very few survivors of the massacres by the *Einsatzgruppen* and allied killers. In part, this was because of the care they took to ensure that none should survive, and, in part, Jews who managed to flee the killings in the Soviet Union in 1941 faced several years of dire circumstances, not least murderous German anti-partisan sweeps.

In terms of finality, the killings in late 1941 were 'final' for large numbers of Jews and for many important Jewish communities, not least that of Kiev and many of the communities in Belarus and the Baltic states. The relationship between these killings, the 'Final Solution' and the general perception of the Holocaust is, therefore, significant. The extent to which the murders of the second half of 1941 can be disentangled from the industrialised killing that followed them can be questioned. This is not least because these murders encouraged bringing ideas for the industrialised killing to fruition.

Although there was no difference in goal, these mass murders in late 1941 did not, though, provide a model for the destruction of the Jews across much of Europe. However docile, collaborationist and anti-Semitic the Dutch or French may have been, it is difficult to imagine most of their authorities cooperating in marching the Jews of Amsterdam and Paris into the surrounding countryside and slaughtering them there. Furthermore, in organisational terms, there was a contrast between killing Jews in, or close to, where they lived in newly conquered lands with the cooperation of part of the local population, as happened in the Soviet Union in late 1941, and, on the other hand, moving them across much of Europe in order to be slaughtered in specially created killing facilities.

The emphasis on the later events is not simply one on the centrality of the extermination camps, but also that they were designed to ensure the slaughter of all of Europe's Jews, whereas the killings in the field in late 1941 were a partial genocide, if such a term can be employed. This contrast is important not only to what happened but also because of the subsequent memorialisation of the Holocaust. The killing of Jews in the field was more 'total' than the comparable slaughter of peoples in eastern Europe (e.g. Serbs by Croats or Poles by Ukrainians) because, although their treatment was brutal, a smaller percentage of the latter was killed in this manner. A difference in the manner of killing, however, was more the case with the extermination camps: the overwhelming percentage of those killed in Auschwitz and the other camps were Jews. As a result, these camps represented the uniqueness of the Holocaust as a genocide to a degree that the killings in the field could not.

Nevertheless, this is misleading, because, as already indicated, for Jewish communities involved in the latter, the experience of violence and destruction was comparable. Indeed, there is a need to devote more attention to these killings than they generally receive in public reference to the Holocaust. Moreover, these killings did not stop when the extermination camps were established. Instead, they remained important, especially in 1942 but also after that.

A focus on these killings also qualifies the notion that the Holocaust was in some respects an aspect of modernity,[33] more specifically of new technology – railways, gas, applied knowledge – the planning of camps and killing, and efficient administration. Aside from the moral dimensions of this issue, as modernity is usually seen as in some way positive, there are also fundamental empirical qualifications to this thesis. For example, far from being modern, the coerced labour of malnourished Jews in the concentration camps was far less effective than the labour used in the essentially free-market USA, or even the Soviet Union, where controlled and coercive labour systems were dominant. Subsequent events have also indicated that controlled labour forces are less effective than free-labour markets.

Moreover, the slaughter by the Germans of so many intelligent and productive people scarcely suggests a search for efficiency, although, as a key purpose of this labour was to kill the workers, a different, and warped, type of effectiveness was at issue. Instead, anti-Semitism was the determinant drive. Furthermore, it is not clear how the brutality of the treatment of the victims prior to slaughter is supposed to relate to modernity. The killings in the field, moreover, indicate that the model of industrialised killing seen in the extermination camps was not applicable to all of the slaughter, and, indeed, taking this further, alongside the murderous use of gas, there were large-scale shootings at Auschwitz.

The activities of the *Einsatzgruppen* lowered restraints on mass killing of Jews elsewhere. These activities also reflected the degree to which restraints on slaughter had already collapsed in key sectors of the regime, with, in addition, important complicity by others – particularly the Army. The chaos of campaign and the euphoria of a triumphant advance provided an opportunity for what was clearly a killing that, in goal and practice, was pursued in a fashion which was methodical and far from chaotic. This ethos of killing could then be generalised. In practice, as far as the *Einsatzgruppen* were concerned, there was a fair amount of inconsistency and much chaos in the detention and slaughter of Jews alongside, of course, the fundamental chaos represented by the very process.

'EUTHANASIA' AND GAS

Alongside the earlier killing of Jews in Poland and during Operation Barbarossa, a key background to the new form of slaughter was provided by the 'euthanasia' programme for the slaughter of mentally ill and disabled Germans unable to work. Authorised verbally by Hitler in July 1939, and later that year by a private written authorisation, and reflecting his long-standing support for 'euthanasia', this programme indicated that mass murderers could be found.

Much of the practice of the Holocaust, such as its secrecy, could be seen in these killings. The 'euthanasia' programme also provided experience in such killing in specially designated mental hospitals such as Hadamar, with its gas chamber and crematorium, in which over 10,000 people were slaughtered in 1941, as well as, in the east, through shooting or gassing in gas vans. The gas used was carbon monoxide. Initially, lethal injection was employed, but, from January 1940, gas was used as it was better suited to slaughtering large numbers. Aside from gas vans, converted shower rooms were also employed. The centrally directed killing of the mentally ill and handicapped was officially halted in August 1941, as a result of the growing popular concern as news of the killings leaked out and in response to a critical sermon by Clemens von Galen, the Catholic Bishop of Münster. However, the murder of the mentally handicapped and ill continued, particularly from the summer of 1942, although now by injection and starvation and not gas.[34]

As with the slaughter of Jews, there was no shortage of willing killers, while a perverted view of progress through racial purification led to enthusiastic support for the policy, rather than any sense of dull acceptance of some sort of necessity contributing to it. As a parallel to the different means of slaughtering Jews, alongside the structure for killing the physically and mentally ill that turned to the use of gas, the so-called 'T-4 Programme', there was, in 1939–40, a large-scale killing by the SS of considerable numbers of psychiatric patients in Poland and north-east Germany. In total, about 212,000 Germans were killed in 'euthanasia programmes', as well as at least 80,000 others from psychiatric institutions in German-occupied areas.

The development of German policy towards Jews also led to experiments in how best to kill people. The Germans sought to find a means of gassing that would give Jews little warning of their fate, so that they had no opportunity to resist. The Germans were confident that they could overcome any resistance, but did not wish to see disruption to the planned processes of predictable slaughter. The Germans also wanted a method that required relatively few operatives. Furthermore, mass killings in the field were considered to be too public and traumatic for the personnel involved, as well as expensive; for example, in the use of ammunition.

At the camp based on a converted barracks at Auschwitz (Oswiecim), west of Cracow in Poland, on 5 September 1941, Zyklon-B (prussic acid) poison-gas crystals were used as a test on 600 Soviet prisoners, instead of the lice for which they were intended in the fumigation of clothes and housing. From September 1941, the Germans also had a gas van that was more deadly than their earlier model, which had used carbon monoxide from bottles. The gas used in the sealed rear compartments of the vans was exhaust fumes (carbon monoxide, not Zyklon B), and the victims suffocated to death. Having been tested on Soviet prisoners in the concentration camp at Sachsenhausen, these vans were used at Poltava in Ukraine in November as part of the *Einsatzgruppen* killings. Other gas vans were then used in Belarus, the Baltic republics and Serbia.

From at least 8 December 1941, Jews were killed in gas vans en route between the newly opened extermination camp at Chelmno and nearby woods where the corpses were buried. Gas vans were a method already employed earlier that year by the Soviet NKVD when killing political prisoners, but not on the scale that was to be employed at Chelmno and elsewhere. Furthermore, in turn, gas chambers were to be more effective in killing large numbers. At Chelmno, most of the Jews who were transferred there from the Łódź ghetto were gassed as soon as they arrived. About 1,000 people could be killed there daily. Eventually, over 150,000 Jews were killed at Chelmno. Other camps swiftly followed.

A NEW GEOGRAPHY

The killing of those deemed unwanted was central to German plans for the future of Europe. The Nazi leadership planned a 'New Order', with Germany central to a European system and the Germans at the top of a racial hierarchy. The economy of Europe was to be made subservient to German interests, with the rest of Europe providing Germany with labour, raw materials and food, on German terms, and also taking German industrial products, both processes contributing to German prosperity. Moreover, Jewish assets were to be seized.[35] Indeed, the despoliation of Jews, first, in Germany, and then throughout Europe, was a vital component of the

Nazi war economy. This was the case in both the narrow, but crucial, sense of funding the production of armaments as well as providing forced labour,[36] and in the wider sense of injecting cash or goods into the economies of Germany and allied and occupied countries, in order to stave off the worst effects of shortages and to cement the Axis system.

This despoliation was not simply a matter of state action. Members of the regime also participated actively. Furthermore, many 'ordinary Germans' sought to benefit from the property and other assets owned by Jews, and also from opportunities for promotion or employment created by their removal. This was an important aspect of the extent to which participation in the Holocaust was far more extensive than that in the actual deportation and killing.

Hitler was increasingly committed to a demographic revolution of slaughter and widespread resettlement, a revolution that was to be accompanied by the economy of plunder that was to lubricate Germany's war effort. His remarks about Jews became more frequent and more vicious, and, in order to demonstrate, to himself and others, his own sense of purpose, he returned to his prediction in January 1939 that another world war would lead to the destruction of European Jews. There was, thus, not only a consistency of attitude on his part but also one that was brought to the fore by circumstances.[37]

The development and implementation of policy led to a geography of killing in pursuit of what was presented as a spatial purification.[38] This was a key aspect of Nazi population policy,[39] although the idea was on record already in the 1920s. Much of the former Soviet Union was designated for occupation, its population classified for Germanisation, extermination or forcible transfer to Siberia, which was not intended for occupation. Like the Madagascar option, however, the possibility of transfer to Siberia was thwarted by Allied resilience and was not to be the direction of the war on Jews. Indeed, whatever the long-term possibilities for German policy, a sense of racial geography as already and increasingly under pressure was suggested by the deportation of western European Jews to already-crowded Polish ghettos.

Such deportation also reflected suggestions from officials seeking to address issues either of anti-Semitic policy, such as sustaining the rate of rounding up French Jews, or other problems, for example housing, at the expense of Jews, Germans displaced by increasingly prominent Allied bombing.[40] These officials did so within the context of an increasingly brutal anti-Semitic ideology, encouraged and legitimated by Hitler's rhetoric and instructions. The deportation of Jews could, thus, be seen as the solution to more problems than that which was fundamental for Hitler; namely, their very existence.

AN IMPORTANT TURNING POINT

Terrible as the killing in the field was, a still more comprehensive and drastic 'Final Solution' was being planned from late 1941. Initially, Poland was seen as a destination, indeed dumping ground, for Jews from elsewhere in Europe, one where they could be treated harshly and made to work; but this soon became the site for a total slaughter.

Mid-September 1941 proved a crucial moment, as these issues were referred to Hitler and, in an important turning point, he determined on the deportation of Western European Jews. On 17 September, it was decided by Hitler to deport the German, Austrian and Czech Jews at once to Łódź. This was seen as likely to lead to the death of many of them that winter, and, indeed, the idea of deportation was both a means to an end and a deception about what was intended. This decision, to implement the long-held plans for a new racial order, was taken in the midst of euphoria about the progress of the war. Indeed, on 16 September, the Germans completed their encirclement of the Soviet South-West Front forces near Kiev, an encirclement that was to yield 665,000 prisoners, the largest number in any encirclement that year. In accordance with Hitler's decision, mass deportations from outside what had been Poland were to begin, even though the war was not yet over.[41] Both Łódź and Chelmno were part of the expanded German territory, and German (and Austrian) Jews transported there were technically still subjects of the Reich, but such points were of no importance before the murderous intent of Hitler's policy.

The decision in mid-September was a crucial one, not least as it established the policy of moving Jews rapidly from throughout German-controlled Europe and thus put more Jews into position for mass slaughter. Eichmann, who was in charge of the Race and Resettlement Office of the Reich Security Main Office's Amt IV, was ordered to prepare the details for a new policy. He used the term 'Final Solution' to refer to the Jewish problem in October, and it appeared thereafter in many documents.

THE INTERNATIONAL CONTEXT

In place of the left-wing tendency, both during the war and subsequently, to emphasise the struggle between fascism and Communism, and, thus, between Hitler's Germany and Stalin's Soviet Union, it is pertinent to note that opposition to Britain, the USA and the liberal values represented by both societies was a key to the policies of Hitler and Stalin. In each case, there was not only hostility to Britain's political position but also a rejection of its liberalism. This was a product not only of a rejection of liberal capitalism, which anti-Semites associated with Jews and decried as plutocracy, but also hostility to Britain for its encouragement of an international agenda focused on opposition to dictatorial expansionism. Moreover, Hitler's cooperation with the Soviet Union from August 1939 until June 1941 can be linked to an anti-Western turn in Nazi anti-Semitism in 1938–41, such that 'the war in the West against Churchill and Roosevelt was no less an ideological war than the war for Lebensraum in the East'.[42]

As Germany's allies and enemies changed, so the threat from Jews remained a constant in Hitler's views and rhetoric. In his broadcast to the German people on 22 June 1941 to mark the launching of Operation Barbarossa, Hitler had managed to blame Jews for both British and Soviet policy. This approach influenced some of his closest supporters such as Robert Ley, who, from 1933, was Head of the German Workers' Front. Before he committed suicide in 1945, he wrote of the Allies as being tools of the Jews and of the war as being a conflict with the latter. Publications and the media had spread this theme.

The extension of the war to include the USA in December 1941 may have influenced Hitler's attitudes to Jews, encouraging him to push forward European mass murder; and it has been suggested that the announcement, on 14 August 1941, of the Atlantic Charter agreed by Churchill and Roosevelt had already contributed to the same end. Hitler claimed that American policy was dictated by Jewish financial interests, an inaccurate argument he also used about Britain.

Japanese forces attacked Pearl Harbor on 7 December, the USA declared war on Japan on 8 December, and Germany and Italy declared war on the USA on 11 December. To Hitler, the American focus on war with Germany, Roosevelt's 'Germany First' policy, confirmed by the Washington Conference that began on 22 December 1941, demonstrated the role of Jewish interests and thus justified and made necessary his escalation of his war with Jewry.

This war was not separate to military and international policies for Hitler but part of the same equation. His speeches and meetings, and references by other Nazi leaders, all from mid-December 1941, make this apparent and suggest that Hitler had decided to instigate genocide. Indeed, Hitler's speech of 12 December to the Gauleiters and Reichsleiters has been seen as crucial for the Wannsee conference. He was happy to anticipate the end of Jewry when speaking on the radio in January, February and November 1942.

With reference to the argument by David Irving that Hitler did not order the Holocaust, but, instead, that it was a product of a momentum or dynamic latent within Nazism and its anti-Semitism, Hitler, in fact, was central to the Third Reich, and no major initiative would have been possible without his direct support, while lesser actions were taken in a context in which his approval was explicit.[43] The idea of 'working towards the Führer' helped provide a dynamic in which, in order to justify their position and fulfil their potential as Germans, large numbers sought not only to execute what they knew to be Hitler's will but even went further to anticipate his objectives. This helped produce an integration of society with state, an integration to which Hitler's influence in both was crucial.[44] This was directly relevant to the treatment of Jews. For example, the *Gauleiters* competed to be first to tell Hitler that their *gau* had no Jews. Individual *Gauleiters* pushed through deportations. Thus, in the autumn of 1940, Josef Bürckel was a keen supporter of the *Aktion Bürckel*, the deportation of Jews from the Saarland and Palatinate.

There is no sign of Hitler having issued any written order for the Holocaust, but Göring and Heydrich cited him as their authority for mass murder. The early autumn of 1941 was the key period.[45] Aside from authorising the deportations, Hitler allowed the SS to gain the control in Poland that made the organisation of genocide there possible. He was also kept informed of the mass slaughter and 'made *ad hoc* interventions in it'.[46] On 18 December 1941, Hitler told Himmler that Jews were to be killed 'like partisans'.

Hitler himself never witnessed any of the killings. In contrast, in August 1941, Himmler saw a mass shooting in Minsk and, in July 1942, he saw a gassing at Auschwitz during his inspection. In 1943, he had quarters prepared for himself in the House of the Waffen-SS at Auschwitz, but he never occupied them, although he visited the extermination camp at Sobibor in July 1943. Three years later, Joachim von Ribbentrop, German Foreign Minister under Hitler, told Leon Goldensohn, an American Army psychiatrist responsible for monitoring those charged at Nuremberg, that:

Hitler was off balance in regard to the Jewish question. He told me often that the Jews caused the war, and that there was a complicity between Jewish capitalism and Jewish Bolshevism [. . .] I know for a fact that this idea of the Jews causing the war and the Jews being so all-important is nonsense. But that was Hitler's idea, and as time went on he became more and more obsessed with this idea.

He also said that in the long view, historically, the Jews' extermination would always be a blot on German history, but that it was in a way attributable to the fact that Hitler had lost his sense of proportion and, because he was losing the war, went 'wild' on the subject of the Jews.[47]

The typically self-serving Ribbentrop felt it unnecessary to add that he had told the Hungarian Regent, Admiral Miklos Horthy, in April 1943, that Jews should either be slaughtered or put into concentration camps, before Hitler pressed on to say that Jews faced the choice of work and death and then compared them to tuberculosis bacilli, which left no doubt of the context and nature of the choice.[48] At Nuremberg, Hans Frank denied knowing about the extermination camps.

The nature of German policy formation, with partially autonomous bodies implementing Nazi beliefs and responding to problems and their perception of problems in light of them, ensures that there was no one moment when the Holocaust of all European Jewry was settled, although Hitler appears to have given a verbal order in 1941. Specifically, although the decisions reached in mid-September were clearly very important, there was no single moment when the mass killings of men, women and children in the field in the Soviet Union were, it was determined, to be a stage in the comprehensive and industrialised slaughter of all of Europe's Jews, which was to be a prospectus for the fate of all Jews in the world. Instead, policy-making was more ad hoc and killing incremental and cumulative, but, accepting that background, the shift occurred in late 1941, as ideology, opportunity and need were brought together, with Himmler and Heydrich as key coordinators. They were instrumental in introducing a new policy, as well as generalising regional policies of murder and turning them into a strategy, but this was dependent on Hitler's approval.[49]

INITIATIVES TOWARDS SLAUGHTER

Ian Kershaw indicates, with his study of the Warthegau (Wartheland), that there was also a complex relationship between central direction and local initiatives, with the latter reflecting a range of factors. The Warthegau was the part of Poland annexed by Germany, as part of the Greater German Reich in 1939, and included the Łódź ghetto. Arthur Greiser, the *Gauleiter* of the Warthegau, agreed to take large numbers of deportees, but, in return, received approval for the establishment of the killing facilities at Chelmno. This was to be administered by the *Gauleiter*, who was to be answerable to Himmler. Similarly, in the region of the German-created General Government of Poland (which included Cracow, Lublin and Warsaw), the demographic situation shifted, not, initially, as a result of deportation thither from elsewhere in Europe, which took a while to become large-scale, but because of the end of the expectation of moving Jews from there into what had been part of the Soviet Union.

This shift helped lead to an accentuation of the already extremely harsh treatment of Jews in the General Government, as well as particular violent initiatives. The beginning of the construction of an extermination camp at Bełzec in November 1941 was a consequence. This camp was the result of an initiative by SS Brigadier Odilo Globocnik, the Head of the SS and Police in Lublin district, and he had presumably been authorised to do so when he met Himmler on 13 October. Knowledge of such policies helped ensure that, when those at the centre spoke of deportation to the East, they meant slaughter and not, as earlier, a territorial, albeit harsh, solution to the Jewish issue. Deportation was eliding into destruction and allowing to die into killing.

Kershaw argues that Hitler was content to permit others to turn the ideological imperatives he expressed into practical policy objectives and, in doing so, to please him.[50] Officials rationalised their policies by claiming that Jews posed a threat, whether as partisans, black marketeers or spreaders of infection, or posed a problem, as consumers of food and housing and as inefficient workers. These claims were preposterous, and that of Jews as consumers of food was a stark contrast to their sub-minimal rations. These rationalisations, indeed, reflected the concerns of officials, but these concerns, and their context, were not simply bureaucratic. Instead, ideological imperatives ensured that issues and problems were interpreted in a violently anti-Semitic fashion.

Nazi propaganda, determined at the most senior level, emphasised that Jewry was to be destroyed. A press briefing by Alfred Rosenberg, the highly anti-Semitic Minister of the Eastern Territories, on 18 November, made after he had seen Himmler, referred to the 'biological eradication of the entire Jewry of Europe', while Goebbels, in the newspaper Das Reich on 16 November, wrote of the annihilation of World Jewry. This article, entitled 'The Jews Are Guilty', was reprinted elsewhere in the German press, which is instructive with reference to the question of German popular knowledge of the Holocaust. There should have been little doubt about the intention of government policy. No qualification, on grounds of occupation, geography, religion or any other criterion, was offered. The Jews were to be destroyed as a race, and without exception.

WANNSEE

The Wannsee meeting, of fourteen senior administrators from relevant agencies, on 20 January 1942, in a suburban villa on the outskirts of Berlin which was a guest house of the Security Police, helped coordinate the organisation of what was intended as a Final Solution. In this, all European Jews, including those not hitherto under German control, were to be deported to death camps and slaughtered. Such an interministerial gathering of specialists was important because Hitler did not use cabinet government. This meeting has been seen as definitive in policy-making by a few scholars, but as more transitional by others; for example, Peter Longerich.[51] For the latter reason, Christian Gerlach argues that the first invitation to Wannsee, for 9 December, was to discuss only deportations to the east, forced labour and selective mass murder.

The eventual Wannsee protocol (minutes), however, indicated agreement on genocide, although the decision was not taken there. At the Wannsee meeting, Heydrich announced that Jews were to be deported to the East and worked to death, with those who survived dealt with. They indeed were seen as a threat because the survivors were presented as likely to be stronger. Thus, their slaughter was regarded as particularly necessary in Nazi race warfare. The fate of those unable to work was left unstated.[52] The minutes suggest that much of the proceedings, which may have lasted between an hour and ninety minutes, was taken up by a lecture by Heydrich in which he pressed for the coordination of an effective response to the task of the Final Solution, a task to which he pointed out he had been entrusted by Göring, the minister nominally responsible for policy towards the Jews.

Heydrich underlined the central role of the SS, and of himself personally, by pointing out his instructions, and the conference thus established that Himmler, the Head of the SS and Police, and Heydrich, as his representative, were in charge. This was a prime example of the institutional and personal empire-building so important in Nazi governance, but the role of the SS also put pressure on other branches of government to cooperate, and that was important in a governmental system in which cooperation was limited.

The calling of the conference indeed reflected the contrast between the situation in the occupied Soviet Union, where the *Einsatzgruppen* could operate, and that elsewhere in Europe where it was necessary for the SS to take greater account of a range of other branches of government. Indeed, the SS determination to control the situation and the determination to make others complicit in the genocide were probably the key purposes of the Wannsee meeting. It served to make clear the subordination of the fussy Hans Frank, who was in charge of the General Government of Poland, and the zealous Alfred Rosenberg, the Minister for the Eastern Territories.

In his speech at Wannsee, Heydrich reviewed earlier policy, specifically the use of emigration to clear Germany of Jews, but continued that this policy had been stopped by

Himmler in October 1941, because it posed problems and also due to new possibilities. Instead, Jews were to be deported to eastern Europe to prepare for the Final Solution; 11 million Jews were to be affected. Josef Bühler, the representative from the General Government of Poland (the occupying authority of much of Poland), asked for the solution to be rapid and claimed that there was no real need for additional manpower there.

Characteristic of German interest in classification was the fact that the questions of mixed marriages and of their progeny took up nearly a third of the Wannsee minutes. The SS wanted to send the progeny to the east with the other Jews. This was a radical solution at variance with the policies of the Ministry of the Interior, which wanted to protect them. In the event, concerned about the possible implications for public opinion, Hitler decided it was not worth deporting those in and from mixed marriages, especially those with Aryan relations.[53]

GENOCIDE AND THE WAR

Deciding on genocide, on the key issue that all must die, however, still left the question of implementation. Should forced labour to death, either in road-building, such as the projected highway across Ukraine, or in work camps, be the key, as was suggested, not least with the possibility of taking over some of the Stalinist sites of forced labour in the Soviet Union? Alternatively, how far was gassing to be used?

By the Wannsee meeting on 20 January 1942, the flow of the war was increasingly complex. Germany's newly far more active ally, Japan, was doing well, capturing Manila in the Philippines on 2 January 1942 and Kuala Lumpur in Malaya on 11 January. The German attacks on Moscow and Leningrad, however, had stalled in early December, and, on 5–6 December, the Soviets launched a major counter-offensive. This counter-attack revealed the extent to which the Germans were not trained for defence and found it difficult to fight well in that role, but the impact of the Soviet attacks was lessened because, instead of focusing on sections of the front where the

Soviets enjoyed a clear advantage, Stalin mistakenly sought to attack along the entire front. In this context, and with Soviet forces less well prepared than they were to be a year later, Hitler's 'stand or die' order to his forward forces helped stabilise the front, albeit at heavy cost in manpower.[54]

Furthermore, Hitler planned a fresh offensive from 1942, one designed to destroy the Soviet forces west of the Don, to seize the oilfields in the Caucasus and to advance to and capture Stalingrad on the River Volga. These gains, it was suggested, could be exploited by crossing the Volga and advancing to the north-east to outflank Moscow, and, despite logistical problems, by advancing from the Caucasus into Syria and Iran to put pressure on Allied interests in the Near and Middle East. Thus, the auspices could be seen as favourable for the Axis.

OPERATION REINHARDT

The Wannsee meeting helped indicate to a range of officials that genocide was now policy and that the SS leadership was committed to it. It was followed by the escalation of the practice of mass murder by gassing, already seen at Chelmno, as those brought from the Łódź ghetto and nearby towns were killed. Jews throughout Europe, wherever they lived, were to be detained, held in local holding camps and then moved by train to camps far from where they lived, where they would be killed by gassing.

Secrecy was to play a key role, in order to minimise possible resistance or critical reaction. In place of deportation, there was to be 'resettlement', effected by 'special resettlement trains', en route to secret camps. As far as the killing was concerned, gas vans were presented as if transporting Jews to labour duty, while the gas chambers were made to look like shower rooms and thus to appear as the entry, after the disruption, misery and squalor of the rail journeys, to a more predictable and safer environment, albeit an arduous one.

Three more extermination camps (not that this term was employed at the time), Bełzec, Sobibor and Treblinka, were established to give effect to Operation Reinhardt, an SS scheme to kill the Polish Jews and also Jews deported there. At Bełzec, the construction of which had begun on 1 November 1941, the Germans began gassing Jews on 17 March 1942 and could kill 1,500 people daily. Jews from Lublin were followed by those from Lvóv and then Cracow. In the event, over 600,000 Jews were slaughtered there. More generally, in the eleven months from the beginning of the killing at Bełzec in mid-March 1942, over half the Jews who would be slaughtered by the Nazis were killed. In March, also, construction began at Sobibor and in May 1942, the month in which the major Soviet offensive near Kharkov was crushed with very heavy casualties, the new camp opened. About 300,000 Jews, mostly from central Poland, but also from Austria, Bohemia and Germany, were killed in Sobibor. In July 1942, the month in which successes in the Don campaign led Hitler to declare 'The Russian is finished', Treblinka was opened. It was to be the camp in which the second largest number of Jews was killed, over 900,000, mainly from the Warsaw ghetto.

The naming of Operation Reinhardt is attributed to honouring Reinhard Heydrich, Himmler's deputy, who had been fatally wounded by the Czech resistance on 27 May 1942 (he died a week later). The naming has also been attributed to Fritz Reinhardt, a long-standing Nazi and State Secretary, a key functionary, in the Ministry of Finance, which was one of the bodies involved in the system. The operation was commanded by SS Brigadier Odilo Globocnik, who was answerable to Himmler. These camps focused on killing Jews on their arrival, as soon as they had undressed. The camps did not focus on forced labour. Carbon-monoxide gas was used for the killing, a slow way to die. The exhaust fumes were generated by large tank diesel engines.[55] There were also some mass executions as part of Operation Reinhardt, which presumably reflected not only the zeal for killing, but also the extent to which it was impossible for the gassing to keep up with the demand. Moreover, the killers may have been less committed to a reliance simply on gassing than some of the popular understanding of the Holocaust suggests.

THE EXTERMINATION CAMPS

Other extermination camps were not part of Operation Reinhardt. Aside from Chelmno, another at Majdanek, near Lublin, had been constructed as a prisoner-of-war camp, but, in August 1942, it was equipped with gas chambers. About 200,000 Jews were killed there. Auschwitz was where the largest number of Jews were killed. Due to lacunae in the evidence that arose from the German failure to keep accurate numbers of those killed there, the number is controversial, but it was about 1.5 million.[56]

The variety of the operations at Auschwitz reflected the different levels of German oppression. There were three camps: Auschwitz I, opened in June 1940, initially for Polish political prisoners; Auschwitz II or Birkenau (it was built over land that had been that village), on which work began in October 1941 (although not at that stage as an extermination camp); and Auschwitz III, opened in October 1942, which was initially to supply forced labour for nearby industrial facilities run by the company I.G. Farben. The initial gassings, first of Soviet prisoners, and then, on 15 February 1942, of elderly Silesian Jews, took place in Auschwitz I. Then, facilities for killing large numbers – gas chambers, using Zyklon-B gas – and, eventually, crematoria were constructed at Birkenau. The first gassing there, again of elderly Silesian Jews, occurred on 20 March. Birkenau was designed for killing far more than were actually slaughtered there.[57]

This was the industrialised mass murder seen only in German anti-Semitism. Zyklon-B, a hydrogen–cyanide compound, was at least quicker than exhaust fumes, although it still took several minutes to kill. The bodies taken from the chambers left no doubt of the pain and anguish suffered by the dying. Aside from the contortions of the corpses, the bodily fluids on the corpses were also indicative.

In contrast, other than by the Japanese in China, gas was not used in the Second World War. This was different to the situation in the First. Then, gas was extensively employed in conflict from 1915, with chlorine gas, and, from 1917, mustard gas, first used by the Germans. During the inter-war years, a major reliance on gas had been envisaged in the event of a future great-power war. Furthermore, gas was used as a weapon in the inter-war period, by the British in Afghanistan (1919) and Iraq (1920–1), the Spaniards in Morocco (1921–7) and the Italians in Libya (1923–4, 1927–8).[58] Although used as part of military operations, there were civilian casualties, particularly because mustard-gas bombs could not be aimed accurately and also because much of the opposition was by irregulars who could not be readily distinguished from civilians.

The gas masks distributed to British civilians at the outbreak of the Second World War were not made necessary by German bombing, as had been feared, and American tests on the effectiveness of phosgene, hydrogen cyanide, cyanogens, chloride and mustard gas were similarly not taken forward.[59] The British also tested gas bombs as well as anthrax, and briefly considered using them in 1944 in reprisal for the German use of V-rocketry against Britain (the first V-rocket was launched against London on 13 June) but did not do so. Thus, in Europe, the Germans were unique in employing gas.

The use of gas was seen as a necessary way to kill the large numbers assigned to slaughter. It served other purposes as well. In their mass shooting, some members of the *Einsatzgruppen* had made clear their preference for a less obvious way to murder women and children, and the use of gas vans and then gas chambers appeared to provide this. This depersonalisation by the Germans, of both victims and murderers, or at least depersonalisation in their eyes and on their terms, was taken further in the camps when *Sonderkommandos*, Jewish inmates, rather than Germans, were used to move the corpses from the gas chambers to the crematoria. In the pathology of killing, gas also seemed a modern and effective way to kill, and it linked with the Nazi assumption that the Jews were a form of vermin.

Not all Jews were killed at once in the extermination camps, and there were important variations in individual circumstances. Nevertheless, slaughter was the objective, and callousness, brutality, sadism and depravity characterised the treatment of the victims, from their deportation to their slaughter. In the rail journeys, which were lengthy, Jews were denied food, water, light, warmth, sanitation, space and bedding. The use of cattle-cars was emblematic as the camps were abattoirs, albeit not for meat production. Both on the journeys and on arrival at the camps, Jews were exposed to acute levels of pain, fear and disorientation. Moreover, those manning the camps were often thugs, and there were no restraints on their cruelty and arbitrariness. Violence and cruelty built up group identity among the guards and thus helped encourage their brutal treatment of the victims.

The degradation and humiliation already commonplace in the deportations were carried forward into an attempted depersonalisation and dehumanising of the victims. This was a matter not only of the living, and acutely so, both in the camps and during the killing, but also of the dead. Their bodies were treated as raw materials or rubbish, with hair, for example, shaved off to be used in textile production in Germany. Spectacles, shoes, watches, wedding rings and false limbs were among the items systematically collected. The smell from the crematoria lay over the camps.[60]

This sadism and degradation followed on from that of the killings in the field. There, it became the practice to make the victims take their clothes off. In part, this was in order to derive use from their belongings, and use without any restraint for privacy or other reasons, but there was also a wish to demonstrate the weakness of the victims and to humiliate them. This was clearly important to the killers. Other forms of humiliation included cutting off beards, often a sign of Orthodox belief, forcing Orthodox Jews to dance and urinating on captives. Particular pleasure seems to have been taken in humiliating the Orthodox and those who, in German eyes, were most clearly Jewish.

If not killed on arrival at the camps, women were stripped and shaved, and some were sexually abused. Their crowded barracks were particularly neglected. Women also had to face the loss of children and husbands, both being parted from them and the likelihood of their death. Any babies they gave birth to were killed at once, commonly being drowned in a bucket.

There is an emphasis in the literature on the disorganised, and frequently incoherent, nature of Nazi administration and policy-makers. Variation, even contradictions, in the treatment of Jews, for example between the goals of slaughter and labour, provide an instance. Nevertheless, the establishment of the camps, and the related logistical, technical and procedural steps, indicates the high degree of central coordination involved in the launching of the Holocaust and the extent to which it was not simply initially dependent on local initiatives by middle-rank officials, although such officials were not without considerable significance.

Aside from Jews, large numbers of Gypsies were also killed in the extermination camps.[61] Homosexuals, in contrast, were not targeted for mass destruction and were not killed in extermination camps. However, they were sent to concentration camps where they suffered particularly brutal treatment from which many died. The same was true of Jehovah's Witnesses, who were actively persecuted because of their opposition to military service and to the Nazi system. Moreover, about 3.3 million Soviet prisoners died in German captivity, largely from starvation and the resulting exposure to disease – in complete defiance of international conventions on the treatment of prisoners.

In 1942, therefore, the cruel treatment of Jews was increasingly focused not on their killing in the field (although that continued), but on their deportation from the ghettos that had been created by the Germans, as well as from western Europe, to camps, which were run by the SS and which helped to increase their centrality in the Nazi regime. As the latter became a killing machine, so it needed killers who could be trusted not to ask questions. The SS was certainly unwilling to accept bureaucratic restraints and constraints; for example, the status of mixed marriages and the role of other agencies. On 29 January 1942, Himmler wrote:

all measures with respect to the Jewish question in the eastern territories are to be carried out with a view to a general solution of the Jewish question in Europe.

In consequence, in the eastern territories such measures which lead to the final solution of the Jewish question and thus the extermination of Jewry are in no way to be obstructed.

He followed up on 28 July:

I urgently request that no ordinance be issued about the concept of the Jew with all these foolish definitions. We are only tying our hands. The occupied eastern territories will be cleared of Jews. The implementation of this very hard order has been placed on my shoulders by the Führer. No one can release me from this responsibility in any case, so I forbid interference.[62]

Later that year, the German Minister of Justice, Otto Thierack, handed over his remaining responsibility for Germany's Jews to the SS, deliberately so that they could be exterminated.

The camps included not only the extermination camps where gas was used but also slave-labour camps. These camps were important to the Nazi economy, specifically the key need to supply the military, and, in the spring of 1942, the organisation of the camps was changed in order to reflect the emphasis on economic needs and labour. Jews, however, were treated more viciously than the other forced labour on which Germany so heavily depended. Most of the harshly treated Jews in these labour camps died, as a result of serious malnutrition, physical violence and disease, or were killed. Aside from the harsh working conditions, the lack of sufficient and adequate food, clothing, bedding and shoes, and the frequent epidemics, there were brutal punishments, including public floggings and hangings for minor infractions of arbitrary rules. The SS assumed anyway that most prisoners would die in these conditions in under three months, and they were frequently correct.

The distinction between those judged able to work, in other words to be worked to death, and those chosen for immediate killing, many of whom, of course, were able to work, was an aspect of the degree to which what were seen by the Germans as rational considerations, especially attitudes towards age and gender,[63] played a role in slaughter. Jews were allocated to one or the other category. The differentiation was carried out in a number of locations, including the ghettos, where it proved the base of deportation to the camps. Moreover, trains carrying deportees from Germany and Slovakia were stopped at Lublin in 1942 and able-bodied Jews removed for work. At Auschwitz, doctors inspected the deportees, already driven by whip-carrying guards from the rail transports, as they were lined up for entry. Those chosen for immediate slaughter included pregnant women, young children and the unfit. As a result, some children arriving at the camps who understood what was going on tried to appear as tall as possible. The killing of children and pregnant women was not simply an issue of usefulness, but also underlined the genocidal character of the slaughter, which contrasted with that of non-Jewish Polish and Russian victims. More generally, Jewish children were a prime target for murder throughout the Holocaust.

Another aspect of supposedly rational criteria, and, in practice, planned viciousness, was seen with the calculation of food availability. This led to a conviction that killing Jews, as well as other Soviet civilians and, indeed, prisoners, would free foodstuffs for the German army and later settlers. These and other ideas, however, were subordinated to the logic of anti-Semitic murder.[64] This war against Jews took precedence over utilitarian considerations, such as the provision of labour,[65] or the use of rail transport for military ends, while the course of the Second World War helped further radicalise Hitler's anti-Semitism.

The year 1942 saw renewed German advances, largely as part of Operation *Blau* (Blue) launched on 28 June, in which German forces captured besieged Sevastopol in the Crimea on 4 July, overran the eastern Ukraine and advanced to Stalingrad on the River Volga and into the Kuban and the north Caucasus, capturing Stavropol on 5 August and Maikop four days later. On 23 August, German tanks reached the Volga north of Stalingrad. As far as Hitler was concerned, his forces were fighting Jewry, because Communism was one of its products. On 26 April 1942, in his speech to the Reichstag on what was to be its last meeting, Hitler presented the war as a struggle with Jews.

German advances in 1942 brought a large number of Jews under German control, although far fewer than in 1939, 1940 or 1941. In the Northern Caucasus, for example, there were killings of over 1,000 Jews each at Essentuki, Kislovodsk and Piatigorsk. They were killed rather than being used for slave labour, their killing in part excused by the German identification of Jews with 'bandits' opposing their activities, an identification that was inaccurate. The German army played a major role in this killing. The advance into the Caucasus was intended to provide the opportunity for killing even more Jews, including the 'Mountain Jews', which Himmler's 'scholars' had been trying to classify.[66] This killing in the field in 1942 tends to be underrated in the literature on the Holocaust.

At the same time as advancing, German forces slaughtered Jews in the field without sending them to distant extermination camps, which were not readily accessible from eastern Ukraine and beyond, so the same process was seen in areas already under control. In part, this reflected the extent to which, although very murderous, the *Einsatzgruppen* in 1941 had not been sufficiently numerous to kill all Jews. This was the case in particular in Belarus and eastern Poland, which lacked the system of concentration and extermination camps seen further west. For example, at Tuczyn in eastern Poland, where Jews had been confined to a ghetto in the summer of 1942, a local resident described their slaughter that autumn:

> For the span of a few days I observed the massive influx of Ukrainian militiamen and German gendarmes, not SS but the regulars with those brown collars, who cordoned off the ghetto [. . .] The militiamen led the Jews out in large groups to the village of Rzeczyca [. . .] There they

were told to dig ditches, to get undressed, and as they were kneeling along these ditches, they were shot in the back of the head.

The ditches, filled to the brim with bodies, were then covered with lime and a thin layer of earth. The stench from the decaying cadavers which pervaded the entire area was simply indescribable. No one knows from where came the myriad of hungry dogs that circled these massive graves and fed on the human flesh.[67]

In Belarus, ghettos destroyed included Baranowicze on 5 March 1942 and Lachwa on 3 September 1942, the latter after resistance: 3,300 and 1,000 Jews respectively were killed. In eastern Poland, there were major massacres at Brest Litovsk in October and Bialystok in November. In Lithuania, where large-scale killings continued at Ponary,[68] the large Vilnius ghetto was destroyed on 16–22 August 1943: the women, children and old men were murdered there and the younger men taken for slave labour. When I visited it in the mid-1990s, the rebuilt site of the ghetto gave very few indications of its earlier identity.

Jews were also killed in anti-partisan sweeps which became increasingly important and large-scale for the German army in early 1942, with some of them involving several divisions. These sweeps brought the German army into areas it had only passed through perfunctorily, if at all, hitherto and also led to the slaughter of large numbers of civilians who had fled to the forests and marshes. Thus, over 8,000 Jews were killed in 'Operation Swamp Fever' in the Pripet Marshes in August–September 1942. This killing of Jews in anti-partisan operations continued during the war, as these operations served as an opportunity for the slaughter of all judged unacceptable and within a context in which brutality and indiscriminate violence were to the fore.[69]

The slaughter of Jews also played a role in strategic and operational planning by the military. Thus, had the Afrika Korps under Erwin Rommel driven the British from Egypt, as they unsuccessfully attempted to do in July and September

1942, it was intended that it should advance into Palestine, in part in order to destroy the Jewish settlements there before the area was handed over to Italy: there were about 470,000 Jews in Palestine. Earlier, the Germans, had they advanced, would have slaughtered the Jews of another cosmopolitan city, Alexandria. In the event, there was no capture of Alexandria and no invasion of Palestine, while Jewish soldiers, earlier, played a role in strengthening the British position in the Near East, including in the conquest of Vichy-run Syria and Lebanon in 1941. Had the Afrika Korps advanced, it would have found itself in conflict with the Haganah, the Jewish defence organisation. The plans to slaughter the Jews in Palestine, where there were not the alleged pressures of food and deportations encountered in Poland, underlined the truly genocidal character of German policy.

CHAPTER 3

GENOCIDE

Hitler tried hard to give force to his prediction in a speech of 24 February 1943 that: 'it is not the Aryan race that will be destroyed in this war, but rather it is the Jew who will be exterminated.' This prediction was not new, but now German policy was clearly designed to give it immediate effect. Indeed, alongside the slaughter of Jews from elsewhere in Europe, a major effort had been made in 1942 to wipe out Polish Jewry, the largest population under German control. That year, about 1.7 million Jews were killed at the camps at Bełzec, Sobibor and Treblinka alone as part of Aktion Reinhardt (Operation Reinhardt), the attempt to clear the General Government area of Jews judged unfit for labour.

WARSAW

The pace of slaughter was pushed forward from July 1942, after a meeting between Himmler and Hitler on 16 July. All Jews in the General Government were to be killed by the end of 1942.[1] In July–September 1942, 300,000 Jews were deported from Warsaw alone, mostly to the death camp at Treblinka, about sixty-five miles away. The process by which Jews were removed from Warsaw indicated their limited options in the face of SS power. On 22–30 July 1942, the Jewish Police played a significant role in persuading, and forcing, Jews to go to the Umschlagplatz for 'resettlement'. The Jewish Council (*Judenrat*) and the ghetto police, the *Ordnungsdienst*, cooperated voluntarily, believing that the Germans were only after the 'surplus', or unemployed and indigent, Jews, although, on 23 July, Adam Czerniakow, the

Head of the Jewish Council, concerned by his failure to save the orphans, committed suicide. During the first half of August 1942, information and rumours began to trickle into the Warsaw ghetto. There was great confusion about the meaning of the deportations, although there were many stories of the worst happening, and it was no longer credible to believe that somehow normal life would resume at the end of the German occupation. The Jewish Police was now working with the SS and their auxiliaries. From mid-August, apprehension hardened as the truth about Treblinka became known to Warsaw's Jews, and it therefore became more difficult to round up Jews for removal. The Nazi commanders, in turn, relied more on SS units and sheer terror. The Germans used sanctions against the Police so that the role they played was not at all voluntary. If they failed to deliver a certain quota, they and their families were sent to Treblinka. In the last phase, from early September, the Jewish Police played a minor part. In the last days of the action, the 2,000 *Ordnungsdienst* were reduced to about 400.

By the second phase, in the first half of August 1942, the newly formed Jewish underground had declared war on the Jewish Police. On 21 August, leaflets were distributed against the Jewish Police, on the grounds that they had aided the mass execution of Jews, although there is the question of whether any other conduct would have altered the outcome.[2]

RESISTANCE

Underlining the variety of Jewish responses to German persecution, the Jewish Fighting Organisation in Warsaw resolved to resist and, accordingly, stockpiled weapons. Created on 28 July 1942, this organisation was seriously disrupted by German action in August and September 1942. Nevertheless, after armed resistance to forcible removal by Warsaw Jews in January 1943 – an attack on German escorts – the Germans initially withdrew. This was also a period when the Germans needed all available troops to shore up their collapsing Eastern Front. On 2 February, the last German troops besieged in Stalingrad surrendered, while on 13 January the Soviets had launched a new offensive, seeking both to advance on Kharkov, moving into Ukraine, and also to seize Rostov, cutting off German retreat from the Caucasus. The Soviets were swiftly successful, capturing Voronezh (26 January), Kursk (8 February) and Kharkov (16 February).

Benefiting from Soviet exhaustion, Field Marshal Erich von Manstein, however, stabilised the front and counterattacked from 20 February, recapturing Kharkov on 15 March and Belgorod on 18 March. On 19 April 1943, the Germans also launched a campaign to destroy the Warsaw ghetto. Although in a hopeless situation, outnumbered and with few arms, the 1,000 Jews of the Jewish Fighting Organisation and the Jewish Military Union, fighting from bunkers and underground positions, resisted until 16 May, killing about 400 Germans. They received scant support from the Polish Resistance, either directly or in terms of diversionary attacks on the Germans. The following year, the Warsaw Rising was to indicate not only the strength of the Resistance but also its vulnerability to German counter-attack. After the Jewish resistance was suppressed by the Germans in May 1943, the surviving Jews of Warsaw were sent to slaughter in Treblinka and Majdanek, and the synagogue was demolished. This was followed by the flattening of the ghetto.[3]

Jews also employed armed resistance in the Bialystok and Minsk ghettos, as well as in at least eighteen other ghettos, including Cracow, Lublin, Lvóv, Lutsk and Vilnius. It was at the last that the United Partisans Organisation was formed in January 1942 in response to a manifesto by the poet Abba Kovner, which declared that the Germans were aiming to kill all Europe's Jews and called for armed resistance. This was a rejection of the claim that the massacres were a retaliation for alleged Jewish support for the Soviet Union.

Most resistance was unsuccessful, but some Jews were able to escape and to join partisan groups in the countryside. In the face of German attacks, survival rates there were not high, but they were far higher than in the camps.[4] In August 1942, for example, many Jews were able to flee into the partisan-dominated countryside after a partisan brigade defeated the Germans in and near Kosov, in eastern Poland: the brigade included a Jewish unit formed that summer.

On a smaller scale, Jews also resisted elsewhere, including in the extermination camps at Auschwitz, Sobibor and Treblinka. Given the disparity of forces present, it was not surprising, however, that the resistance was suppressed. At Treblinka on 2 August 1943, fifteen guards were killed in a major revolt, and about 400 fled, but most were captured. At Sobibor, on 14 October 1943, a revolt led to the killing of a few guards and the escape of about 600 prisoners, but most were swiftly captured, in part due to the assistance of anti-Semitic Poles. A large-scale revolt at Auschwitz II on 7 October 1944 by the *Sonderkommandos*, the Jews forced to work in disposing of the bodies, led to the blowing up of a crematorium and escape of about 250 inmates, but they were all killed. There were also revolts in the camps at Chelmno and Ponary.

Options only improved as the Nazi regime collapsed, and in Buchenwald the inmates successfully revolted on 11 April 1945 just before the American troops arrived.[5] This independent activity continued as the regime collapsed, not least with guards killed in some camps (e.g. Bergen Belsen) after their power ended. This was resistance eliding into retributive justice.

In the majority of cases, however, the swiftness and completeness of German dominance ensured that there was no possibility of armed Jewish resistance. This helps answer the question of why there was not more resistance. The German practice of brutal reprisals, particularly mass shootings, may also have acted as a restraint. There was, however, not only no proportion between resistance and retaliation but also no suggestion that retaliations ordered from the top of the German regime were intended to be seen by Jews as a cause of compliance. Instead, the drive was to kill Jews.

The explosion of a small incendiary device in the Lustgarten in Berlin on 18 May 1942, the work of the pro-Communist Herbert Baum group, which had Jewish members, led to the execution of the group and the shooting, as a reprisal, of 250 Jewish men held at Sachsenhausen. It also led Hitler to heed Goebbels' advice that the Jews be deported from Berlin, including those involved in munitions production whose retention had been pressed. In 1943, the Warsaw, Treblinka and Sobibor risings led Himmler to press for the killing of Jewish workers, including 18,400 held in Majdanek, slaughtered on 3 November.

Instead of resisting, most Jews, including the *Sonderkommandos*, adjusted to a harsh and destructive environment in which their options were pitifully few: 'The misleading assumption is that people had the power to choose whether or not to be robbed of their dignity in the first place.'[6] German deception also played a role. The Jews being transported to extermination camps or marched out of towns in order to be shot were not told that they were going to be killed. Instead, they were informed that they were being moved to work. Thus, the shower chambers at the extermination camps were presented as a disinfection stage for Jews prior to their allocation to labour tasks, while, before the 'disinfection', clothes and shoes were hung on numbered hooks, implying that they would be retrieved.

Alongside the ending for most of any option for life, there were also, for a comparative few, possibilities for survival, although the opportunities to postpone, even evade, or escape, were all too few. Chance played a role: some potential victims were able to hide or flee, but these were options for very few, and each was made risky by murderous German action. Suicide, which was frequent, was another avenue used by Jews to reject the German attempt to control them and, thus, an act of resistance. So also were attempts to pass on news of the killing to the outside world and, moreover, to record what was happening. Indeed, keeping diaries were seen as a means to testify against, and thus reject, German control. Vandalism and sabotage in industrial works were also important. Resistance of some type was more frequent than is often appreciated. In the ghettos, it occurred more easily than in the camps, as German control, though pernicious, was indirect, and it was possible to maintain central aspects of Jewish culture, especially education and religious observance.[7] The latter was a way to testify belief, the former to ensure continuity, and each affirmed Jewish identity.

The absence of large-scale Jewish resistance was one that was to trouble later commentators, many of whom were confused by the apparent fatalism of the victims, a fatalism that could be linked to strong religious belief or to a failure to understand what was going on. As a result, the resistance that is known is celebrated. Martin Gilbert, in his *Atlas of Jewish History* (1969), produced a map of Jewish partisans and resistance fighters, followed by another on Jewish revolts, in which he described them as 'among the most noble and courageous episodes not only of Jewish, but of world history'. He followed with an *Atlas of the Holocaust* (1988).

The scale of the German oppression was a key factor in limiting resistance. The Holocaust is not the sole instance for which it is pertinent to consider this factor when assessing the extent of Jewish resistance to threats to their communities. For example, pogroms in Russia in the early twentieth century, such as the brutal one at Kishinev in 1903, led to the organisation and arming of Jewish self-defence units, but, in 1919–21, when the Russian Civil War resulted in a fresh bout of pogroms, the White armies that helped carry them out, especially in Ukraine, were relatively so strong that self-defence against them was not an effective option.[8]

There was also very little effort by non-Jews to forcibly disrupt the deportation and killings, although a large number of individuals were responsible for helping Jews to avoid capture by giving them shelter and contributing to their disguise or escape. On 19 April 1943, unusually, a train carrying deportees, in this case en route for Auschwitz, was attacked near Boortmeerbeek, between Mechelen and Leuven in Belgium. Three young men used a hurricane lamp covered with red paper to bring the train to a standstill before employing wire cutters to open one of the goods wagons, releasing seventeen prisoners. Such action, however, was exceptional.

THE PACE OF SLAUGHTER

At the same time, the Germans were driven on not only by their vicious ideology but also by a sense of the challenge posed by the large numbers and extensive areas they now controlled. Thus, paradoxically, the weakness of Nazism played a major role in the Holocaust. Slaughter was intended both to effectuate and to overcome a racist paranoia which ensured that the Germans lacked the willingness and ability to elicit consent from other than the few groups in occupied eastern Europe designated for collaboration, a situation already seen with the army in Serbia in 1941.[9] This sense of challenge also reflected a belief in the potential strength of Judaism, as in October 1940, when the Reich Security Main Office issued a decree banning the emigration of Jews from Poland on the grounds that this threatened a 'lasting spiritual regeneration of world Jewry', by enabling Jewish religious leaders to reach the USA.[10] This decree was instructive in seeing the USA as the key safeguard for Jewry and also because the religious dimension was presented as crucial to Jewish viability.

Hitler's linkage of Jewry and Communism reflected his fears about both. In particular, he was anxious that a Jewish-led and inspired Communism might lead to a repetition of the challenge posed by the Communist risings in Europe in the late 1910s. Agitation then in Germany provided a warning, in Hitler's eyes, as it had led to defeat in the First World War and showed that Germans could be infected by Communism, a threat that Hitler argued required Jewish intermediary action. Fear about the internal threat allegedly posed by Jews was a response to any sign of opposition with which Jews could be linked – for example, the small explosion in the Lustgarten in Berlin on 18 May 1942, which was the responsibility of the Herbert Baum group. Indeed, this attempt and the assassination of Heydrich in Prague (which was not carried out by Jews) appears to have encouraged Hitler and Himmler to press on to complete the 'Final Solution'.[11]

It was not only Polish Jews that were to be slaughtered, with the ghettos in Cracow and Lvóv destroyed in March and June 1943 respectively. The extermination camps in Poland were also used for Jews deported from elsewhere in Europe, with 'evacuation to the East' employed by the Germans as a euphemism for slaughter. In June 1943, Himmler ordered the destruction of the remaining ghettos in Belarus and the Baltic republics, with the deportation of Jews to the extermination camps. The Jews of Belgium, France and the Netherlands, already rounded up and held in camps (Malines/Mechelen, Drancy, Westerbork), were deported to be killed in the extermination camps in Poland, as well as in Kovno and Riga. Deportations from western Europe had become more important in 1942, with French Jews deported to Auschwitz from March, Dutch from 14 July, Belgian from 4 August and Norwegian from October. Greece followed in March 1943, and Italy that October. Most of the French and Dutch Jews killed in the war were slaughtered that year.

In most cases, gas chambers were used in killing the Jews, but at Chelmno, Riga, Zemun near Belgrade and Maly Trostenets, an extermination camp near Minsk, gas vans were used. At Bełzec, Maly Trostenets, Sobibor and Treblinka, the vast majority of Jews were killed as soon as they arrived, even if they were able to work. Only a small number of very fit Jews were kept, under heavy guard in special detachments, in order to help sort the effects of the slaughtered or to move their bodies for cremation. In turn, they were killed.

SLAVE LABOUR

When Auschwitz II (or Birkenau) and Majdanek were established in 1942, however, there was a different priority. They were both concentration camps and extermination camps. By then, it was clear that the war would not be rapidly settled with a German victory, as had seemed possible, and to optimists likely, in the autumn of 1941. Instead, Germany was now at war with a Soviet Union that had been capable of mounting a major winter counter-offensive in 1941–2, as well as with the industrial might of the USA. This suggested that the conflict would be attritional, which put a focus on industrial production and, thus, on labour.

Auschwitz had a place in this new military and geopolitical prospectus, because, unlike the other extermination camps, it was located in a key economic zone, that of coal-rich Upper Silesia. Aside from the coal mines, this was a major area of industrial location and one that required a large slave-labour force, not least because the Germans were increasingly conscripting their own men for the army. Auschwitz, thus, acted as a nexus of the cooperation between Himmler and Albert Speer, Minister for Armaments and Munitions from February 1942, that was to be so important to the German ability to sustain the conflict in the face of American and Soviet power.

The large plant constructed near Auschwitz of the industrial concern I.G. Farben, for the manufacture of synthetic rubber and oil, was one of the largest German industrial projects. This Buna Works deliberately drew on local slave labour, which Himmler used to persuade the company to locate there, as well as local coal.[12] Moreover, the exhausted nature of the workers, and specifically the impact of the daily march to the Buna Works, led the managers to have Auschwitz III constructed nearby in late 1942. The SS had not been keen on this additional facility, but they accepted this outcome, guarding what, in effect, was a private concentration camp. Workers who fell sick and did not recover speedily were sent to the gas chambers at Auschwitz II, and the arduous and cruel nature of work and life in such camps was such that many fell sick.

If Auschwitz represented the culmination of Nazi extermination policies, it is also pertinent to note that the use of slave labour there was the end result in another narrative of the brutal treatment of Jews. Forced labour had become an important theme from 1938, not least because in Germany, Nazi persecution, in seizing Jewish businesses and closing down Jewish employment opportunities, made it possible to direct Jewish labour. Having made Jews unemployed, they were given state welfare only on condition that they accepted employment in difficult and demeaning conditions that were designed to remove them from fellow Germans. Thus, Jews were made to work on processing rubbish or in projects in which they were segregated in camps. From 1939, this programme expanded, in response to the need for non-Jewish German manpower for the Army. The Reich Labour Office recruited Jews for skilled work, a process that continued to be important, and not under SS control, until large-scale deportations from Germany occurred in 1941. Even after that, some Jewish workers were retained in Germany by influential employers, for example the armaments division of the German Army, until they were finally all seized for deportation in February 1943. That June, Germany was declared 'judenfrei'.

In practice, possibly 10,000–12,000 German Jews had gone into hiding, of whom 3,000–5,000 survived the war. Known as U-boats (a reference to submarines), they faced hazardous conditions. While some Germans provided shelter, in many cases knowing that those they sheltered were Jews, others denounced hidden Jews, for whom the Gestapo searched. Hiding in dangerous circumstances, short of food and without medical attention, other Jews died. Some were killed by Allied bombing, while, for others, it provided an opportunity to explain their loss of papers identifying them as Jews.

The use of Jewish labour was a more important issue, as it became clear that the war would be a difficult one. Jewish labour was significant in both the Warthegau part of Poland, which was annexed to Germany, and the General Government of Poland. Aside from the prominent role of the SS, large numbers of Jews were used for forced labour in Poland and under labour agencies that were not under SS control; although in Upper Silesia, the eventual site of Auschwitz, the SS controlled and profited from Jewish forced labour from the outset. SS control of Jewish labour elsewhere became dominant, as the 'Jewish question' moved towards the Final Solution, with the allocation of Jews for slaughter or work a central means and display of SS power. This allocation was increasingly insistent and immediate for the Jews in Poland, as well as for those deported there.[13]

In some respects, as with the slaughter, forced labour was a continuum that did not only include Jews. Millions of foreign workers, especially Soviet, Polish and French, were brought to Germany, while, elsewhere in occupied Europe, workers were forced to work in their home countries in often brutal conditions, in order to produce resources for Germany. Aside from prisoners of war, 5.7 million foreign workers were registered in the Greater German Reich in August 1944; combined with the prisoners of war, they provided half the workforce in agriculture and in the manufacture of munitions.[14] Moreover, German prisoners categorised as asocial or social misfits were allocated to the SS from 1942 and deliberately worked to death. Many were petty thieves, the work-shy, tramps and alcoholics.

This perspective might seem to diminish the specific issue of Jewish suffering. Such an argument can particularly be taken if the focus is on 1940 or early 1941, not least because it was not clear at that stage that this forced labour would not be the final solution for Jews, at least until forced emigration could be resumed at the close of the war. However, in the case of Jews, although SS attitudes with regard to the choice between murder and slave work moved back and forth from 1941, there was to be a major shift, in 1941–2, towards both killing at once and working the remainder to death. The latter, moreover, was presented as an explicit goal and not as a by-product of exploitation.

In contrast, the need for the labour of prisoners led the Germans to cease being so murderous to Soviet prisoners in October 1941, although their working conditions, which, from 1944, included less than 1,000 calories of food daily (in comparison to the official German civilian ration of 2,100 calories), were such as to lead to high death rates, and knowingly so. However, Jewish prisoners of war were automatically slaughtered.

The labour force at Auschwitz was not simply Jewish, but Jews were important in it. As a result, although those deemed unable to work hard were gassed on arrival, fit men and women were selected for labour. With a serial number tattooed on their forearm, subsequently an emblematic feature of the suffering, they were sent to crowded barracks where they lived while they worked. Most were subsequently killed, gassed when ill, or worked to death. The treatment of Jews, both by SS guards and by non-Jewish prisoner-overseers, most of whom were convicts, was generally worse, indeed far worse, than that of other prisoners.[15] The relatively harsher treatment of Jews was seen across the entire system of Nazi brutality and incarceration, not simply in issues of life and death but also, for example, in the opportunities for music-making in the concentration camps.[16]

The deliberate and deadly neglect of Jewish workers is a major reason why the term 'slave labour' is problematic, not least because it can be made to imply a comparison with other systems of slavery, such as those of African slaves in the European, Islamic and, indeed, African worlds. Such a comparison is inappropriate as these slaves had a clear financial value, expressed in sale and purchase, and, for that reason, as well as to fulfil productive tasks, it was important to keep them alive. Indeed, there was added value from slaves having children, and castration of slaves was only normal in the Islamic world. Some racists, such as the Nazi Manfred Sell in his *Die schwarze Völkerwanderung* (*The Black Migration*, 1940), opposed the slave trade because of the possibilities it offered for intermarriage and deracination.

Nor is the comparison with governmental slave systems, such as that of Communist North Korea, pertinent. Such comparisons may be relevant up to a point in the case of much of the forced labour deployed by the Germans, and also capture the emphasis on productivism not capitalism, goods not profit; but, in the case of Jews, there was a distinct genocidal intent. Slave labour thus describes the very one-sided nature of control experienced by Jews, but does not suggest any equivalence with other slave systems.

Profit from Jews was not simply sought in the form of slave labour. A large number of German companies also profited from the construction, maintenance and supply of the camps. Some, such as Topf and Sons, crematorium specialists of Erfurt, had a readily apparent role, but hundreds of companies were in fact involved, as were their bankers, suppliers and insurers.[17] This underlines the extent of German knowledge of, and profit in, the Holocaust. Profit and knowledge were frequently linked. Auschwitz was also a major transport centre and, like Chelmno, an annexed part of Germany, not a site in the supposedly obscure 'East'. Knowledge of the slaughter could scarcely have been limited. Moreover, the bodies of the murdered were burnt in the open air at Auschwitz until the crematoria came into service in 1943. Burnt flesh has a distinctive smell. Families visited or lived with SS guards and presumably observed and understood at least part of what was going on.

Aside from providing labour, the system at Auschwitz was also designed to ensure that there were no Jewish children. Nearly 1.5 million Jews under fourteen were killed in the Holocaust. It is the accounts of the slaughter of children that are most affecting. In order to ensure that there were no Jewish children, Himmler pressed doctors to develop an easy method of sterilisation.

This was a brutal example of the conflation between Nazism and medical murder. It was not the only aspect of a more general perversion of reason. Other sciences were also used to forward Nazi themes. For example, the anthropologist Bruno Beger was sent to Auschwitz in 1943 to undertake research on Jewish skulls, to forward which eighty-six Jews were killed. Medical experiments, such as those by Josef Mengele at Auschwitz and Kurt Heissemeyer's injection of Jewish children (aged five to twelve) to further his work on tuberculosis, were also cruel and totally unnecessary. The role of 'experts' on race policy in German planning and administration was another aspect of the extent to which an allegedly rational dimension characterised German policy towards Jews. In practice, this was the very opposite of the case, and both ends and means were murderous in intent and barbaric in character, however rational their apparent language.

Auschwitz II was solely for Jews and Gypsies, an aspect of the way in which they were treated more harshly than other victims of the Germans. Alongside the huts and barracks, Auschwitz II contained gas chambers and linked crematoria. It was expanded rapidly after Himmler inspected the camp on 17–18 July 1942. This camp was fed by train with Jews from throughout occupied Europe, the first from Slovakia arriving on 26 March 1942. Prominent groups killed there included the large community of over 40,000 from Salonika, a key step in German anti-Semitic violence in Greece.[18] Italian diplomatic representations on behalf of some of the Salonika Jews were rejected. This was also a fundamental blow in the decline of Salonika as a multi-ethnic community, a character that had helped give it a particular vibrancy and cultural importance.

Aside from the specific viciousness of German intentions, the position of Jews, segregated by the Germans in ghettos, made them far more vulnerable to attack, deportation and murder than the non-Jewish population, particularly if the latter were dispersed across the countryside. This helped explain the contrast in levels of resistance, but, however much levels of race violence were different, a common feature was the total failure of the Germans to negotiate any outcome, or seek any meaningful compromise, with those they despised.

This also helped ensure their more general failure. Particularly from 1942, the German inability to deal with the practical difficulties stemming from insufficient resources, over-extended front lines and the strength of their opponents' war-making and fighting quality owed much to the extent to which the Nazi regime had lost its way, with decision-making warped by ideological megalomania and strategic wishful thinking.[19] The Germans were not alone in failing to consider adequately the nature of the likely response to their policy and in not matching operational planning to feasible strategic goals, but their war-making proved particularly flawed under both heads. The harsh treatment of the conquered, not least, but not only, the slaughter of Jews, was a central aspect of this megalomania and wishful thinking, as it presupposed that cooperation was unnecessary and that a new order did not need to be grounded in acceptance, however coerced.

Yet, this critical point is unhelpful in this context, because it presupposes for Nazi Germany a functional end and analysis for what was in fact ideological, and also with this ideological dimension far from being an optional add-on. To point out, as I did, when having to listen in Afghanistan in 1976 to the remarks of a German veteran that Germany might have done better had they not turned on Jews served my purpose of riling him, but was also knowingly foolish as that attack was a central aspect of German policy. Indeed, it took precedence over the tensions and rivalries between German agencies because they cooperated in the slaughter, even though that made it more difficult to fund the slave labour to pursue the goal of constructing a new Europe.[20]

The killing went on to the close of the war. Although, in August 1941, refugee Polish Jews were detained by the Hungarian Police and handed over to the SS for slaughter, it was not until the summer of 1944 that the Hungarian Jews were killed: from 15 May, 435,000 Jews were deported by the Germans to Auschwitz. Some were used for labour there, but about three-quarters were killed at once as the result of a very high rate of deportation and slaughter: an average of over 8,000 daily. Indeed, a rail spur was constructed so that the trains could go directly to Auschwitz II. This rail spur helped reflect and ensure the preponderant role of this camp in the killing. Already, from the spring of 1943, when large new crematoria there came into operation, the mass factory killing at Auschwitz II was at an unprecedented rate. Partly as a result, other extermination camps were closed down, while facilities at Auschwitz II were maintained.

The lack of opportunity provided by the attitude of the Hungarian Government, ensured that there was no comprehensive slaughter of Hungarian Jews until 1944. The deportations from Hungary occurred after Germany occupied the country on 19 March 1944 in order to prevent its defection to the Allies, a potential defection that reflected the collapsing position of the Germans on the Eastern Front and also so that the Germans could make more effective use of the Hungarian economy.[21]

The flow of the conflict was indeed moving strongly against the Germans. In the right-bank Dnieper/Ukraine campaign, launched on 24 December 1943, the Soviets proved very successful. Breakthrough attacks in Ukraine in March 1944 forced the Germans back, and in April–May the Crimea was conquered. Hitherto, Soviet advances had largely been achieved without the encirclement and destruction of German forces, but, from June 1944, there was to be much more success in pushing encirclements through to destruction, in large part because Soviet forces had acquired the means and doctrine to fulfil these goals. This was not simply an advance on one axis but one along the entire front, from the Black Sea to the Baltic, as well as in Finland. Soviet advances increased the sense of threat on the part of the Germans.

The treatment of Hungarian Jews, however, reflected the continuing synergy between Hitler's war strategy and the war against Jews, and his attempt to ensure a synergy. Hitherto, despite serious anti-Semitic acts, the Hungarians, who were allied to Germany and had joined in the war with the Soviet Union in 1941, had refused to carry out a variant of the Final Solution, but, once occupied, Hungarian officials cooperated eagerly, motivated, as in part the Germans were, by the benefits sought from the seizure of Jewish assets. The post-war Communist regime, typically, refused to return the seized assets.[22] Elsewhere also, the seizure of assets played a role in encouraging active cooperation with the Holocaust. This was the case, for example, with the bounty hunters responsible for the capture of nearly 40,000 Dutch Jews, most of whom, having been transported to Poland, were killed in Auschwitz or Sobibor.[23]

The seizure of assets paid the costs of the Holocaust, as German officials were keen to calculate and demonstrate to each other. This seizure was also designed to aid the Nazi economy, an economy under tremendous pressure from the growing strains of a war that was becoming more difficult as the Soviet Union and USA deployed their economic strength. As such, the Holocaust was an aspect of the attempt to transform the socio-economic structure of eastern Europe. This does not make the vicious policy an aspect of some sort of perverted modernisation but, rather, underlines the extent to which part of the context for the mass slaughter was the drive for plunder on the part of a regime that, despite its preposterous claims to culture, was very primitive in its methods.

The distribution among the German population of goods seized from Jews was designed to help bind further the public to the regime as well as to provide the public with compensation for the burdens of the war, not least Anglo-American bombing. In July 1943, Hamburg was heavily damaged, and, that November, the air offensive on Berlin, which was to last until the end of March 1944, was launched. The distribution of seized goods indicated the range of the spoil system, led to pressure from below for more plunder and underlined the extent to which Jews were being mistreated. Clothes taken from Jews were provided to Germans who had lost everything in Allied bombing. Watches taken from Crimean Jews were used for the military.

The plunder was a matter not only of the seizure of the goods, jobs and property of Jews but also the use of their bodies. Personal jewellery, such as wedding rings, was seized, as were gold fillings from teeth, which were extracted with pliers. Moreover, the hair and skin of the dead was used. The bodies were burnt to ashes, which were thrown away or used as fertiliser. The detailed lists kept of the goods that were plundered, both in the camps and in other stages of the treatment of the Jews, indicated a concern to profit as well as a conviction that such records were acceptable as well as necessary. Yet, although such listing may seem to show administrative sophistication, that was far from the case.

The use of slave labour was also an aspect of a primitive plunder of resources, not least because it was obtained as part of a system that included the destruction of skilled manpower and, more generally, the deliberate elimination of the Jewish role in the economies of Europe. This slave plunder became more important to the Germans as the war continued and that, in turn, became a more prominent factor in the treatment of Jews.[24] With German forces no longer advancing after late 1942, there was no more prospect of obtaining forced labour, Jewish or non-Jewish, by conquest, and that meant that existing sources of slave labour had to be used more carefully, including the undesirable categories of Jews and Russian prisoners of war.

Nevertheless, care is a very relative term. Jews who were moved to labour camps were treated in a particularly brutal fashion, and, to ensure that they could be, they were segregated in distinct teams. The food was limited and poor quality; the barracks were not heated; sanitary facilities were limited; the clothing was inadequate; and the work was hard. Shifts were long; there was no concern with safety; many of the workers lacked relevant experience; and there were frequent beatings and shootings. Those who were ill or who collapsed through exhaustion were shot.

This was true not only of Jews working under the control of the SS, but also of those working under other German agencies, not least the Organisation Todt (OT), which was the key construction agency for the German war machine. Headed, from 1942, by Albert Speer, the OT was responsible for the underground facilities built to safeguard weapons production from Allied air attack. Jewish workers were sent in 1944 from Auschwitz and directly from Budapest to build facilities at Kaufering and Mühldorf, which were satellite camps of Dachau, near Munich. The workers were mistreated, many were killed, and, in September–October, the remaining Jews were sent to Auschwitz for gassing. The following year, Jews from Auschwitz were sent to the Mittelbau concentration camp, in order to work in the underground Nordhausen factory manufacturing V-weapons. A large number of Jewish slave labourers were employed in private industry, where death rates were also high.

Both as individuals and as a group, Jews suffered what Germans, albeit to very differing degrees, intended as a deliberate retribution for their Judaism. Sadism, thus, was supposedly sanctified in the cause of racial justice and necessity. The imposition of suffering thus appeared a duty as much as it clearly was a pleasure to the large number of sadists whom total power called forth.

The European assault on Jewry included a deliberate destruction of Jewish knowledge, culture and locations, for example prayer books and synagogues, both of which were destroyed. Cemeteries were not so much desecrated, as still happens at the hands of neo-Nazis today, but destroyed, with the gravestones used for construction purposes. In Salonika, this was for road-building and the creation of a military swimming pool. There were also assaults on the memory and culture of other communities, for example the German and Soviet treatment of Ukraine, part of a larger mistreatment of the Ukrainians,[25] but not on this scale. The Yiddish culture of Eastern European Jewry was particularly hard hit, and it is appropriate that the Holocaust is known in Yiddish as the *Churban* (Destruction).

The Jewish role in European culture was also destroyed. This ranged from the attempt to extirpate the major Jewish contribution to European science and the arts to the renaming of buildings and streets that carried Jewish names. The burning of books was particularly symbolic. There was also an attempt to obliterate the legacy of philo-Semitism. Thus, in 1942, the Germans destroyed the statue at Lunéville, in Lorraine, of Abbé Henri Grégoire (1756–1837), a key figure in late Enlightenment thought who had made efforts on behalf of the Jewish emancipation.

Having demonised Jews, Germans, like other anti-Semites before them, were in the dangerous position of feeling both strength and weakness towards them. A belief that Communism was led by Jews helped make the latter appear more diabolical. The killing of Jews was excused by some perpetrators, particularly among Hitler's allies, such as Ukrainian and Lithuanian nationalists, by reference to the alleged Jewish role during Soviet occupation, as well as with reference to Communist atrocities – alleged or projected. Germans were able to plan and execute a barbarous rolling massacre that reflected the one-sided nature of a power relationship, in which the perpetrators of slaughter were in no physical danger.[26]

As Hitler's reliance on will was revealed as inadequate in German war-making, not least with this reliance leading to a failure to set sensible military and political goals, so the slaughter of Jews was left as a vicious way to convince himself that he still had will-power and could achieve something with it, as he felt he had to do so. Fearing, from the late summer of 1942, that final victory might be, if it was not already, out of reach, Hitler was determined to fight on in order to destroy Europe's Jews, as well as to achieve a moral victory for his concept of the German people.[27]

Furthermore, increased difficulties led to the radicalisation of the military, as Nazi commitment came to play a greater role in appointments and promotions. After the unsuccessful July bomb plot of 1944, in which a group of German officers failed to kill Hitler and to overthrow his regime, the bulk of the military command rallied to Hitler, and Nazification was pushed by General Heinz Guderian, the new Chief of the General Staff. Moreover, the repression of disaffection and of any sign of 'defeatism' by the Nazi surveillance system, presided over by Himmler, helped ensure that there was no repetition of the German collapse of 1918, while the judicial system willingly responded to Hitler in dramatically increasing the harshness of its sentences.[28] Reflecting the mobilisation for total war ordered in July 1944, the *Volkssturm*, a compulsory local defence militia for men between sixteen and sixty, was placed under the control of Himmler and Martin Bormann, not the Army. This militia was designed to inflict casualties on the advancing Allies such that their morale – it was believed – could not tolerate, and also to indoctrinate the civilian population for a total struggle.

Indeed, it has been argued that, imbued by Nazi ideological assumptions, the German leadership, or at least part of it, continued to believe that it could win even after the summer of 1944. Victory was held to depend on stronger will, as well as on new technology, such as rockets and jet aircraft, to be built in underground factories in murderous conditions by forced labour, and improved tanks and submarines. This will was seen as within the racial potential of the Germans.[29] The counter-offensive launched by the Germans in the Ardennes on 16 December 1944, which led to the Battle of the Bulge, was designed to lead to the defeat of the Anglo-American armies and possibly to the collapse of their will to fight, which was a serious misjudgement of German prospects. This provides another context within which the continued slaughter of Jews appeared pertinent: not only to create a Jew-free Europe if Germany lost, but also one if they won.

The number of Jews who could be killed, however, diminished as the war continued. In part, this was because so many had already been slaughtered, and this was the key element in Poland. Deportations from there to the extermination camps, however, continued into 1944, as the Germans slaughtered those they had already confined. Over 67,000 Jews were deported from Łódź to Auschwitz II in the summer of 1944, the ghetto being liquidated at the end of August in accordance with orders from Himmler on 10 June. In response to this policy, nearby Chelmno was also reopened.[30]

More generally, the frenetic, yet methodical, pace of the killings in 1944 reflected the collapse of the German Empire, but also the still potent determination to kill Jews. In their breakthrough attacks in Ukraine in March and April 1944, the Soviets drove the Germans back across the Bug, Dniester and Prut rivers. Operation Bagration, the attack launched on Army Group Centre on 23 June, led to the conquest of Belarus and the pushing back of the Germans into central Poland. Lublin was captured by the Soviets on 23 July and Lvóv on 27 July. Further north, they took Tallinn on 22 September and Riga on 15 October. Romania surrendered to the Soviet Union on 23 August (and had already downplayed its anti-Semitic policies), Finland signed an armistice on 2 September, and, threatened by the advancing Red Army, Bulgaria declared war on Germany on 5 September. On 11 October, Hungary concluded a preliminary armistice with the Soviet Union.

Yet still, Germans continued their killing and, indeed, on 26 May 1944, Hitler pressed the necessity of doing so in a speech to National Socialist guidance officers. Aside from the slaughter of the Łódź Jews, 10,000 Slovak Jews, for example, were deported to Auschwitz in August–October 1944, while deportations thither from the 'model' concentration camp at Theresienstadt, whose inmates were initially supposed to receive better treatment, continued until the end of October. On the distant Aegean island of Rhodes, an Italian possession until seized by the Germans in September 1943, Jewish women and children were seized in July 1944, in order to be shipped to Piraeus and then taken by train to Auschwitz. Thus, as the farthest tendrils of the Reich collapsed, Jews had to be killed first. It was only on 28 November that there were the last gassings at Auschwitz, and then only in response to the Soviet threat to Upper Silesia. In practice, however, in the face of growing casualties and logistical difficulties after the major advance of the summer, and in response to stiffening German resistance, the Soviet offensive stalled in late 1944.

The driving back of the Germans was also important in reducing the number of potential victims for slaughter. In some areas, this driving-back meant that Jews with partisan groups or in hiding could now come out. That, however, could also expose them to the hostile attentions of the Soviet NKVD, which was intensely suspicious of partisans and those who might be associated with them, not least in Poland.

Other areas where large numbers of Jews had survived were reconquered, most obviously much of Italy in 1943–4 and France in 1944. The German commander in Paris surrendered on 25 August, three days after the last transport of Jews left France for Auschwitz, and on 3 September, Brussels was captured. Rome was captured by American forces on 5 June 1944 and Florence on 4 August. These areas and cities, therefore, were no longer open to German pressure for deportation nor to the possibility that this might become more effective. Changes in allegiance by Germany's allies, or the prospect of such changes, similarly lessened the possibility of any expansion or intensification of the Holocaust. This was the case in Bulgaria and Finland, although, in Hungary, the Germans seized the initiative for long enough to slaughter large numbers.

It was not only killing that continued until the end of the war, particularly mass shootings, but also a neglect of those held in the camps that led to high rates of death through malnutrition and epidemics. The last proved particularly serious. Meanwhile, the Soviet advance led to the overrunning of the extermination camps or their sites: Maly Trostinets, Sobibor, Majdanek and Treblinka being captured in Operation Bagration, the major offensive in the summer of 1944, and Auschwitz on 27 January 1945.

The Germans, however, razed camps to the ground when they finished using them. Although they did not have time at Majdanek to destroy the evidence of their activities, this happened, for example, to Sobibor and Treblinka after they closed in November 1943. This destruction was an aspect of German deception and one pushed forward by the extent to which the war was no longer moving in their favour. At the end of November 1944, Himmler ordered the destruction of the gas chambers at Auschwitz. The SS also destroyed deportation schedules, which made it difficult to reach agreement on the number of victims. In 1943–4, in order to destroy evidence, there was an unearthing of victims who, once killed, had been buried rather than burned, and a burning of their bodies, for example at Ponary near Vilnius from September 1943 to April 1944. On 16 February 1945, a decree ordered the destruction of files dealing with the Holocaust, in order to prevent them from falling into Allied hands.

Already, at Krasnodar in July 1943, the first trial by the Soviets on the charge of participation in German war crimes made public a case of mass murder of Jews. Those convicted were publicly executed.[31] Such action did not lead the Germans to cease killing, but it encouraged them to destroy evidence, although that was not always done. The 'execution book' at Mauthausen concentration camp contained 36,318 entries. Trials in the Soviet Union, combined with a conviction of Jewish influence in each of the Allies, helped ensure that Nazi leaders felt that they were committed to the Holocaust and that there was no turning back from their destiny.

The Allied insistence on unconditional surrender, enunciated at Casablanca in January 1943, made compromise unlikely and underlined this sense of committal. It would, however, be foolish to blame the continued German commitment to the Holocaust in some way on the Allied insistence on unconditional surrender, whether or not that blame is an example of a German narrative of victimhood. In practice, the German commitment was centred on ideological fervour and an unwillingness to accept failure, and both were seen in the willingness to continue fighting and take very heavy casualties. The movement of Jews from areas about to be conquered by Soviet forces was carried out so that their forced labour and the genocide could both continue. That movement from Auschwitz began on 18 January 1945. Although a few risked death by escaping in the chaos, large numbers were shot or died during these moves: aside from the sadism of the guards, especially towards those deemed stragglers, the prisoners were forced to endure a punishing walk on low rations and with little night-time shelter. Their scanty clothes did not keep out the effects of a very harsh winter. The provision systems that had supported the concentration camps, however harshly, collapsed.

Killing, freezing, exhaustion and hunger combined to kill large numbers. The numbers who died on these marches is unclear, in part because the record-keeping apparatus of German brutality was collapsing, but the figure for Jews, who were the majority on the marches, may be between 250,000 and close to 400,000. Aside from marchers, many Jews were put into open rail cars where they froze to death, not least as the trains were frequently stranded in open sidings and their 'passengers' left without food. Some trains, however, carried Jews to concentration camps in Germany such as Buchenwald and Dachau. Jews who were too ill to take part in the marches were slaughtered.[32]

Alongside killing, which included by shooting, bludgeoning and burning alive, there was disease both on the marches and in the camps. Like many others there, Anne Frank died in Belsen of typhus.

Moreover, the killing at this point, both on the marches and in the camps, when victory was impossible for Germany, indicated not pointlessness but, instead, the centrality of race warfare to Nazi policy, particularly as additional options were closed down by defeat. In January and February 1945, plans were still being drawn up to deport Jews in mixed marriages and the children of such marriages to the surviving camps.

As in the concentration camps, Jews were treated more harshly than others involved in the death marches, such as prisoners of war. This treatment in large part reflected the views and determination of officials acting on their own initiative, as the central impetus behind slaughter slackened with the growing collapse of the regime. Killing and maltreatment against Jews on these marches continued into April 1945, as in that from the Helmbrechts work camp to Prachatice in Czechoslovakia, and even into the early days of May.

This reflected the extent to which Nazi activity continued, despite Hitler first being surrounded by Soviet forces in Berlin (25 April) and then, on 30 April, committing suicide as they fought their way through to his bunker. In his 'Political Testament', dictated the previous day, a raving Hitler held Jews responsible for the war and thus for the destructive bombing of Germany, and also for the very killing meted out to Jews. Similarly, even at this late stage, and underlining the role of ideological fervour, German field forces carried out massacres in the field, for example of captured Polish troops, and also tried to break through Soviet forces to relieve Hitler in Berlin.

THE GERMAN PUBLIC AND THE HOLOCAUST

From the outset of the killing, not all German commanders, troops and officials responded to Jews in a brutal fashion, and those who did not comply were not punished. There is no record of anyone being punished for refusing to join the *Einsatzgruppen* or the SS units active in the camps. Similarly, although in most cases, companies sought concentration-camp prisoners as slave labour, those which did not were not punished. This underlines the extent of complicity in the Holocaust. Moreover, beside the executioners, there were planners, organisers and apologists.[33]

Furthermore, in Germany and Austria, local people who did not join in the persecution of camp inmates and, instead, helped them were generally not punished; unlike in eastern Europe, where the punishments were savage and often immediate. This variety in response highlights the issue of individual responsibility and removes from the guilty the argument that they were in some way passive victims of an all-powerful system and ideology. Knowledge and complicity are issues because Hitler did not announce the 'Final Solution' publicly. So also is indoctrination, such as that of the young in the Hitler Youth or the League of German Girls.[34]

A valuable case study makes it clear that the people of the German city of Osnabrück (from which the major deportation of Jews occurred on 13 December 1941) knew of the persecution of Jews that was happening, even if only a minority took part in anti-Semitic acts, and the same is true of the Austrian town of Mauthausen near Linz, near where there was a concentration camp.[35] More generally, widespread public acceptance of a policy of social exclusion also affected those with at least one Jewish grandparent.[36] At the same time, intermarriage complicated the response of many individuals. It ensured that some Jews were helped by fellow Germans, but this did not lead to an openness to the plight of others. At the individual level, however, the wartime career of Oskar Schindler, the subject of a 1980 book, Thomas Kennedy's *Schindler's Ark*, and a very successful 1993 film, Steven Spielberg's *Schindler's List*, exemplifies the possibilities for individual action. Initially as a means for profit, the corrupt Schindler looked after a Jewish labour force, whom he then took expensive and risky steps to save from slaughter. Schindler's strategy worked during the period in which some SS agencies placed more emphasis on slave work than on murder.

A lack of knowledge was pleaded by many Germans after the end of the war. In some cases, this can be shown to be inaccurate. Leni Riefenstahl, who had made key Nazi propaganda films in 1933–6, continued to be a propaganda filmmaker during the Second World War. She was subsequently to deny knowledge of Nazi killings, but the evidence reveals that she was a liar. This has been proved in two cases. In 1939, she saw the killing of thirty Jewish civilians in the town of Konskie after they had dug a mass grave in the town square, a very public act of slaughter. Riefenstahl denied being there, but photographs by a German soldier prove the contrary. In 1940, Riefenstahl used Roma (Gypsy) children from a transit camp as extras, after which they were returned to the camp. She subsequently declared that they all survived the war, when in fact most were killed at Auschwitz.[37]

Clearly, the extent of knowledge varied. Nevertheless, Germans were not segregated during the war: soldiers, in particular, came home on leave, and knowledge or rumours of killings in the east and of the ghettos were widespread. The extermination camps were far less in the forefront of attention, but rumours, nevertheless, circulated widely. The railway workers who transported Jews did not live in a vacuum. Moreover, Jews who worked in public places, as Victor Klemperer (who was married to a non-Jew) did in Dresden, were clearly discriminated against and thus mistreated, and then many disappeared as they were deported. Furthermore, arrests and deportations were often carried out in public, and government propaganda unequivocally presented Jews as enemies to be destroyed. Germans internalised this by ignoring neighbours and others who were Jewish.[38]

The Jewish threat became more, not less, prominent in German propaganda in the closing years of the war. Jews were seen as the source not only of Communism, but also of the British and American plutocracies allegedly responsible for bombing Germany. SD reports indicated that air raids were seen amongst the public as a reaction to German persecution of Jews, a belief that indicated the misleading extent to which Jews were believed to influence, if not dictate, American and British policy. That so many Germans thought the air offensive was a retribution for anti-Semitic measures indicates that they knew what was being done to Jews, if not in detail, then at least in its outlines.

In the spring of 1943, over 70 per cent of radio broadcasts focused on aspects of this supposed Jewish threat, including the likely fate for Germans if Jews took their revenge through the Allies. Thus, Germany was to be united under the threat of Jewish atrocities, a bizarre inversion of the actual fate of Jews. This approach not only looked towards post-war German victimhood, but also testified to the extent to which it was difficult to be able to listen to the radio and not understand that the regime saw itself as involved in an existential struggle with Jews.[39]

From a different direction, the widespread willingness to serve Nazi goals and, in doing so, fulfil a personal role, by denouncing others, including spouses and friends,[40] denunciations that helped the Gestapo in their campaign to catch Jews,[41] suggests that more people would have taken an active part against Jews had they been asked to do so. In mid-1944, Goebbels received a number of unsolicited letters suggesting that Jews be used as human shields within German cities to deter bombing, and that Jews be hanged in reprisal for Germans killed in the bombing. This has been presented as aspects of a more general moral brutalisation of German society, although the extent to which anti-Semitic legislation and violence had been accepted, both before the war and in its early years, suggests that this brutalisation was already present in the years before the war went wrong for the Nazis and encouraged further hatreds.[42] The bombing also encouraged Hitler in his flights of anti-Semitic paranoia, as he blamed it on Jews.

That those who were asked to become killers mostly did so reflects the widespread nature of Nazi loyalties, racist assumptions and willingness to participate in or, at the least, condone killing.[43] Racial-eugenicist ideas were widely held. They were not only common among intellectuals but also widely diffused in society, not least because, at least in some form, they proved readily understandable and could also be assimilated to existing prejudices such as anti-Semitism.

Such ideas were almost a staple of Western thought in the period, with characteristics believed to pertain to particular races, as in the British idea about Indian 'Martial Races' who should be recruited: Gurkhas, Sikhs or Rajputs, but not generally shorter and darker southern Indians. Eugenicist ideas reflected anxiety about the consequences of competition between the races and also about the 'racial health' of particular nations. In particular, urbanisation and its alleged consequences were believed to challenge or compromise racial health, and cosmopolitanism to threaten racial identity. This led to a widespread support for eugenics on the Left, for example in Sweden, as well as on the Right. Resulting policies included the incarceration of those deemed physically and/or medically unfit and also measures to prevent them having children, including, in some contexts, sterilisation.

This was violation and violence, and if it was a violence totally different in nature and scale to that of the Nazis, it also helped explain how barriers against cooperating in the killing were overcome as officials and others adapted willingly, and even enthusiastically, to the murderous treatment of Jews. Moreover, many came to see this brutal treatment as a moral duty that was necessary to the destiny of the German race, and thus to European civilisation. Indeed, those in the field who opted not to kill did not necessarily take this course because of opposition to the idea of the slaughter. Frequently, instead, it was the means of killing that were disliked or, indeed, there was a sense of personal unsuitability for the task.

On 7 July 1944, referring to the German treatment of the Hungarian Jews, the *Times* (of London) claimed 'the responsibility [. . .] rested on the German people'. Only a few thousand Jews survived the war inside Germany with the help of non-Jews, a tiny number that invites the question about whether individual Germans could have done more, although the pressure of a totalitarian police state has to be borne in mind.

The stress here, therefore, is on an argument not only that the Holocaust was central to the Nazi regime, but also that its implementation was dependent on features of the German society of that period. That does not mean that all Germans played a role, but, instead, that social norms and organisation contributed directly to Nazi success in this sphere. Hitler and Himmler orchestrated the Holocaust and benefited to that end from structural forces in, and facets of, German society. As a result, the functionalist interpretation, which stresses initiatives by officials responding to particular problems, appears pertinent as far as the mechanics and, to a degree, timing of slaughter are concerned but, otherwise, as less significant.

The issue of individual and collective German responsibility is highlighted by the post-war rebellions against Communist rule in East Germany, both unsuccessful and speedily suppressed in 1953 and, yet, rapidly successful in 1989. These rebellions indicated the possibilities of resistance to totalitarian rule, even if, thanks to the use of Soviet forces, in Hungary in 1956, this resistance could be swiftly crushed. The 1989 rebellion, moreover, showed that totalitarianism had its weaknesses, a point that invited a reconsideration not only of Communist East Germany but also of Nazi Germany. SD reports indicate that the Nazi surveillance system also had weaknesses. This is an instance of the way in which subsequent events help reformulate the questions asked. Reading back from 1989 to the opposition to Hitler underlines the extent to which this opposition lacked active public support on any scale. If prudence in the face of a brutal totalitarian Nazi regime played a role, with the regime far more brutal and powerful than its Communist counterpart in East Germany in 1989, so also, for many, did ideological support for the regime.

The churches certainly acted in post-war eastern Europe, particularly, but not only, in Poland, to sustain public distance from Communism in a way that they largely failed to in the case of the Nazis.[44] In part, this was because aspects of Nazi ideology and policy reflected the aspirations or at least inclinations of powerful constituencies within the churches, or could be interpreted as doing so. In this respect, anti-Semitism was an aspect of the anti-liberal and anti-Communist nature of much church thought, although there was also a core religious element, with alleged Jewish guilt for the death of Christ playing a prominent part in the liturgical season of Lent. As in Vichy France, an opposition to what were seen as metropolitan and cosmopolitan tendencies lent added bite and direction to anti-Semitic inclinations.

Much of the clergy, moreover, in Germany and elsewhere, was more concerned about its ministry to its flock than about developments elsewhere in society. State terror also played a role. In 1935, Göring declared that clerical interference with state policies would not be tolerated, which led to arrests by the Gestapo. The treatment of clerical opponents became much harsher in Germany once the Second World War broke out. This harshness, which could include being sent to concentration camps, was the response, for example, to German Catholic clerics ministering to Polish labourers. In the majority of cases, there was no need for Gestapo action against priests helping Jews, as such action was unusual and usually restricted to Christians of Jewish descent. Bernhard Lichtenberg was a conspicuous exception in the Berlin diocese.[45]

Clerics tended to be hostile to Communism, an atheistical movement, and to those on the Left who could be seen as crypto-Communist. The association between Communists and Jews, made by the critics of both, thus further helped to marginalise Jews. Nationalism and an emphasis on obedience to secular authority contributed to these attitudes in Germany and its allies. Thus, Clemens von Galen, the Catholic Bishop of Münster, who publicly criticised Nazi policies of 'euthanasia' in 1941, also preached that year, presenting the Jews as denying God's truth, as well as being against the 'Judeo-Bolshevik conspiracy'.[46] In my experience, that is not pointed out in Münster when Galen's opposition to Hitler is emphasised. Catholic intellectuals found many aspects of Nazi policy attractive,[47] while in Austria, aside from the dominant Catholics, the small-scale Protestant Church also welcomed the Anschluss. Earlier, when, in 1933, German Protestants considered the issue of Jewish converts, the report from the theological faculty in Erlangen recommended that the church demand the resignation of Jewish converts from office.

The churches, especially the Catholic Church, can be seen to have played a role not only in terms of their policies (or lack of them) at the time, but also with reference to their longer-term part in encouraging the notion of insider and outsider. Scholarship on the medieval church has argued that this legitimated persecution and made it necessary and legal. This was thus important to later manifestations of persecution.[48]

There is also an instructive parallel with popular support for the Inquisition in the early modern period (sixteenth to eighteenth centuries). Although reviled in Protestant Europe, and criticised by 'progressive' Catholic intellectuals, the Inquisition appears to have enjoyed a considerable amount of popular support. Reflecting the situation across much of Catholic Europe, the frequent autos-da-fé (burnings), organised at the behest of the Inquisition in the lands of the Crown of Aragon in the late sixteenth and early seventeenth century, were popular because those punished were mostly outsiders. In the kingdom of Valencia, which was part of Aragon, the Inquisition's attempts to repress the worst excesses of erroneous doctrine were seen as laudable, and it continued in the eighteenth century to display an impressive capacity to attract fresh recruits.[49]

If anti-Semitic messages still came from the pulpit in the 1940s, they were more systematically pushed through government propaganda. This included not only diatribes, for example on the radio, but also the use of film, especially *Jew Süss* (1940), which had been seen by 1943 by over 20 million Germans, and *The Eternal Jew* (1940), which compared Jews to rats. The lesson of an apparently endless struggle between Germans and Jews was repeatedly driven home. It provided a key background to hostility that was both organised and spontaneous.

Support for the Holocaust is an aspect of the more general issue of backing for Nazism.[50] This is complex because, aside from the pressures of totalitarianism and a police state,[51] Nazism meant very different things to particular individuals and groups and at distinct moments. The same was true, for non-Jews, of the state anti-Semitism that culminated in the Holocaust. This variety ensures that questions about the degree of support are dealing with a moving target. This was even more the case because, however vicious, the disorganised and incoherent nature of Nazism contrasted with the greater consistency and interior logic of Soviet Communism. The latter, moreover, had longer in which to implement its policies, and benefited also from the extent to which it gained total power after victory in a civil war which had permitted the terrorisation of real or alleged domestic opponents. Thus, Communist authority and strength in the Soviet Union started from a different basis to that of the Nazis in Germany.

The incoherent nature of Nazism was also an aspect of its strength, as it ensured that the movement could reach out to a large number of constituencies of support, in part by representing itself directly, or through its intermediaries in these constituencies, in different lights. Furthermore, in reaching out differently, there was an opportunity to respond to what were seen as popular drives and discontents. Although there were core groups and regions of support, not least young men, backing for Nazism was wide-ranging across society, attracting women and older men as well.[52] Moreover, far from limiting support for the Nazis, anti-Semitism provided themes for expanding it, not only with Christian anti-Semites but also as a way to try to appeal to left-wing views, by presenting the unattractive side of business and finance as Jewish.

BRITAIN AND THE USA

There is also the long-standing question of what could have been achieved by Allied pressure to ameliorate, slow down or limit the implementation of German policy. This issue is one that was widely raised after the war, not least over the past decade, with claims that Allied pressure could, and should, have limited the Holocaust. In large part, this debate focuses on whether Allied bombing could have disrupted the rail routes to the concentration camps and, indeed, the camps themselves. In 1961, British secret reports were revealed showing plans to bomb Auschwitz, which were, in the end, turned down.

Discussion frequently underplays the range of demand on Allied air power and the distance of the extermination camps from Western air bases, although the Farben works at Auschwitz were bombed, while in 1944 British planes reached Warsaw in order to drop supplies to help the Rising there. Allied air capability increased in 1944 with the introduction of the P-51D Mustang, a first-rate fighter that, fitted with external underwing drop tanks to carry extra fuel, had an operating range of 600 miles. This extended the range within which bombers could be escorted, but, for UK-based planes, still excluded Hungary and Poland. The superiority of American interceptors had already been demonstrated with the P-47 Thunderbolts and P-51B Mustangs, introduced in April and December 1943 respectively. In late February and March 1944, they used their superiority over German interceptors in raids in clear weather on German sites producing aircraft and oil, not least during 'Big Week' in late February.

Despite the increased range of Allied planes, Hungary and Poland posed serious extra challenges. The normal maximum range for the American B-17 and B-24 aircraft operating from East Anglia was 750 miles, although greater range could be gained by adding auxiliary fuel tanks or reducing the bomb load. Greater range, however, meant increased exposure to interception, as well as less time over the target. There was also no shortage of strategic targets in Germany. Thus, in 'Big Week', Anglo-American air attacks focused on German fighter production.

Had the killing of western Europe's Jews taken place in western Europe, then the situation as far as range, though not targets, would have been very different. The emphasis would still have been on military and military-industrial targets. By 1944, Hungary was easily within the range of Allied air bases in Italy: in November 1943, the 15th US Army Air Force had moved its base to Foggia. It focused on attacking German oil supplies, especially the Romanian oilfields at Ploesti, the aircraft industry, especially at Wiener Neustadt, and transport links. All were crucial to the German war effort. Target, not range, was the key issue. The range of Allied planes was not the reason why the Germans deported Jews to Poland for killing.[53]

Prior to the outbreak of the war, the British Government was already aware of the mistreatment of German Jews. In late 1939, in response to German propaganda about Allied atrocities and concerning the role of the British in establishing concentration camps during the Boer War (see p. 43), the British Government presented to Parliament 'Papers Concerning the Treatment of German Nationals in Germany 1938–39', which were then published by the Stationery Office. They left no doubt of the murderous nature of the treatment of Jews, not least of incarceration in the concentration camp at Buchenwald. The tortures there were detailed at length. Of the 2,000 Jewish prisoners who arrived at Buchenwald on 15 June 1939, the death of 110 in the first five weeks was reported.[54]

It took a while, however, for the outside world to understand the full extent of German policy in the shape of the Final Solution. In large part, the Allied focus was on other issues, primarily, and understandably, the conduct of the war, but it was also difficult to understand that genocide was being carried out, that the killing was in pursuit of a systematic plan and the nature of this plan.[55] For Jewish leaders outside occupied Europe, in Palestine, Britain and the USA, including the Jewish Agency, the organisation headed by David Ben-Gurion for establishing a Palestine national home for Jews, this indeed also took a while to grasp fully. Their experience was of pogroms, not genocide, an experience and assumption that also affected the attitude of some Jews when confronted by German rule.

The Allies were aware of the killing of Jews, in part through the interception and deciphering of German radio traffic, which revealed, from 18 July 1941, that Jews were being killed by German units operating in the Soviet Union. The Gestapo messages could not be read – unlike the ciphers used by the regular police, who played a significant role in the mass slaughter. Whether more public use should have been made of these reports is controversial, but fails to take note of the urgent British need to maintain secrecy in order to retain interception and code-breaking capabilities.[56]

Subsequently, aside from disbelief about the extermination camps and the policy of total extermination, the Allies did not appreciate the scale of the killing, as was shown by the American Government's response in August 1942 to the report by the World Jewish Congress. The Allies were also wary of proposals for deals or rescue ideas, seeing them as possible Nazi ploys.[57] It has been suggested that there was a reluctance, not least on the part of the American State Department, to acknowledge German action in case it provided the basis of demands for action on behalf of Jews, such as relaxed immigration quotas.[58] German deception,[59] as well as conflicting accounts, made it difficult to confirm reports or piece together the entire picture, and the information that arrived in the West was frequently of events and developments that had already occurred.[60] Allied intelligence agencies focused anyway on German strategy and war production.

Information about the killing at Chelmno, supplied by Emmanuel Ringelblom, led to the BBC reporting it on 2 June 1942. On 20 June, *The Times* printed news of the murder of 1 million Jews 'either by being shot or by being made to live in such conditions that they died'. The following month, Edward Schulte, a German businessman opposed to the Nazis, was able to pass on information that the Germans were planning the genocide of Jews, the basis of the Riegner telegram sent by Gerhart Riegner of the World Jewish Congress. In November 1942, Jan Karski (real name Jan Kozielewski), a Polish agent who had entered and left the concentration camp at Bełzec disguised as a guard, arrived in London. He was able to provide an account of the killing to the Polish government-in-exile, Anthony Eden (the British Foreign Secretary) and President Franklin D. Roosevelt. In response, on 17 December 1942, the Allied governments produced a declaration attacking 'this bestial policy of cold-blooded extermination'. By then, the Jewish Agency had also made the facts at its disposal public and had called for action. On 24 November, *The Times* had reported the 'systematic extermination' of Jews in Poland, followed, on 4 December, by referring to a 'deliberate plan for extermination'.

Once the fact of large-scale mistreatment, even genocide, was understood, the Allies were unwilling to focus on this issue, in part because it did not seem central to the war with Germany. The American Government proved particularly reluctant to emphasise the Holocaust. Anti-Semitism in the State Department and other sectors of government, including part of the military leadership, may have played a role, but there were also policy issues. Aside from concern about popular anti-Semitism in the USA, as well as anxiety that the conflict would be presented as a Jewish war, and thus serve isolationist goals, and also the argument that reports about German atrocities in Belgium in the First World War had been misleading or counter-productive, the Holocaust did not correspond to the Government's distinction between Nazis and Germans. This was a distinction important to publicly expressed war goals and to post-war planning, with the desired unconditional surrender of the former designed to lead to the rehabilitation of the latter.[61]

There was also a sense that Jews were one among many victims of the Germans and that attention should not be diverted from the war in which Americans were fighting. Partly as a result of the latter and, more generally, of the range of the war news and the pressures this created for news reporting and layout, newspapers such as the New York Times not only did not wish to, but also could not, focus on the Holocaust.[62] Nevertheless, on 9 March 1943, Congress passed a resolution condemning the 'mass murder of Jewish men, women, and children', and demanding due punishment. At the same time, the State Department issued a report recording the 'cold-blooded extermination' of Europe's Jews.

Among the British public, absorbed with war news and its own efforts to get by, there appears to have been a widespread lack of interest.[63] It was also difficult to understand and credit the full extent of Nazi actions and plans,[64] although, on 11 March 1943, the The Times reported that 2 million Jews had been killed and, on 1 June 1943, that the killing was spreading to the Balkans. That year, the Mass Observation Survey in Britain noted public sympathy for Europe's Jews and concern about an absence of government action on their behalf,[65] although the Government itself was worried that stressing the issue might lead to a rise in anti-Semitism, not least if the Germans were able to present the conflict as a

Jewish war. There was certainly latent anti-Semitism, as indicated by the false rumours that circulated in London during the Blitz of 1940–1 that Jews got into the air-raid shelters first and that others had been successful in leaving London.

There was also British concern about the implications for Palestine. At the Anglo-American Bermuda Conference in April 1943, a conference held at the same time that the Germans were attacking the Warsaw ghetto, the proposal by the Jewish Agency for an approach to Hitler to ease the position of Jews was turned down, as was the plea to ease immigration into Palestine. Indeed, the conference simply decided to open a Jewish refugee centre in North Africa. The British feared that encouraging Jewish immigration to Palestine would stir up Arab antipathy and thus help the German war effort.[66] Indeed, such immigration was seen as a German plan to that end.

As a result, the British Government had no time for the Biltmore programme, announced after a meeting of American Zionists in the Biltmore Hotel in New York in May 1942. This called for Jewish sovereignty over an independent Palestine as a way of providing a post-war refuge. On 6 November 1944, Field Marshal Alan Brooke, the Chief of the Imperial General Staff, recorded in his diary: 'a difficult Chiefs of Staff at which we discuss the problems of the partition of Palestine for the Jews. We are unanimously against any announcement before the end of the war, but our hand may well be forced.'[67]

British governmental concerns led to the refusal to accept Jewish illegal immigrants into Palestine. Instead, many were forced to remain in neutral countries, such as Turkey, or were interned in the British Indian Ocean colony of Mauritius. Their circumstances there, however, were considerably better than those the Germans had intended for Europe's Jews on nearby Madagascar.

More information on the Holocaust was received as the war continued, including, by the summer of 1944, reliable reports of events at Auschwitz. In 1944, indeed, Allied pressure on the Hungarian Government helped persuade it to stop the deportations. By then, Allied successes, not least the range of Allied bombers operating since late 1943 from Italy, made this pressure more effective.

Earlier in 1944, authorised by Himmler after the idea had been agreed by Hitler, Eichmann had initiated an approach over Hungarian Jews. In May, he proposed, via Joel Brand, a key member of the Jewish Relief and Rescue Committee, and the Jewish Agency, to exchange Hungarian Jews, on a pro-rata basis, for lorries, coffee, cocoa, tea and soap – the lorries, he promised, only to be used for the war against the Soviet Union. The British opposed negotiations, seeing them as a way to sow disunion among the Allies, but the Americans persuaded the British to maintain the link in the hope that it might help Hungarian Jews. Without even being aware of the provisions about the lorries, Soviet opposition led to the abandonment of the approach.[68]

In practice, the German proposal was probably intended to divide or discredit the Allies. The willingness of German leaders to trade Jews was only episodic and pales into insignificance beside the general determination to slaughter them. Indeed, Eichmann was to criticise the idea of slowing down for diplomatic ends the slaughter of Hungarian Jews. More generally, Hitler was willing to ally with Stalin in 1939–41, but not to make any deal with or over Jews. This made Himmler's tentative approaches to Jewish organisations and others, in Switzerland and Sweden in late 1944 and early 1945, for some sort of deal involving favourable treatment for at least some Jews unviable.

After the war, Jewish anger and Anglo-American guilt combined, with a concern to establish the facts of wartime policy in discussions of whether the Allies could have done more. In part, there is a misleading tendency to focus on the real or supposed wrongs of Britain and the USA, rather than the evil of Germany or, not that it is so directly pertinent in this issue, paranoid mass murder by the Soviet Government. Whether Britain and the USA should have done more, it has been argued that obtaining victory was seen as of greater importance at the time.[69] Indeed, more specifically, it was generally claimed that this was the way to rescue Jews. For the many Jews saved as Allied forces advanced in 1943–5 (1942 if Morocco and Algeria are included) this was true, although many others were slaughtered by the Germans then. By late 1944, it is unclear what would have been achieved by bombing the camps. Most of the killing had already taken place, and the Germans were preparing to dismantle Auschwitz.

Looking back to before the war, it is possible to note the refusal by both Britain and the USA to take more Jewish immigrants from Germany and occupied territory, and to link this to the wartime failure to do more to help. In the particular case of British policy over migration to Palestine, there is a link, but it is far from clear that this is more generally pertinent. Concerned about domestic opinion, neither the American nor the British governments wished to create the impression that the conflict was being waged on behalf of Jews, not least because it was feared that this would play into the hands of German propaganda. Allied anti-Semitism doubtless played a role in what were presented as pragmatic considerations, but the central fact was that the vast majority of Jews were under German control and received no mercy.

CHAPTER 4

GERMANY'S ALLIES

The anti-Semitic commitment of the Nazi regime helped ensure that the extensive German alliance system registered this hatred. That, however, is not to underplay the strong and autonomous anti-Semitic impulses of many of Germany's allies; for example, Romania under General Ion Antonescu, its dictator from 1940 to 1944. Nevertheless, there can be little doubt that these impulses were encouraged by the Nazis. Furthermore, had the German Government taken a different position, then its strength within the alliance would have led to corresponding pressure that could have affected outcomes. This would also have been the case had Italy under Mussolini been the dominant party in the Axis alliance system, as anti-Semitism was not a key drive or policy for him.

ROMANIA

Of the allies, there was particular support for extermination from the Antonescu Government. There was a long tradition of Romanian anti-Semitism, and it had been an issue in diplomacy in the late nineteenth century. One of the most difficult subjects to settle at the Congress of Berlin in 1878 was Romania's treatment of its Jewish minority. Unlike its Bulgarian and Hungarian neighbours, the Antonescu Government was a keen supporter of the slaughter of Jews. Unlike the case with Bulgaria and Hungary, this was not solely a policy for conquered regions. Instead, the policy was applied in Romania itself with, for example, a brutal pogrom in Iasi in June 1941, in which at least 4,000 Jews were slaughtered. This policy was also followed for the nearby sections of the

Soviet Union occupied by the Romanians from 1941, particularly Bessarabia (now Moldava), Northern Bukovinia and
Transnistria (part of Ukraine between the Bug and Dnestr
rivers). The Jews of Bessarabia were deported to camps in
Transnistria where they were slaughtered.

When Odessa fell in 1941, after a long siege, the
Romanians killed tens of thousands of Jews in a murderous
pogrom. This was a major episode in the Holocaust and one
that receives insufficient attention. The Romanian army
played a leading role. Aside from the mass shootings of
Odessa's Jews, there were also other forms of slaughter
including burning Jews alive. Within Romania, there was no
secret about the killings.

In large part, the Romanian Government was motivated
by anti-Semitism. There was also a political dimension, as in
much of the violence in this (and other) regions. Antonescu,
who stated that 'there is no law' as far as Jews were concerned, claimed, as did colleagues, that Jews were pro-Soviet
and, therefore, a threat to Romania – in fact, traitors. Indeed,
the slaughter in Iasi was planned by Romanian military intelligence. Aside from those killed in the town, many died, from
a lack of food and water, on trains moving them to camps.
On 18 August 1941, Hitler told Goebbels that Antonescu had
taken more radical steps than the Germans had yet pursued.[1]

CROATIA, SERBIA AND SLOVAKIA

Other allies were very happy to cooperate with German intentions. The collaborationist regime of Ante Pavelić and his
Ustasha movement, installed in Croatia in 1941, slaughtered
Jews there and in Bosnia; although, in terms of numbers
killed, Serbs were their major victims. The Croat regime
proved very willing to deport Jews for slaughter by the
Germans, but the majority had already been killed, and in
conditions of great brutality. Jews, like Serbs, were hacked to
death and burned alive in barns. The type of killing was similar to that seen in Rwanda in 1994.

The religious dimension of the slaughter was seen in the
option given Jews and Serbs of conversion and in the support

of some of the Catholic bishops for the Ustasha campaign. Conversion was not an option offered by the Germans. In total, nearly 45,000 Jews were killed or handed over to the Germans, and with no criticism from Pope Pius XII about this genocidal policy of a Catholic state. Instead, it was the Italian military that helped to end it by advancing farther into Croatia in late 1941 and offering protection to Jews and Serbs.

Within Serbia, the collaborationist regime also cooperated in the Holocaust, although the Germans were in control. The Slovak regime of the People's Party under Josef Tiso, a Catholic priest, introduced anti-Semitic legislation and forced labour. From 1942, it also deported its Jews to the extermination camps rather than slaughtering them in Slovakia: 10,000 Jews were sent to Auschwitz from 28 August to 27 October 1944 alone.

HUNGARY

The Hungarian Government of Miklós Kállay, in power from March 1942 to March 1944, was anti-Semitic but only deported a small number of Jews, and, in relative terms, killing then was limited. Indeed, the Hungarian attitude was discussed, as a problem, at the Wannsee conference in 1942. However, after German troops occupied Hungary on 19 March 1944, Kállay was replaced by General Döme Sztójay and the situation changed. A Reich plenipotentiary was installed to ensure that the new pro-German government complied fully. A ghetto was established in Budapest on 16 April, and the Hungarian Police then assisted the SS in deporting Hungarian Jews to Auschwitz. Some 425,000 were deported, with the active support of Hungarian officials. The majority of Jews were killed, but Hungarian policy then switched again.

In part, the change in policy was due to the tide of war in eastern Europe, which had already led Romania to change side. Concern about the fate of Hungarian Jews, accentuated by pressure on Admiral Miklos Horthy, the Regent of Hungary, from the Pope, Britain, the USA and Sweden, led to the end of the deportations, and a new government under

General Géza Lakatos was appointed on 29 August. Nevertheless, many Jews were still killed by the Arrow Cross and other Hungarian fascist movements. There was a particularly serious and murderous pogrom in October 1944, the month in which a German-encouraged coup led to the installation of an Arrow Cross regime under Vevenc Szálasi.[2]

BULGARIA

Not all of Germany's allies persecuted Jews to death. In Bulgaria, as the Government moved closer to Germany in 1940, anti-Semitic legislation was passed. This was designed to make it easier to segregate Jews, who were no longer permitted to have Bulgarian names, nor Jewish ones with Bulgarian suffixes. Jews were also made to wear the yellow star. Moreover, restrictions were placed on their freedom of movement. A Purity of the Nation Act banned mixed marriages. As relations with Germany became even closer, with Bulgaria joining the war in 1941 and annexing territory from Yugoslavia and Greece, in Macedonia and Thrace respectively, so pressure on Jews increased, in part in response to demands on the Government from Adolf-Heinz Beckerle, a committed Nazi, who became German envoy in October 1941. Jewish organisations were banned; Jews lost their civil rights; and their businesses were compulsorily purchased. In August 1942, Jews in the occupied territories were deprived of their Bulgarian citizenship, and, the following March, they were deported to the extermination camps.

There was also a plan drawn up for the secret deportation of 6,000 Jews from pre-war Bulgaria by Aleksandŭr Belev, the head of the Commissariat for Jewish Affairs, with the connivance of the Cabinet. The secret was not kept, however, in part because Belev's outraged mistress informed the press, and there was a chorus of outrage, which contrasts markedly with the situation in Germany, France, Romania and most of occupied or allied Europe. The Orthodox Church attacked the proposed step, as did a range of workers' organisations, including railway workers, and such middle-class professional groups as doctors and lawyers. Government supporters in

Parliament signed a petition against the deportation. Once submitted to King Boris III, he vetoed the deportations of Jews from pre-war Bulgaria, i.e., Bulgaria excluding the wartime conquests.

Another secret attempt to deport Jews from pre-war Bulgaria was unsuccessful in May 1943, with Metropolitan Stefan of Sofia prominent in the opposition. For Boris III and others, a key issue was national sovereignty and the need for Bulgaria to retain control of its citizens.[3] Bulgaria's Jews, instead, were sent to work camps within Bulgaria, camps that did not compare with the concentration camps of the Germans and Croats. It is possible that concern about post-war punishment by the Allies was also an issue, as the war was now moving against the Germans; indeed, in March 1943, Boris admitted that he no longer thought German victory likely.

Beckerle finally backed down, arguing that the Bulgarians were used to multi-ethnic life, lacked the anti-Semitism found across much of Europe and that Germany would be unwise to compromise its political influence in Sofia by trying to force the Bulgarians to yield.[4] All Bulgarian anti-Semitic legislation was repealed on 17 August 1944, as Soviet forces advanced into the Balkans.

ITALY

Elsewhere, as with other aspects of complying with a new order increasingly based on German notions of their own superiority, there could also be a notable lack of zeal in implementing persecution. This was the case in Fascist Italy, with Mussolini, who had a Jewish mistress, lacking commitment to the killing, although recent scholarship has emphasised his racism.[5] It was acceptable in Italy in 1938 to ban Jewish teachers from teaching and to forbid marriage between Jews and non-Jews,[6] but there was relatively little anti-Semitic feeling among the population and scant support for deportation and mass murder.[7] Italian Fascism sought a stronger state: there was not the commitment to race seen with Germany.

Indeed, Italy and Italian-occupied territory, such as Dalmatia, Nice and parts of Greece, were safer for Jews than other German-allied states, for example Vichy France and Croatia, and, as a result, many Jews took refuge there, while others sought to do so. The Italian treatment of Jews varied, and issues of control and status played a role in the unwillingness to deport them, but, notably in response to Croat atrocities, 'the Italians eventually devoted special attention to the rescue of the Jews'.[8] The Italians also refused to deport foreign Jews from Italy. The Italian Government and military, not the Vatican, were the key elements in this situation, although they were also the bodies with power.

The situation did not change until Germany seized Italy and Italian-occupied territory, following the overthrow of Mussolini on 25 July 1943 and the Italian armistice with the Allies on 3 September 1943. The position of Italy's Jews then deteriorated in those areas which the Allies were unable to conquer. On 16 October 1943, the Jews of Rome were rounded up by the Germans. The Fascist Salò republic, created in northern Italy, was a German puppet state headed by Mussolini whom the Germans had rescued in September. This republic collaborated in deporting Jews to slaughter in the extermination camps. Although 8,000 Jews were deported from Italy, 35,000 survived.[9] In the former ghetto in Venice, the list of names of those killed is a poignant memorial.

FINLAND

A more distant ally, Finland, was unenthusiastic about the Holocaust. Himmler visited Helsinki in July 1942, to press for the handing over of foreign Jews (who numbered 150–200). The Finnish Secret Police drew up lists, but there was opposition in both the Government and among the public. Eight foreign Jews were handed over in November 1942, of whom only one survived the war. The Finnish Government did not cooperate thereafter, and no further Jews were deported. Finnish Jews fought alongside their compatriots against the Soviet Union in 1939–40 and 1941–4, and against the Germans in 1944–5.[10]

JAPAN

Japan also proved unwilling to implement German pressure for participation in the Final Solution. The Jewish population under Japanese rule increased from 1931, as a result both of Japanese conquests and of Jewish emigration from Europe. The first brought under Japanese control areas where some Jews already lived, such as Manchuria, where they were part of the large Russian population that had left Russia as a result of Communist victory in the Russian Civil War, as well as Shanghai (conquered in 1937). Jewish emigration from Europe ensured that more Jews came to areas conquered by Japan, such as the Philippines (conquered in 1941–2), which had taken about 700 refugees, as well as to Japan itself. About 19,000 Jews were confined in Shanghai, but the Japanese rejected German pressure for their slaughter. This contrasted with the murderous Japanese policy towards the Chinese.

DENMARK

The range of response scarcely glimpsed in Germany but seen far more among its allies was also witnessed in occupied Europe, although it is necessary to note the pressures the German occupiers imposed on the collaborating governments and authorities in occupied countries. Cooperation was minimal in Denmark, which was conquered in 1940, and most of its Jews survived. Denmark indicates that a willingness to rescue Jews could exist and be overwhelmingly successful in a country that was not removed from the anti-Semitism and racism seen elsewhere in Europe. The refusal of the Danes to cooperate set a standard the Norwegians failed to meet. In Norway, collaboration was more common.

POLAND

In Poland, however, admittedly in very adverse circumstances, there was active or complicit hostility to Jews, including a massacre of between 200 and 400 at the town of Jedwabne on 10 July 1941. What happened there is controversial. Claims that 1,600 Jews were killed, and by the Poles, have been qualified by research indicating, instead, that a smaller number of Poles, encouraged by anti-Semitic priests, cooperated with the German killers. In 2001, President Aleksander Kwasmiewrski laid a wreath at the site of the massacre, before apologising for it.[11]

In Poland, there was anti-Semitic hostility that preceded the war and that continued after it. There was also, nevertheless, much help on the personal level, particularly sheltering Jews.[12] Indeed, aside from killings elsewhere, 1,500 Poles who tried to assist Jews were killed in the extermination camp at Bełzec. Due to their own hatred of the Poles, the Germans did not give the Poles the opportunity to collaborate in killing Jews that they offered to Ukrainians, for example of the ONU, and Balts.[13] However, a post-war pogrom at Kielce in July 1946, against Jews trying to return home from Auschwitz, led many of the few thousand Jews in Poland who had survived the Holocaust to emigrate.

LITHUANIA, LATVIA AND UKRAINE

There was also active and large-scale cooperation in the Holocaust across much of occupied Europe, for example from the police from the Baltic republics (Estonia, Latvia, Lithuania). Such cooperation was useful to the Germans, and many of the tasks of deportation and murder were allocated to local collaborators. In some cases, this collaboration in the Holocaust began before the German invaders arrived in 1941 or in their absence. This was true of Latvia, Lithuania and Ukraine, with some of the vicious hatred for Jews attributed to the allegation that they had allied with the Communists, as a small number had done. As such, slaughtering Jews was an aspect of the collapse of Communist control. Thus, in Latvian towns such as Daugavpils and Riga, before the arrival of German troops in 1941, Jews were seized by Latvians and killed without anyone stopping the armed gangs. These were particularly vicious pogroms. The same occurred in Lithuanian towns, such as Kaunas where 2,500 Jews were killed, and in Ukrainian towns such as Lvóv and Tarnopol. This was a killing very different to the standard conception of the

Holocaust as carried out by Germans in extermination camps. Moreover, the Lithuanians and Ukrainians were just as willing as the Germans to kill women and children. At Kovno in Lithuania, the killing was applauded by the local people. Elsewhere, there was less cooperation, for example in Brest Litovsk, where neither the Poles nor the Belorussians supported the killings in 1941.

Subsequently, Lithuanians and Ukrainians were prominent in supporting the German war effort. This involved Lithuanians as concentration-camp guards and also killing Jews in the field, for example in Belarus in 1941. Lithuanian units, moreover, took part in anti-partisan operations, in which Jews were killed, and also in suppressing the Warsaw ghetto. Ukrainians were prominent among the guards at several of the extermination camps, particularly Bełzec, Sobibor and Treblinka. Ukrainian anti-Semitism looked back on a long tradition. For example, the Golden Charter of the 1768 rising in the western Ukraine ordered the killing of all Jews and Poles.

OCCUPIED EUROPE

Most of those occupied, however, focused on their own concerns, a feature of the extent to which defeat, occupation and totalitarian rule leads a demoralised populace to atomise and to concentrate on their own private concerns. If these excluded Jews, whether neighbours or not, the process also excluded many non-Jews, but there was a contrast. In part, this was a matter of anti-Semitism and, in part, a response to the new political environment. This was a compound of powerlessness and a determination to secure the most acceptable position under occupation. Both led to an attempt to continue government as usual, an attempt that played into the hands of the Germans. This was a general situation, but, in the specific case of the Holocaust, it led to large-scale cooperation in aspects that were necessary to German purposes, not least in segregating Jews and then deporting them. Anti-Semitism was an aspect of the collaboration with, indeed active role in, the Holocaust across allied and occupied Europe. Other factors also played a role. These included the desire to benefit personally by seizing the property of Jews. Thus, the war helped precipitate the dissolution of what had been multi-ethnic communities, as the fault-lines of earlier tensions were exposed in a totally one-sided fashion. At the same time, the situation did differ across Europe, in part as a result of the nature of civil society and in part due to the particular impact of German policy.

NETHERLANDS

This was seen, for example, in the Netherlands. Three-quarters of the 140,000 Dutch Jews were deported and killed, and, if some of this activity rested on the individual initiative of bounty-hunters, much was due to the cooperation and efficiency of the Dutch civil service and police.[14] The ratio of Jews deported and killed was far higher than in Belgium or France, and the total number was also higher. The Dutch also provided more volunteers for the SS than the French or Belgians.

The post-war conduct of the Dutch was similarly shameful, with a callous indifference to returning Jews, and a reluctance, until the mid-1960s, to acknowledge what had been done. It is instructive, however, that the Dutch have not shared a popular opprobrium for wartime conduct comparable to that of the French. The dockers strike in Amsterdam on behalf of their fellow Jews gave the Netherlands a reputation for resistance to German demands, which survived the true facts of collaboration until fairly recent times.

BELGIUM

In contrast, there has been less work in English on the deportation of the Jews from Belgium to Auschwitz.[15] Almost 25,000 Jews, 40 per cent of Belgium's total, were deported, with twenty-seven trains sent from Mechelen to Auschwitz between 1942 and 1944, and another 5,000 Belgian Jews were sent to Auschwitz from Drancy. The role of the SS in Belgium was limited by the determined opposition of the German Military Administration, which was focused on military and economic goals.[16] The Belgian civil authorities proved accommodating to German measures, for example the regulations of 28 October 1940, which decreed the registration of Jews and their exclusion from public functions.

As a reminder of the importance of local variations, the civil authorities of Brussels refused in the summer of 1942 to distribute yellow stars or to use the police to arrest Jews, while, the same summer, those of Antwerp did both. On 14 and 17 April 1941, Flemish fascists had moved into the Jewish quarter in Antwerp and burnt two synagogues, the sort of riot not seen in France or the Netherlands. Flemish collaboration in Antwerp was in part due to well-devised German propaganda hailing the different, Aryan, character of Flanders as distinct from the French-speaking Walloon in the rest of the country. In the latter, the authorities of Liège were more compliant than those of Brussels, not least in drawing up a list of Jewish-owned enterprises before the Germans asked for them. Such contrasts contributed to the character of the Holocaust as the interplay of an ever-more brutal, insistent and oppressive German drive to control and kill, with a response ranging from eager cooperation to successful defiance.

FRANCE

The situation in France exemplified the room for contrasts. Once conquered, France was divided between a German-occupied zone and a zone left under the control of a pro-German French government, voted into office in July 1940 and based at Vichy. In the former, the trajectory seen elsewhere in occupied Europe was followed, with a move eventually towards large-scale deportation to the extermination camps in eastern Europe. These round-ups were entrusted to the French police, and they focused on foreign Jews. Alsace-Lorraine was annexed anew by Germany, and Jews were deported from there in October 1940.

In Vichy France, there was, from the outset, a willingness to discriminate against Jews, and one that did not require much German prompting, let alone pressure. The agrarian, ruralist, Catholic values advocated by the government of

Marshal Pétain were directed against metropolitan and liberal values with which Jews were associated, as Vichy strove to create an ostentatiously Christian France. In doing so, it took forward the anti-Semitic revival in France in the late 1930s which had been linked to opposition to Jewish refugees.[17] In 1940, the citizenship of many naturalised Jews was revoked and foreign Jews were interned. There was also legislation to define who were Jews and to exclude them from government posts, including teaching. The issue of definition, not least the competing criteria of race and religion, led to fresh legislation in 1941, as did further limitations on employment. In both zones, Jewish property was subject to confiscation, with the relevant measures introduced in Vichy in July 1941. A separate Police for Jewish Affairs was established by the Vichy Minister of the Interior. Such measures were intended to demonstrate a desire to cooperate with the Germans. Vichy attitudes were displayed in France's colonies, where German oversight was very limited. Thus, there were major purges of Jews in Guadeloupe, which was under Vichy from 1940 to 1943 and in Madagascar (1940–2).[18]

In 1942, Vichy handed over foreign Jews for deportation to the camps. This was very different to the restrictions on immigration displayed pre-war, not least because now the policy was explicitly anti-Semitic (as well as being murderous in effect). The extent to which these deportations were handled by the French authorities was concealed post-war, but most of those deported in 1942 were not under German control until handed over for movement out of the country. Vichy, however, resisted handing over French Jews, in part because of a critical public reaction, and, in 1943, the deportations fell in number and the round-ups were mostly by the SS, not the French police. The Vichy Government knew that Jews were being sent to slaughter, and, indeed, fewer than 3 per cent of the 76,000 deported survived, in comparison to the 59 per cent of 63,000 French non-Jews deported, mostly to Ravensbrück and Buchenwald. This contrast underlines the problematic nature of the post-war commemoration that failed to distinguish Jewish from non-Jewish victims, for example the Day of Remembrance of the Deportations that was instituted in 1954.

The killing did not trouble Vichy, but the Government was concerned that being seen to back German policy over French Jews would compromise Vichy's position in its contest with anti-Vichy forces within France. In the event, French Jews were rounded up in 1943–4, despite the wishes of Pierre Laval, the Prime Minister, and, in 1944, a more extreme government, which, as in Hungary, was imposed by the Germans, encouraged the *milice* (Far-Right militia) to round up Jews, including French ones. In the event, nearly one-third of Jews deported from France were French Jews.

The French public itself was split. There was protection for the Jews, particularly in the Protestant-dominated Cévennes mountains, and, at the individual level, there was much help from French people for Jews, both compatriots and, albeit to a lesser extent, foreign Jews. The Catholic Church included those willing to take risks to help Jews alongside others who preferred to accept, indeed support, Vichy, which also benefited from widespread anti-Semitism. The majority of French Jews, especially if children, survived the war within France, but foreign Jews found the situation far bleaker.[19] This contrast was more generally the case across Europe, with officials being more willing to give over foreign Jews in order to assuage German pressure. Furthermore, these Jews had far fewer links with, and in, local society, and, in practical terms, were also less able to evade seizure.

NEUTRALS

French action serves as a reminder of the extent to which imperial systems depend on consent and cooperation. Much of this is provided within a context in which coercion, overt or implicit, plays a role,[20] but they are, nonetheless, important. Moreover, consent and cooperation reflect not only the hard power on which coercion is based, but also aspects of soft power, including cultural and ideological influences. These could be seen, for example, in the international alliance structure that supported Germany. In the case of both Sweden and Switzerland, each of which was neutral, important economic and financial benefits accrued to the Nazi system, as well as to both countries.[21] These benefits included profit at the expense of Jews: for example, the expropriation by banks and insurance companies of money belonging or owed to Jews and dealing in gold seized from Jews. Revelations about Swiss practices led to widespread international criticism and became the focus for demands for restitution in the 1990s, with the D'Amato inquiry on the Swiss banks and the Volcker Committee's report on dormant accounts. Revelations about the Swiss also affected public culture, as with the depiction of the crooked Swiss banker in the James Bond film *The World Is Not Enough* (1999). During the war, the Swiss National Bank purchased large amounts of gold from the German Reichsbank in order to maintain its gold reserves.

Few Jews were given refugee status by these neutrals: Switzerland took in only 7,000 before the war and another 21,000 during it. The neutrals' support for Germany reflected not simply 'realist' considerations of relative power, but also ideological factors. In the latter, racism was prominent, and, alongside pan-Aryanism, there was, in Switzerland and Sweden, a degree of anti-Semitism that led to a reluctance to help Jews, although a Swedish diplomat, Raoul Wallenberg, made major efforts to save Hungarian Jews and did so for about 4,000 by handing out Swedish visas. Italian Jews deported to slaughter were not moved by train via Switzerland; on the other hand, the best route to Auschwitz lay further east. In the statistics prepared for the Wannsee conference in January 1942, Eichmann included as Jews to be slaughtered those from the neutral countries, such as Ireland, Portugal, Spain and Switzerland, as well as the 330,000 British Jews once Britain had been overcome. There was space at Auschwitz for such slaughter.

In Ireland, there was a reluctance to heed the plight of Jews that in part reflected the strength of anti-Semitism in a strongly Catholic country, as well as the Taoiseach, Eamon de Valera's pro-German and anti-British attitudes. He was aware of the slaughter of Jews by 1943, but showed little interest in their plight. After the war, the Irish Government was not helpful to Jewish refugees, while films of the concentration camps were treated critically as propagandist.

Alongside neutral states came neutral international organisations such as the Papacy (see p. 156) and the Red Cross. Each found it difficult to understand the nature and scale of the problem, and both were subsequently criticised, and understandably so, for lacking moral courage and for their inability to produce a credible response. In the case of the Red Cross, concern about the consequences for Switzerland may also have played a role. The World Jewish Congress found the role of the Red Cross unsatisfactory.[22]

The extent of cooperation and collaboration across Europe was concealed after the Second World War, but it helps ensure that the Holocaust was far more than an episode that can be discussed simply in terms of German causes and actions. They were the key, but their wider impact was in part dependent on a degree of cooperation that constituted a more general crisis of European culture.

CHAPTER 5

MEMORIALISATION

The scale of the German killing did not become public knowledge until the liberation of the concentration camps pushed it to the attention of the outside world in 1945. For the first time, photographic evidence of the killing was available in the West. Bergen-Belsen was liberated by the British on 15 April, and Buchenwald, Dachau and Mauthausen by the Americans on 11 April, 29 April and 5 May respectively. For the British, Bergen-Belsen, where over 10,000 unburied dead were found, was a shocking revelation, one spread round the world by BBC filming and by cinema newsreels. The victims, however, were not generally presented as Jews. Plans to use Bergen-Belsen as a camp for displaced persons were hastily discarded. The camps indeed lent urgency to the cause of displaced persons, but not specifically to that of Jews.

The liberation of the camps also led to pressure for action against those responsible in, and through, international law. Genocide, a term coined in 1944 by the Polish jurist Raphael Lemkin, was not a charge used in the Nuremberg trials of German leaders; 'Holocaust' was not a term employed in the trials; and Jewish survivors of the Holocaust had not been called as witnesses there. Nevertheless, the 'mass murder' of Jews was an aspect of Count Four of the indictments at Nuremberg, while, in 1948, genocide was made into a crime by a United Nations convention. At Nuremberg, figures of between 4.5 and 6 million Jewish victims were given by the prosecution. The use of a documentary film *Nazi Concentration Camps*, shown to the court in November 1945 as proof of criminal wrongdoing, was a major juridical innovation,[1] and also provides a background for the role of film in the understanding of the Holocaust.

The war was also followed by a series of trials of those directly responsible for the Holocaust, especially the commandants of concentration camps. For example, Max Koegel and Martin Weiss were tried, convicted and executed in 1946, while Rudolf Höss was executed outside Auschwitz in 1947. The Nuremberg Military Tribunal tried twenty-four *Einsatzgruppen* leaders in 1947–8, sentencing fourteen to hanging, although some sentences were later reduced. The Holocaust, however, then receded from attention, as efforts were made to forget the war and as Germany was reconceptualised with the Cold War. Further trials were downplayed or abandoned.

There is no best way to discuss the legacy and memorialisation of the Holocaust. In this chapter, the organising principle is geography, by state or group of states, but that implies a failure to employ a typology in terms of perpetrators, victims and bystanders. This has an unfortunate legacy, as perpetrators and victims are considered in the same vein. This poses problems, not only on moral but also on methodological grounds. Memorialising the Holocaust and dealing with its legacies means different things to the descendants of perpetrators and survivors. On the other hand, memorialisation is focused in terms of specific states and expounding their wartime conduct and legacy. That the particular priorities of the public reflect national issues is not simply because the frame of reference is national.

GERMANY

Having fought to ensure unconditional surrender and the destruction of German militarism, the USA and Britain now sought a new Germany. The Cold War with the Soviet Union, which became readily apparent from 1948, and the desire, first, to get their occupation zones to work and then to 'normalise' West Germany, and to revive it as a pro-Western democracy, ensured that other issues were stressed. Partly as a result, relatively little attention was paid to the Holocaust in the 1950s. This also reflected the nature of the earlier prosecutions, which had focused on proving a Nazi conspiracy to aggression, and thus war guilt, rather than on detailing the actual Nazi crimes. With the emphasis on Nazi perpetrators, not victims, the notion of collective Jewish suffering was downplayed. Furthermore, in the trials, the Anglo-American emphasis on documentation led to a stress on the concentration camps they had liberated and on Auschwitz, rather than on the extermination camps for which less documentation was readily available, particularly Bełzec, Sobibor and Treblinka. This emphasis on documents was at the expense of eyewitness accounts, although using German documentation ensured that the Nazi state was exposed by its own records. There was also a failure to bring out the role of the German Army and Police, and of collaborators in the Holocaust.[2]

The West German Government preferred to ignore the Holocaust and to downplay the Nazi era. One of the first laws passed by the newly constituted *Bundestag* (Parliament) in 1949 was a widespread amnesty. The Government paid compensation, with the first Federal Compensation Law with Israel being passed in 1953, but there was considerable reluctance to do so, and American pressure was important in order to secure the measure. The Social Democrats were readier to engage with the issue of Jewish reparations, whereas the more reluctant Christian Democrats, who were the governing party, tended to emphasise aspects of what they saw as German victimhood. Many voted against the reparations which, in the end, came to over 100 million Deutschmarks.

Both West Germany and East Germany, created as a rival by the Soviet Union from its occupation zone, publicly rejected the Nazi system and its works, including the Holocaust. Nevertheless, many West Germans were inclined to criticise what they saw as the Allies' verdict on the war, not least complaining about what they claimed was the 'victors' justice' of the Nuremberg and other trials. This was a key aspect of the self-serving presentation by Germans of themselves as victims of the war. Issues of widespread German responsibility were widely shunned, and, instead, Hitler and the Nazi regime were held accountable for the Second World War, as they also were for the failure of the attack on the Soviet Union in 1941. Polls indicated that many Germans thought the Jews partly responsible for what had happened to them.[3]

In many senses, this shunning repeated the experience of the years after the First World War, when there had also been a German rejection of war guilt. Many Germans developed a long-standing account of victimhood that looked back to 1918–19, and then to the experience of being bombed by the Allies in the Second World War[4] and, subsequently, to the brutal post-war driving of Germans from eastern Europe. Not only individual German responsibility was shunned but also the damage done by Germans to others, most blatantly the Holocaust. This reluctance deserves as much attention as the Western repositioning of West Germany as an ally in the Cold War.[5]

Indeed, during the Chancellorship of Konrad Adenauer from 1949 to 1963, many former Nazis were employed in responsible positions in West Germany, while few were tried for war crimes, and the even fewer who were convicted received very light sentences. Reintegration and amnesty were key themes in government policies that enjoyed much public support. The governing Christian Democrats were particularly sympathetic towards ex-Nazis, in part because their electoral constituency included many former Nazi sympathisers, but so also were the other parties, although some prominent Social Democrats, such as Kurt Schumacher, had been held in concentration camps. Schumacher publicly accepted German responsibility for the Holocaust.[6] Most West Germans, however, proved very willing to ignore or downplay the evidence of the extermination camps, which were now in Communist-run eastern Europe.

Conversely, the German attitude after the Second World War was also very different to that after the First World War. While it is true that there was not much discussion about German war crimes after the Second World War, this was also due to the fact that most Germans were busy surviving, finding their relatives or getting jobs. When plans for the creation of a new German army became public, the strong reaction against it in Germany showed that lessons had been learned. After the First World War, most Germans had quite a different perspective on the issue of rearmament.

Seeking to integrate West Germany into the West as the front line against Communism led, from the 1950s, to the reformation of German nationalism, with the creation of a 'new' free West Germany and, in particular, a new West German army. This required an acceptable presentation of recent history in which Nazism was seen as an aberration, while resistance to Nazi policies was emphasised. There was a particular stress on the military plotters who unsuccessfully sought to kill Hitler in July 1944. They were emphasised as part of a positive evaluation of the German army, which was seen as a background to the German contribution to the Cold War. This did not encourage a scrutiny of the actual conduct of the Army during the Second World War. In practice, moreover, these plotters were scarcely democratic, while the non-military resistance enjoyed only limited support. Nevertheless, this resistance was important for the construction of an acceptable post-war German identity.

Within the West, not only the exigencies and ideological suppositions of the Cold War, both of which were influential,[7] but also the pressures for western European integration, encouraged an overlooking of a German self-image as victims of Nazism. Conversely, the experience of National Socialism and the desire to neutralise German economic power and nationalism by integrating it into a supra-national structure were the driving forces behind European integration. European integration was popular in West Germany because many Germans realised that it was the only way back into the international community, after what Germans had done during the Second World War.

Pressures for integration included ideas of a Western bloc, western Europe or United States of Europe, that looked towards the plan for a European Defence Community and, more successfully, to the establishment of a European Coal and Steel Community in 1951, and of the European Economic Community (EEC) in 1958. This was the result of the Treaty of Rome of 1957, which, in pledging to work for 'an ever closer union of the peoples of Europe', understandably did not leave room for the recollection of German popular support for Hitler.

Ironically, aspects of the EEC in part looked back to wartime talk of a new economic order that was advanced by collaborators with Nazi Germany, especially in France. Yet, at the same time, the EEC owed much of its genesis to anti-Nazi Catholic politicians such as Konrad Adenauer, the West German Chancellor from 1949 to 1963. In 1940, Robert Schuman, later, as French Foreign Minister (1948–52) and the President of the EEC Assembly (1958–60), a key figure in the creation of the EEC, had voted, as a member of the National Assembly, for the fall of the Third Republic.

A comparable integration occurred in eastern Europe, with the formation of the economic bloc of Comecon (1949) and the security bloc of the Warsaw Pact (1955). The continuity between Nazi Germany, and both the Soviet occupation and East Germany as totalitarian regimes, was indicated when the concentration camps at Buchenwald and Sachsenhausen were used for detaining political prisoners. East German scholarship tended to neglect the Holocaust or to mention it either as a product of capitalism, specifically needs for labour and capital, or of an attempt to divert attention from the failings of capitalism and the Nazi system. Compensation was not paid to Jews. This was because East Germany perceived itself as an anti-fascist state, and not in the tradition of previous German states, whereas West Germany saw itself explicitly as the legal successor of the German Reich. In East Germany, the victims of Nazi killing were presented as opponents of fascism and not as Jews.[8]

The situation subsequently changed, both in Germany and in other states that had played a role in the Holocaust, either as sites for murder, sources of collaboration or, allegedly, as overly disengaged observers. The attempt to contain the effects on Germany's image by blaming the atrocities specifically on the Nazis, and thus presenting the bulk of the population as victims, was eventually challenged in West Germany, especially in a debate about the complicity of the military, which was indeed pronounced and cumulative.[9] In occupied Serbia, for example, the mass killing of Jews was pushed by the Army from 1941.[10] By the late 1950s, there was a willingness to engage with misconduct by generals, although not yet with responsibility for the Holocaust.[11] Similarly, in 1960, Theodor Oberländer, a cabinet member, was dismissed in response to reports of the mass murder of Jews by Ukrainian forces under his command in 1941, although it was alleged that the evidence used against him was fake and, indeed, part of the East German attempt to discredit West Germany as a new Nazi state.

In West Germany, the pressures on the collective myth of general social and cultural changes were important, specifically the rise, from the 1960s, of a generation that did not feel responsibility for Nazism, the decline of deference towards the former generations and the need to explain what had happened to those who had not lived through the war as adults. The political and cultural agenda was no longer shaped by the pressures of post-war reconstruction, as well as by the evasion of responsibility through presenting wartime conduct as that of uninformed bystanders. Indeed, an aspect of the critique by the generation of 1968 of their predecessors was the charge that the latter did not mark a break from the wartime cooperation with Nazism and had not accepted individual responsibility. The radical Left accused their predecessors of being the 'Nazi generation'. It was now argued that coming to terms with the past was an aspect of anchoring democracy in Germany. Human rights became increasingly important in the political agenda. This argument also reflected the rise of the Social Democrats who, from 1969 to 1982, occupied the Federal Chancellery. Visiting Warsaw in 1969, the new Chancellor, Willy Brandt, knelt before the Ghetto Monument, a powerfully symbolic gesture of official atonement.

In part, the shift in German attitudes was due to a growing awareness of the atrocities committed by the Nazi regime, not least the trial that opened at Frankfurt in 1963 of twenty-three men involved in Auschwitz. Witness statements left no doubt of what had occurred and also provided an opportunity for public testimony by survivors. A wall of silence was broken. In December 1964, members of the court made an official visit to Auschwitz. The trial had a Cold War dimension, with Friedrich Kaul, the lawyer for the East German civil plaintiffs, being instructed by the East German Government to use it as a propaganda opportunity, while the visit to Auschwitz was encouraged by the Polish authorities. Both despite, and because of, this dimension, the West German authorities and the court, both under the spotlight, did not allow the trial to be used to discredit the idea of trying war criminals, as the key defence lawyer, Hans Laternser, wanted. However, in what, in some respects, proved an unsatisfactory outcome, it proved difficult to bring together collective responsibility and individual guilt.[12]

Moreover, Holocaust survivors such as Simon Wiesenthal directed attention to surviving Nazis who had been involved in atrocities. Among those Wiesenthal tracked down was Franz Stangl, the Austrian-born Commandant of first Sobibor and then Treblinka, who was tried in West Germany and given a life sentence. This shift was matched by an increased focus on the Holocaust from outside Germany.[13]

Within West Germany, eventually, there developed an influential determination to treat the Holocaust as the defining moment in public responsibility. Thus, in place of the notion of the Germans as in some ways victims of the Nazis[14] (an idea that continued to be pushed especially hard in Austria for the Austrians), came the view that the Germans had collaborated. A recognition of this was seen as important to the health of German democracy and as crucial to public education. From 1962, the *Länder* (provinces) extended the teaching of history to cover the Hitler years, including the Holocaust. Becoming effective from 1967, this was a major step in a process of public education over the Holocaust and one that ensured that the Germans became better informed on the Holocaust than other Europeans, although there were still important lacunae and a lack of agreement about how best to interpret the information. Moreover, there was a reluctance to commemorate key sites. The Bavarian Government, for example, was opposed to spending money to maintain Dachau as a memorial, and the same was true of the local council. On the extreme right, Holocaust deniers were active, such as Wilhelm Stäglich, author of *Der Auschwitz-Mythos* (1979). The presence of such deniers and, more generally, of neo-Nazis, who were responsible for acts such as the desecration of Cologne synagogue in 1959, as well as the electoral success of the Far-Right NPD during the 1960s, led to support for an emphasis on the need for public education about the Holocaust. This also encouraged a more positive response to foreign representations of the Holocaust, as, crucially, in 1979, when the American television series of that name was broadcast to an audience of about 20 million, over half the adult population.

The emergence of the Holocaust as a central issue in Germany, France and the USA from the 1970s, and more particularly in the 1990s, rested on complex social, cultural and political reasons.[15] These included, and not only in Germany, a reaction against Holocaust denial by the resurgent Extreme Right. This denial had become central to the mythology and discourse of the Extreme Right.[16] Growing interest in, and reference to, the Holocaust marked an important change in how people saw the Second World War, while the Holocaust also became a legitimate academic subject.

Moreover, a wider frame of reference developed. This was seen, for example, in the USA, with the opening, in 1993, of the large United States Holocaust Memorial Museum on a prominent site in Washington, and with the passage of the Nazi War Crimes Disclosure Act in 1998. To implement the latter, the Nazi War Criminal and Imperial Japanese Records Interagency Working Group was established.[17] Developments within individual countries encouraged pressure for action elsewhere, while a general atmosphere of scrutiny encouraged institutions to open archives in response to criticism. Thus, in the early 1980s, the International Committee of the Red

Cross opened its wartime archives. Businesses found it necessary to demonstrate and make amends for their relations with the Third Reich.

In German historiography, there was a bitter controversy about the relationship between the Nazis and the longer-term trends in German history, and this had a direct relevance to heated debates over the legitimacy of the West German political system and was linked with challenges to the dominant conservative (and, to an extent, gerontocratic) character of post-war West German historical scholarship. The *Historikerstreit* (controversy among historians) of 1986–7, which linked discussion of the Holocaust to the question of how best to present national history, was played out in a very public fashion, with many articles appearing in prominent newspapers. In part, this was a product of the attempt to 'normalise' German history, made by historians close to Chancellor Helmut Kohl, the leader of the conservative Christian Democratic Party, which gained power in 1982. This normalisation was taken to mean making German history more acceptable in order to ground national identity and seek inspiration. Kohl, who remained Chancellor until 1998, saw such a normalisation as a necessary basis for patriotism, national pride and spiritual renewal, a theme taken up more generally on the German Right, but one that scarcely focused on issues of ethical concern. Kohl himself had earlier voted against abolishing the statute of limitations for murder, an abolition that left ex-Nazis vulnerable to prosecution.

In the controversy, the degree to which Nazism could be seen as a historical episode, rather than inherent in longer-term trends, and to which the Holocaust arose from specific German characteristics, rather than being an aspect of more widespread violence, were debated. So also was the extent to which the German state had a historical mission, specifically to resist advances from the east, i.e., the Soviet Union, an approach pushed by conservatives such as Andreas Hillgruber. This led to the claim that German iniquities had to be considered against this background, with Ernst Nolte arguing that the Nazis were a reaction to Communism and presenting

Hitler as trying to thwart what he saw as a Jewish–Communist threat. Furthermore, Nazi activities were presented as in part emulating the Communists.

The argument that the Germans had to fight on to resist the Soviet advance was also that of German generals in the final stage of the war. This self-serving argument did not stop them also mounting a fierce resistance to Anglo-American forces, including directing the reserves involved in the Battle of the Bulge counter-offensive against them, rather than against the Soviets. Fighting on, of course, also provided more time for the Holocaust, not that this was the main purpose of the generals, although it was a factor for Nazi leaders.

Kohl's attempt at a re-evaluation was unsuccessful in that it led to much criticism both within Germany and internationally. Nolte and others were attacked by a number of prominent scholars, including Jürgen Habermas. They argued that Nolte was trying to relativise or historicise Nazi activities and thus limit them and reduce the collective and individual responsibilities of Germans. Instead, the Nazi enterprise was presented as unique in its criminality.[18] An essential issue in the *Historikerstreit* was the fact that the Holocaust was seen as implying the problem, indeed issue, of the legitimacy of West Germany. This legitimacy was challenged by East Germany, and that was a reason why the controversy petered out once German unification became a prospect, which ended this challenge.

Meanwhile, scholarly work on key aspects of Germany during the war, particularly the Army, the Police and the Judiciary,[19] presented them critically as actively supporting Nazi aims. The greatest controversy was caused by the Wehrmacht exhibition, arranged by the Hamburg Social Research Institute which toured Germany and Austria from 1994, drawing 800,000 visitors in thirty-three cities by 1999. The photographs of Wehrmacht soldiers involved in atrocities had a major impact on the public and led to much discussion and contention, including hostile demonstrations in Dresden and Munich and a terrorist attack by right-wing extremists at Saarbrücken in 1999. The thesis that the Army, instead of solely the SS, had been active in the Holocaust cut across the argument that they were patriots fighting for their country.[20]

In the same period as the *Historikerstreit*, Kurt Waldheim became President of Austria (1986–92). He was elected and served despite wartime involvement in anti-Jewish atrocities in Yugoslavia and Greece: the intelligence staff of Army Group E, of which he was a member, played a role in the deportation of Greek and Yugoslav Jews to slaughter, as well as in brutal anti-partisan operations. In response to criticism, Waldheim publicly claimed that Jews were trying to ruin the reputation of his generation. Taking up earlier Nazi themes, Waldheim linked this to a purported international conspiracy, with Jewish pressure against him being presented as centred in the USA, where the former Secretary-General of the United Nations was now treated as an undesirable alien.

Waldheim's persistent evasions and downright lies symbolised the extent to which this episode was seen as a key aspect of the Austrian reluctance to accept the legacy of the Holocaust, and one that contrasted markedly with the greater engagement in Germany. Indeed, on 8 May 1985, in the ceremony held in the Bundestag marking the fortieth anniversary of the end of the Second World War, Richard von Weizsäcker, the West German President, recognised the Holocaust as an aspect of the war and emphasised individual and collective responsibilities, while also presenting defeat as a liberation for Germany.[21]

Austrians, in fact, had played a prominent role in the Holocaust. From January 1943, the Reich Main Security Office was headed by Ernst Kaltenbrunner, formerly Head of the SS and Police in Austria;[22] Eichmann was brought up in Austria; Globocnik was born in Trieste when it was Austrian and became active in Austrian Nazism, eventually becoming *Gauleiter* of Vienna. Austrians were regarded as being particularly cruel concentration-camp guards (and became guards out of all proportion to their numbers) and had also, for example, been very active in the deportation of Jews from the Netherlands. Judging by public-opinion polls, anti-Semitism, which was potent during the Nazi years,[23] remains strong in

Austria, although Holocaust memorialisation has become more prominent, and, from 1991, a 'Commemorative Service' financed by the Government has existed to provide guides at Holocaust sites. A reluctance to accept the implications of wartime action was also seen in Germany in Nuremberg in 1997. Criticism of the granting by the City Council that year of honorary citizenship to Karl Diehl, a local industrialist who had used concentration-camp workers, led to a bitter controversy in which the majority of the council supported Diehl.[24] Conversely, and more generally, there has been a major debate about compensation for forced labourers, which, in many respects, has been a cornerstone for a new way the German Government and companies have tried to come to terms with their past. Class actions brought against German actions in the USA in the late 1990s encouraged restitution, most centrally through a public-private foundation.[25]

The capacity of totally different historical works to ignite public interest in this field was shown by the response to Daniel Goldhagen's depiction of a large number of Germans as *Hitler's Willing Executioners* (1996), and also with the 2000 libel trial in Britain arising from David Irving's work. The former episode juxtaposed an often-critical scholarly response, with a more engaged populist reception accepting Goldhagen's somewhat simplistic and ably marketed case, especially in the USA, although also with young German listeners in his 1996 tour.[26] Anti-Semitism has been seen at work in the critical reaction among important sections of German opinion and in German-controlled publications,[27] although the prejudices this reaction drew on were more complex and, in part, reflected institutional, historiographical and political drives within Germany.

Conversely, criticism also focused on what was presented as an over-simplistic thesis, poor methodology, questionable conclusions, combative manner and the desire to build a career on presenting himself as a taboo-breaker. This ensured that there was scholarly criticism of Goldhagen from the Left as well as, more prominently, from the Right. In contrast,

Christopher Browning's *Ordinary Men* was very well received by German historians. German Jewish commentators were divided in their response to Goldhagen. There is indeed a lack of consistency in his running together evidence of Germany wishing to exclude Jewishness and the determination to kill Jews, not least because the former could be achieved by assimilation or forced emigration. Goldhagen also provided the Holocaust with an inherent past in German political culture and society that exaggerates the earlier centrality there of anti-Semitism. The scholarly criticism of Goldhagen, by those on the Left as well, more prominently, as on the Right, was to be repeated in the early 2000s, in discussion of the simplistically critical German response to the Allied bombing campaign.

The Irving libel trial arose from a case brought by Irving against Deborah Lipstadt and her publisher Penguin, because Lipstadt had claimed that Irving had falsified history in order to advance a particular agenda. Irving was presented by supporters as being denied the ability to present his views, but the exact opposite was in fact the case. Irving is frequently described as a historian, but this is only so in so far as he writes about the past. He has not been trained as a scholar and has not held an academic or other related post as a historian. Irving had appeared for the defence in 1988 in the second trial in Toronto of Ernst Zundel for Holocaust denial. The prosecution called Christopher Browning, who, in the face of attacks from the defence on the methodology of history, underlined the role of facts as opposed to simply opinions. Zundel was convicted.

The Irving libel trial of 2000 indicated anew that historical evidence could be deployed effectively within the constraints of legal cases, as the trial served as an opportunity to assert and demonstrate historical truths, in this case the horrors of the Holocaust, which was done, in particular, by the historian Richard Evans. This demonstration, both of the truths and of Irving's misuse and denial of them, ensured that Irving lost his case. The judge, Charles Gray, remarked that Irving's ideological slant was 'anti-Semitic and racist';

and the case led to the publication of a number of reviews of the evidence, as well as accounts of the trial. Irving was subsequently arrested, tried and imprisoned in Austria in 2006 for Holocaust denial on an earlier visit, again an episode that led to extensive coverage. In this trial, Irving accepted that the Holocaust involved the murder of millions of Jews and that Hitler knew about it, a point he had earlier denied in his *Hitler's War*. Holocaust denial is a criminal offence in Austria (since 1992), as also in Germany, where, in 1994, it was made a form of racial incitement.[28]

The very different Goldhagen and Irving controversies indicated that the Holocaust remained an issue capable of engaging much interest and generating much comment, the first in the USA and Germany in particular, and the second in Britain. Indeed, the saliency of the Holocaust, both in its own right and not least as a touchstone for wider tensions, emerged powerfully in both cases.

Separately from, but related to, debates among historians, the controversial nature of the recent German past has a direct impact in German domestic politics and, possibly, on German foreign policy. The former was seen in October–November 2003, when a controversy arose over a speech by Martin Hohmann, a backbencher from the then opposition Christian Democratic Party, declaring that Germans should not, as a result of their support for Hitler, be treated as a 'guilty people'. Hohmann's comparison was indeed designed to deflect criticism onto those whose brutal treatment under Hitler formed the prime charge, Jews, because he claimed that they were themselves guilty of a prominent role in Communist atrocities, a claim also made on behalf of anti-Semitic nationalists in eastern Europe. After a fortnight's controversy, Hohmann was expelled from the party.

Hohmann lacked the significance of Philipp Jenninger, who had to resign as President of the German Parliament in 1988, but his argument was resonant in a country in which part of the population, an increasing percentage of which had had no experience of the war, was fed up with being urged to remember the Holocaust. This remembrance was central in

German education, with the Nazi period a compulsory subject. However, as the response to Goldhagen's *Hitlers willige Vollstrecker* (1996) (the translation of *Hitler's Willing Executioners*) indicated, some German historians and senior journalists were unwilling to move from a form of abstract condemnation and a depersonalisation of the Holocaust, to confront, as well, the argument of widespread German willingness to engage in a slaughter characterised by sadistic anti-Semitism. The popular response to Goldhagen's book tour in 1996 was far more positive.

In policy terms, the German Government had taken a more significant step when, for thirteen years after the fall of the Iron Curtain, it offered all Jews from the former Soviet Union automatic residency. As a result, by 2006, there were 115,000 Jews in Germany, most from a Soviet background. In comparison, over 1 million moved from the Soviet Union to Israel in the same period, although possibly as many as 100,000 returned to the Soviet Union, in large part to take advantage of the greater economic opportunities there.

The official federal-government memorialisation in Germany was reflected powerfully in the Memorial to the Murdered Jews of Europe, which was finally opened in May 2005 after long controversy, and four years after the Jewish Museum in Berlin opened. A large work, the size of two football fields, built close to the Brandenburg Gate and the site of Hitler's bunker in Berlin, its design, however, was a source of dispute, as was the extent to which it represented a real break with the past. The need to coat the stones (designed to represent a Jewish cemetery) with anti-graffiti spray reflected anxiety that they could be defaced by neo-Nazis. Similarly, the Ohel Jakob synagogue, a complex comprising synagogue, Jewish museum and community centre, which opened in Munich in March 2007, faced neo-Nazi opposition, including, in 2003, a plot to bomb the construction site. The synagogue's dedication in 2007 was protected by 1,500 police and by metal-detecting gates.

As another cause of controversy over the Berlin Memorial, the anti-graffiti spray was manufactured by Degussa, a subsidiary of which had produced the Zyklon-B gas used in the extermination camps. The memorial was presented not simply as a response to the past, but also as a warning. In July 2004, Wolfgang Thierse, the Speaker of the German Parliament, praised it not just as a memorial to mark the Holocaust, but also for being 'about the future: a reminder that we should resist anti-Semitism at its roots'.

This, indeed, was an urgent issue for a Germany where racism was resurgent, especially in the former East Germany. Racism there can be seen not only as an aspect of the failure of the Communist system in public education, but also as a consequence of the fall of that system. Concern helped lead the German Government, in January 2007, to propose to make Holocaust denial a crime across the European Union (see p. 193), Brigitte Zypries, the Justice Minister, claiming: 'We should not wait until it comes to deeds. We must act against the intellectual pathbreakers of the crime.' In part, the resurgent racism of the 1990s and 2000s was a product of the economic difficulties that followed German reunification, particularly high male unemployment in the former East Germany, but there were also powerful cultural and ideological currents of hostility and fear that led, for example, to attacks on Jews and Africans, synagogues and asylum hostels. These currents reflected the persistence of neo-Nazi beliefs, agitation and symbols, although the Extreme Right was scarcely specific to Germany.

At the same time, the Jewish community in Germany greatly increased, in large part due to large-scale immigration from Russia. As a consequence of this, and of the earlier devastation in the Holocaust (followed by the emigration of Jews, who had ended up in Germany as a result of the enforced population movements of displaced persons in 1945–6), Germany came to have the fastest growing Jewish community in the world. It is estimated at 100,000 by the World Jewish Congress. That in Munich, for example, is now over 9,000 strong, an instance of the total failure of the Nazis even in their heartland. In 2001, a new synagogue opened in Dresden, the first to be built in the former East Germany since the Nazi years. In 2006, the first rabbis to emerge from rabbinical training since the Nazi years graduated.

Furthermore, Jews became more central in German life as an aspect of public absolution. This was both symbolic and also played a role in particular crises. Thus, in April 2007, when Günther Oettinger, the Christian Democratic Premier of Baden-Württemberg, landed himself in controversy for his funeral eulogy for a predecessor, Hans Filbinger, who had had to resign for his wartime role as a military judge in occupied Norway, he met Charlotte Knobloch, the Head of Germany's Central Council of Jews, as part of the process of apology.

Reflecting different national issues, memorials and cemeteries are important sites for contestation, as well as commemoration.[29] This is not only true of specific Holocaust sites, such as Auschwitz, which became a World Heritage Site in 1979. Thus, President Ronald Reagan of the USA caused a stir on a state visit to West Germany in 1985 when, joining the German Chancellor, Helmut Kohl, he visited the military cemetery at Bitburg. The controversy arose because the cemetery contained the graves of forty-nine members of the Waffen-SS. They were not SS concentration-camp guards, and, by the time they died, the Waffen-SS was no longer a volunteer army. Only fifteen of the forty-nine were registered in the SS personnel files. Nevertheless, the Waffen-SS was a vicious organisation (indeed, a criminal one in clear breach of international law), and Reagan had been advised not to visit Bitburg. However, he heeded Kohl's pressure to do so. Reagan, indeed, described the soldiers as being as much victims of the Nazis as those who had suffered in concentration camps, a bizarre equivalence, but one that reflected the sense that he had to say something about the camps.[30] Reagan also visited Belsen.

FRANCE

Germany's wartime allies and collaborators also came to grips with the Holocaust, although only with some difficulty. This was most contentious in France, where the Vichy legacy proved difficult, not least because of a determination not to accept what had happened, and also due to the strength of the Gaullist myth about a powerful and unifying French resistance. Moreover, aside from active anti-Semitism in the shape of organisations and demonstrations, there was only limited governmental support for the restitution of goods and buildings seized from Jews or for indemnification.

The French role in the Holocaust was neglected, both in the French account of the recent past and in the French treatment of Germany. Thus, at Nuremberg, François de Menthon, the French prosecutor, did not refer to the Holocaust, while, in France, prominent figures from Vichy were criticised and tried for treason but not for cooperation in mass murder. In Alain Resnais' documentary about the deportation, *Nuit et brouillard (Night and Fog*, 1955), a film commissioned by the Comité d'Histoire de la 2e Guerre Mondiale, with the support of the Ministry of Veterans' Affairs, the French licensing authorities censored a shot briefly showing the kepi of a French policeman among those guarding deportees who, furthermore, were not identified as Jews.[31] The film was also withdrawn from the Cannes Festival as a result of a formal protest by the German Foreign Ministry to the French Government.

This process of denial was given added force by the search for assurance and prestige that finally culminated in the formation of the Fifth Republic in 1958, and the presidency of Charles de Gaulle from 1958 to 1969. His refusal to collaborate during the war was presented as the quintessential cause of the new France, and the fact that he was now president apparently vindicated the French of 1940–4 and, more generally, French history, as did the widespread exaggeration of the popularity and effectiveness of the wartime Resistance. This idea of a national resistance also had no particular place for Jews.

This situation was to change, in part because of developments specific to France itself, but in part due both to the greater weight that the Holocaust came to play in the collective Western consciousness and to the less reverential approach to the past that was an aspect of the cultural changes of the 1960s. Scholarship played a role, not least the book *Vichy France: Old Guard and New Order, 1940–1944* (1972), by the American Robert Paxton. In place of the presentation of Vichy and collaboration as something forced on France by the Germans, Paxton, by extensively employing German archival material (the French archives were closed to him), argued that the Vichy regime had been popular and also keen to collaborate, in order to win German support for a reconfiguration of French society that was to mark the triumph of Vichy's anti-liberal ideology.

Paxton's approach, however, was unacceptable to many of those in academic authority in France, and there were difficulties in publishing a French translation of his book. Similarly, Marcel Ophuls' documentary about the occupation in Clermont-Ferrand, an industrial centre near Vichy, *Le Chagrin et la pitié (The Sorrow and the Pity)*, eventually released at the cinema in 1971, was not shown on French television for twelve years. The Government, in 1969, had already banned the television transmission of this tale of collaboration, which, however, was shown that year on television in Germany, Switzerland, the Netherlands and the USA. The lengthy documentary was largely based on interviews.

De Gaulle himself had publicly indicated his critical view of Jews on 27 November 1967 in a press conference, when he called them over Egypt, Jordan and Syria, 'a people sure of themselves and domineering'. While a response to Israel's sweeping success in the Six-Day War earlier that year, this remark was also all-too-indicative of the role of anti-Semitism in the unwillingness to face the French past.

Sympathetic post-war views about wartime conduct, indeed, continued to be expressed, as in François-Georges Dreyfus' *Histoire de Vichy* (1990). Nevertheless, growing interest in Vichy's complicity in the Holocaust, and the less deferential character of French society, especially after the unrest of May 1968, combined to provide a more conducive atmosphere for the pursuit of the truth by journalists, scholars and others. Documentaries, films, memoirs and novels were published. Louis Malle's film *Lacombe, Lucien* (1975) created considerable controversy because it made fascism seem attractive and presented its French protagonist as working voluntarily for the Gestapo.[32] Marcel Ophuls' documentary *Hotel Terminus: Klaus Barbie* (1988) won an Oscar. Research by journalists also played a role. In October 1978, the news-magazine *L'Express* published verbatim an interview with Louis Darquier de Pellepoix, who, in 1942, had been appointed Commissioner for Jewish Affairs, thanks in large part to German support for this virulent anti-Semite. Darquier claimed in this interview that the Holocaust was a 'hoax' and that only lice were gassed at Auschwitz (which provided the title for the interview 'In Auschwitz, They Only Gassed Lice'). Darquier also claimed that the research by Serge Klarsfeld on the names of Jews deported from France was a 'Jewish invention'. Klarsfeld's research, which showed the large numbers deported, had been published that year as *Le Mémorial de la déportation des Juifs de France*.

This interview caused a sensation, with the National Assembly (Parliament) debating it the following month. In part, there was anger that Darquier was living in Spain, where he had been given refuge, like many Nazis, by Franco. Sentenced to death in France *in absentia* in 1947, Darquier had not been hunted down. Moreover, in 1978, he could not be extradited because his sentence, for collusion with the enemy (rather than for mass murder), had lapsed in 1968, as a result of the statute of limitations. In part, the anger rebounded more widely because Darquier himself drew attention to the more favourable fate of his wartime rival, René Bousquet, Chief of Police in the Occupied Zone of France from 1942. Bousquet had been able to stay in France and even to pursue a successful career, despite having agreed to use French police in arresting Jews and having pressed for the deportation of foreign Jews to eastern Europe.[33]

This interview, and the resulting consideration of Bousquet's position, helped encourage a sense that France had failed to address the issue of Vichy's complicity in the Holocaust, specifically rounding up Jews for deportation to

Auschwitz. Further journalistic research provided fresh light on the same process. In 1981, the press first revealed the major role of Maurice Papon, wartime Secretary-General at the Préfecture of the Gironde, in the deportation of Bordeaux's Jews. Post-war, Papon had become a government minister and a key member of the French establishment. As Police Chief of Paris under de Gaulle, he had also been responsible for the violent suppression of post-war demonstrations.

Politics also played a major role, as scores were settled with those who could be tainted for their role under Vichy. Most prominently, although only indirectly, this included François Mitterrand, President from 1981 until 1995. A civil servant under Vichy, Mitterrand was a friend of Bousquet, who, indeed, was assassinated in Paris in 1993, just before he could be tried for his role in rounding up Jewish children for deportation to slaughter in Germany. Judicial proceedings further helped encourage interest and controversy, especially the capture and trial in 1994 of Paul Touvier, Head of the collaborationist *milice* in Lyons, and the trial, in 1997–8, of an unrepentant and aloof Papon. Evidence of the role of Vichy in the Holocaust was thus publicised. Paxton gave evidence, a responsibility several French historians refused to accept.[34] In 2003, Kurt Schaechter took legal action against the SNCF, the French railways, for deporting his parents to Sobibor and Auschwitz, a symbolic case designed to highlight the range of responsibility.

The Holocaust helped focus a more complex refashioning of the recent French past, creating a demand for the recognition of events and memories that had been ignored in the public account,[35] and that were challenged by Holocaust deniers.[36] In 1994, Serge Klarsfeld published his *Le Mémorial des enfants juifs déportés de France*. Pressure for a new public memory was grasped in 1995 when, on 16 July, the anniversary of the major round-up of Jews in Paris in 1942, Mitterrand's long-time opponent and eventual successor, Jacques Chirac, accepted national responsibility for the wartime treatment of Jews. This was a major condemnation of the Vichy regime and a step that Mitterrand had refused to take in 1992. Indeed, Papon had only been arrested after Mitterrand's death. The contrast that Mitterrand, following his predecessors, had sought to make between the true France, which did not commit crimes, and Vichy, was shattered, and it was also clear that there had been a serious cover-up.

The responsibility was more seriously Mitterrand's than his predecessors because of the extent to which by the 1980s, and even more 1990s, other governments were coming to grips with wartime collaboration and post-war moral cowardice, not to say, in many cases, complicity; although, in his refusal to accept collective responsibility, Mitterrand shared the attitudes of his friend and political ally, Kohl. Chirac, in contrast, referred to Holocaust denial as a crime against truth and a perversion of the soul. In 2004, the French education ministry distributed to schools DVDs with excerpts of *Shoah* (1985), Claude Lanzmann's influential (and nine-and-a-half-hour-long) film about the Holocaust (in eastern Europe, not France), as part of its attempt to combat anti-Semitism.[37] It was certainly a blow against French Holocaust deniers. The use of *La Shoah* in France to describe the Holocaust is a potent testimony to the impact of Lanzmann's work and, more generally, of film.

The weight of the past continues to play a role in current French politics. With the Right divided between the Gaullists and the far-right National Front, under Jean-Marie Le Pen, both struggled for appropriate historical references. The Gaullists argued that the National Front looked back to Vichy, and, indeed, it did make such references, not least in the 2002 Presidential Election when the Vichy slogan 'Work, Family, Country' was deployed. Le Pen, who came second to Chirac in that election, was also accused of minimising the Holocaust, a serious charge in France.

The relationship between past and present was at stake in France in 2004 when Chirac sought an appropriate context for a call to act against a rising wave of anti-Semitism and racism. He travelled to Le Chambon-sur-Lignon, a village in the Massif Central that had sheltered Jews from the Holocaust, in order to declare:

Faced with the rise of intolerance, racism and anti-Semitism [. . .] I ask the French to remember a still recent past. I tell them to remain faithful to the lessons of history, a so-recent history.

Praising Chambon (where the Catholic Church was weak) as a model for modern France, because its people had rejected 'the infamy of the Vichy regime', Chirac linked a call for modern vigilance to a demand that the horrors of the past be understood. The Holocaust Memorial opened in Paris in January 2005. Alongside Vichy, although as a lesser topic, German actions in France were also at issue.

BELGIUM

Holocaust denial is currently a criminal offence in France (since 1990, the Gayssot Law), as it also is, in western Europe, in Austria, Belgium, Germany, the Netherlands and Spain. In 2007, the Belgian Prime Minister Guy Verhofstadt apologised in Parliament for the role Belgian officials played in denouncing Jews to the Germans and/or deporting them. This was the first apology by a senior Belgian governmental figure in Parliament and was an occasion that was different to the inauguration, in 1970, by the then Prime Minister, Gaston Eyskens, of the Mémorial National des Martyrs Juifs. Verhofstadt had, as Prime Minister, apologised for this first in 2002 at Malines/Mechelen, the deportation centre, and now the location of the Jewish Museum of Deportation and Resistance; and then, in 2005, at Yad Vashem in Jerusalem. His speech included the need for information on the Holocaust to be part of school education – although, in Belgium, responsibility for that subject rests with the regional, rather than the federal authorities.

Verhofstadt also attended the unveiling in the Mont des Arts, the centre of Brussels, of memorial plaques to the 'Just', non-Jews who helped Jews to escape capture. The unveiling took place on 8 May, the day that commemorates the end of the Second World War for Belgium. Verhofstadt paid tribute to the 'Just' and argued that their contribution was a reminder of the need for tolerance at all times. As an instance of the manner in which the Holocaust could now conflate different forms of public memorialisation, the town authorities agreed to name the path containing the plaques as the Alley of the Just; the Minister of Defence, whose responsibilities include war victims, unveiled the plaques, one in French, the other in Dutch; the national anthem followed by the Last Post was played by a military band; and, after a minute's silence, the European 'anthem' from Beethoven's Ninth Symphony was played. Whether this was an appropriate choice, not so much because of Beethoven's national background as due to the European theme, is left to the reader to consider. All the Belgian radio stations put the ceremony as the first item on their lunchtime news programmes.

In his speech, Verhofstadt noted that the Ceges (Centre d'Études et de Documentation Guerre et Sociétés Contemporaines) report, commissioned by the Sénat in 2003, describing the role of the Belgian authorities during the Nazi occupation, had been received and that it had described them as docile at best and with some directly collaborationist activities. The closing remarks of the report were that 'the Belgian state had adopted a docile attitude in providing, in different but crucial sphere, a collaboration unworthy of a democracy towards a policy that was disastrous for the Jewish population, both Belgian and foreign.' In response, Verhofstadt announced an expansion of Holocaust compensation.

In 2002, the Buysse Commission had been set up to work with Jewish representatives in Belgium in directly allocating public and private funds. In 2007, an additional fund was established to help those not covered by the original grant. In total, the Belgian Government had already contributed to the establishment of a fund of 110 million euros for compensation for Holocaust sufferers.

THE NETHERLANDS

Dutch public understanding of cooperation in the deportations essentially dated from the mid-1960s, particularly the publication of the historian Jacob Presser's study *Ondergang*

(1965). That year, but not earlier, the Government offered to pay towards the Auschwitz memorial. Only in 1995, however, did the monarch, Queen Beatrice, acknowledge the fate of Dutch Jews.

ITALY

In Italy, the treatment of Jews, particularly after the anti-Semitic legislation of 1938,[38] was, and is, an issue in the contest over the reputation of Benito Mussolini, not least over the popularity of the Fascist Salò republic in northern Italy in 1943–5. This issue also relates to that of the Italian position in the Balkans, part of which was occupied by Italian forces in 1941–3. The contest over the Italian past is directly linked to the legitimacy of current political groupings that look to the past for evidence of their probity and of the iniquity of their opponents. The Italian Social Movement (MSI), the Fascist Party, has, however, tried to break with its past in order to move from the political margins. As late as 1992, the MSI marked the seventieth anniversary of Mussolini's seizure of power by donning black shirts and giving the Fascist salute, but, in 1994–5, the leader, Gianfranco Fini, changed the MSI into the more moderate Alleanza Nazionale. This sought acceptance, not least by a rejection of anti-Semitism. A more positive appraisal of Mussolini was also offered by Silvio Berlusconi, when Italian Prime Minister, but was rejected by the Left.

THE PAPACY

Serious questions have also been raised about the role of Pope Pius XII, who had been elected Pope in March 1939. He has been accused of anti-Semitism and of failing to act against the Holocaust, not least in Rolf Hochhuth's play *Der Stellvertreter* (*The Representative*, 1963). The Pope has been criticised, more specifically, for failing to block the deportation of Jews from Rome, and also for his stance over the treatment of Jews in Croatia, France and the Netherlands.[39]

Conversely, it has also been claimed that Communist misinformation played a role in such charges, and that Pius XII was more sympathetic to Jews than is generally believed and also active on their behalf.[40] In responding to the Germans, the Catholic Church was also aware of the hostility to religious interests of Communism, an atheistical movement. The Church also feared that criticism of the Germans would lead to problems for Catholics. Indeed, in May 1943, Dutch Jews baptised as Catholics were arrested and deported to their deaths in response to a Pastoral Letter from the Dutch Catholic bishops opposing the deportation of Jews. In contrast, Protestant Jews were not deported.

The previous Christmas, the Pope used his radio message to criticise the Final Solution, as he did again in June 1943, but he did not respond when the Germans rounded up Rome's Jews that October. Later that year, the Vatican indeed, in response to German raids in Rome on Church properties, instructed that only Jews who had been baptised as Catholics should be given shelter. Already, in 1939, Pius had shown a failure to respond to the Germans and to provide leadership when he said nothing about their killing of Polish Catholic clergy.[41] In his apologia of June 1945, the Pope argued that his radio messages had been the sole effective means he had to influence German Catholics in the face of the power of evil.

Nevertheless, the Papacy, like other church authorities across Europe, did little to oppose the Holocaust, by influencing either Germans or others, both those active in the Holocaust and those who did nothing, and this remains a serious moral failing. The extent to which the Holocaust was dependent on the cooperation of non-Germans, many of whom were Catholics, underlines the importance of this issue. Pius XII, for example, did not match the denunciations of Alojzije Stepinac, the Archbishop of Zagreb in Croatia. The Papacy failed to pass on the knowledge of the Holocaust that it had from the winter of 1941–2 and did not provide the leadership of the Church that the hierarchy, clergy and laity expected and needed. In contrast, foreign Protestant churches, while primarily concerned about the plight of co-religionists in Germany, were increasingly aware of the nature and immorality of Nazi anti-Semitism.[42]

Blaming Pius XII for not having done enough to criticise the Holocaust may be fair (in retrospect), and Pius would have been regarded as more heroic had he suffered detention as Pius VII did under Napoleon. Yet, alongside underlining the complexity in the relationship between Pius XII and Hitler, the Vatican and the Nazis, it is necessary to underline the extent to which church authorities outside Germany receive blame for something that individuals and secular institutions within the country were better placed to prevent.

After the war, however, Pius XII devoted scant attention to the aftermath of the Holocaust as far as Jewish victims were concerned, while he was also not interested in improving relations between Christians and Jews. Instead, he sought to ensure that no blame was attached to the German Church. An opponent of de-Nazification policies, Pius XII was keenly anti-Communist, while the Vatican helped German and Croatian war criminals to escape to Spain and South America.

In contrast, Pius's successor, John XXIII (1958–63) favoured a better relationship with Jews. This led to the Second Vatican Council's decision in 1965 to absolve Jews from responsibility for the death of Christ, a key thesis in Christian anti-Semitism. Paul VI (1963–78), who had served in the Vatican diplomatic service in wartime, was considerably less positive but did not reverse this step.

The Vatican was sufficiently affected by the greater centrality of the Holocaust in public discussion to take a role in the debate over Pius XII. In 1998, its Commission for Religious Relations with the Jews issued a defence of the Pope in its report 'We Remember: A Reflection on the Shoah', but this is a one-sided approach to the evidence and less than convincing in its judgement. Five years later, the Vatican declassified archival material relating to Pius XII in an attempt to indicate his 'great works of charity and assistance' towards those persecuted by the Nazis.

EASTERN EUROPE

In eastern Europe, Communist totalitarianism was presented by the Communists as very different to its Nazi rival, although, in fact, there were echoes, including the use of some of the same apparatus of oppression.[43] For example, in East Germany, Sachsenhausen concentration camp was employed anew as a detention centre, as was Mühlberg. Communist criticism of the Nazi regime and its collaborators was often matched, in practice, by anti-Semitic policies. In part, these reflected attempts to ground Communist governments in a populist nationalism and, in part, rifts within Communist regimes as a result of which Jewish Communists, who had been influential, were widely purged. In the Soviet Union, Jews were presented as unpatriotic cosmopolitans, the wartime Jewish Anti-Fascist Committee was suppressed under Stalin in 1948, and its leaders were executed in 1952.[44]

The satellite states followed suit. Zionism was a major charge against Jewish Communists who were purged, but, with a macabre twisting of truth, all too characteristic of both Communists and Nazis, some Jews were accused of wartime collaboration with the Germans. Factions within the Communist Party used anti-Semitism and the charge of Zionism against rivals, for example in East Germany and Romania, and, very prominently, in the Slánský trial in Czechoslovakia in 1952, where there was a marked upsurge in anti-Semitic propaganda.

The following year, Soviet Jewish doctors were denounced in *Pravda* as a 'Zionist terrorist gang', anti-Semitic attacks occurred, and it is possible that this would have led to the deportation of Soviet Jews to the east, a distant Soviet homeland in Birobidzhan; but Stalin's death cut short the idea. However, the support shown to Israel by the USA from 1967 and, conversely, Soviet backing for Egypt, Syria and pan-Arabism, strengthened Communist anti-Semitism, which was seen, for example, in the anti-Semitic purges in Poland in 1968. Indeed, in the bizarre world of Soviet propaganda, Zionists were accused of cooperating with the Holocaust in order to give birth to Israel.

Linked to this was a practice of downplaying the extent to which Nazi atrocities were aimed at Jews.[45] This was seen in the memorialisation at the camps. For example, Auschwitz was presented as a symbol of Christian, Polish resistance. Jewish victims were not mentioned, and the museum there, on which work began in 1947 as a memorial to the 'martyrdom of the Polish nation and other nations', was used to disseminate a Communist view of events, which was also the case with the International Auschwitz Committee established in 1954. Polish and Soviet works made mention of the large numbers killed, without identifying the fact that many were Jews. In part, this reflected the argument that Communism, a movement that supposedly was axiomatically opposed to religious or racial prejudice, took precedence over other identities. In this light, Jews should not be treated as separate to other Poles and other Soviet citizens. Nationalism played the same role in France.

There was also a deliberate attempt to minimise the extent to which the killing had been aimed at Jews. Babi Yar was presented as the slaughter of 'peaceful Soviet citizens', and the inscription there did not mention Jews.[46] Auschwitz I, not Auschwitz II, the site of the killing of most of the Jews, was for a while the only part of Auschwitz that could be visited. The *Historical Atlas of Poland* (1981) claimed that over 6 million Polish citizens were killed during the war, without giving a figure for the Jews. It also stated that in Auschwitz, 4 million people 'of various nationalities' perished.[47] The extermination camps as the site for the slaughter of non-Jews as well as Jews were presented to Hollywood viewers in Alan Pakula's film *Sophie's Choice* (1982), which was based on William Styron's novel of 1979, and which used flashbacks to Auschwitz.

It would, however, be misleading to suggest that the Communist period was one of unchanging indifference or even hostility. There were signs prior to the fall of the Communist system, for example, in the early 1980s in Poland, of greater interest in Jewish perspectives,[48] and there were efforts to bring academics together in order to find a basis for discussion.[49] As noted earlier, there were also parallel tendencies elsewhere. In the case, most obviously, of Oradaur in France and Lidice in Czechoslovakia, national sites commemorating German atrocities were villages rather than ghettos.

The fall of the Iron Curtain led to the publication of new sources from former Communist states relating to the Holocaust, but the key emphasis was now not on Nazi killing but on Communist and Soviet oppression. For example, in Belarus, the mass graves at Kuropatny, where the Soviet NKVD (Secret Police) had slaughtered at least 100,000 people between 1937 and 1941, were exhumed from 1988,[50] reviving and popularising Belarussian nationalism in the crucible of anger. As eastern Europeans came to see themselves as victims of Communist rule, who had played no role in the regime (a largely misleading view), while Communism was presented as a foreign ideology, so the sufferings of others, such as Jews, was neglected. Moreover, the tendency seen earlier in the century to link Communism with Jews, a tendency very much pushed by Nazi Germany and its allies, was revived in the 1990s, with anti-Semitism playing an explicit or implicit role in some populist nationalism. Furthermore, the long-held tendency to emphasise Christian victims of Nazi persecution as much as, or more than, their Jewish counterparts continued. This was seen, for example, in the contest between Catholic and Jewish interpretations of Auschwitz,[51] which had been visited by over 20 million people by 1997. The fall of the Iron Curtain was followed in Auschwitz's museum by an emphasis on the German killing of Poles.

Throughout eastern Europe, there was also a reluctance or failure to acknowledge the degree of local complicity in the Holocaust.[52] Furthermore, in Bulgaria, Croatia, Hungary, Romania and Slovakia, wartime regimes that had collaborated with Hitler received far more sympathetic attention than had been the case under the Communists. Ion Antonescu, dictator of Romania from 1940 until 1944, had actively persecuted Jews and collaborated with Hitler, being executed for war crimes in 1946, but, in the 1990s, he was proclaimed as an anti-Soviet nationalist, and cities rushed to name streets after him. Although not seen as anti-Semitic acts, this process was an aspect of the expression of traditional themes that included anti-Semitism. Indeed, it was not until 2004 that the Romanian President, Ion Iliescu, made the first official acknowledgement of the country's role in the Holocaust. The previous year, he had established an international panel to report on the subject, which did so in 2004. Iliescu was an ex-Communist, and it is unclear whether a right-wing leader would have made the same decision. Indeed, it is improbable, while Iliescu had scarcely been eager to take the step.

In 1996, when the Polish Foreign Minister apologised to the World Jewish Congress for anti-Semitism and the Kielce pogrom, the apology was by an ex-Communist, Dariusz Rosati. Only in 2004 did the Polish President officially acknowledge that maltreatment by Poles was an aspect of the wartime devastation of Poland's Jews. This was followed in June 2006, when President Lech Kaczynski joined Jewish leaders in breaking ground for the Museum of the History of Polish Jews in the heart of what was once the Warsaw ghetto. The museum, scheduled to open in 2009, will have exhibits on the Holocaust, but its primary purpose is intended to be the large Jewish community that once flourished there.

In 2001, Hungary established a Holocaust Memorial Day, followed in 2004 with a Holocaust Memorial Centre. As a reminder of the variety of national memories, the Hungarian Holocaust Memorial Day is on 16 April, the date on which the Budapest ghetto was established in 1944.

In Lithuania, the process of exonerating anti-Communists extended to include celebrations of 'heroes' who fought with the SS, and, in 1991, Lithuania gave a general pardon to wartime collaborators. The Germans had won considerable support among those who had been ruled by the Soviet Union since the Russian Civil War, particularly from non-Russians,[53] and this made the issue of post-Communist commemoration and history more problematic and troubling. Denial of the Holocaust is currently a criminal offence, in eastern Europe, in the Czech Republic, Lithuania, Poland and Romania, but that is only a limited guide to the diverse complexity of public memory about the Second World War and its place in national historical narratives. Thus, in Lvóv in the 1990s, Ukrainian nationalists freely expressed anti-Semitic sentiments.

Aside from tensions within countries, the Holocaust also became an issue between them, although less so than the more widespread pattern of occupations, killings and forced movements that eastern Europe experienced in the 1940s. Responsibility for actions was the main topic for debate, or, more usually, diatribe, but there was also dissension as to the national identity of the victims. In particular, wartime territorial divisions became an issue, as commentators strove simultaneously to inflate the number of their own victims and also to assert territorial interests. This dissension continues to this day, with Russia keen to use the territorial gains made by Stalin in 1939 (eastern Poland) and 1940 (Estonia, Latvia, Lithuania and part of Romania) and to describe victims from these areas as 'Soviet citizens'. These areas, which were conquered by the Germans in 1941, and reconquered by the Soviets in 1944, indeed, largely became part of the Soviet Union in 1945. Others reject this interpretation, and it has become critical at Auschwitz, where the Polish Government refuses to permit Russia to reopen its exhibition unless it acknowledges the Polish viewpoint. This has led to a war of words.

The determination of ex-Communist states to win international acceptance, not least in order to provide a degree of protection against a resurgent Russia, led them to face up to the international significance of the Holocaust, particularly in the USA, the key to NATO membership, and western Europe, the key to European Union membership. This encouraged a symbolic process of apology. Thus, in 1995, Algirdas Brazauskas, the President of Lithuania, addressing the Knesset (Israeli Parliament), publicly apologised for the Lithuanian role in the Holocaust. In May 2007, seeking to make all the correct gestures at a time of great sensitivity about memorialisation, the Estonian Prime Minister, Andrus Ansip, attended ceremonies at a Holocaust memorial outside Tallinn, as well as at a cemetery commemorating soldiers who had died in Estonia fighting for the Soviets and the Germans and at the recently, and controversially, moved monument to Red Army casualties in the Second World War.

Discussion of the Holocaust was not only a question of memorialisation in eastern Europe, where, for example, cinema engaged with the Holocaust from the history and memory angle.[54] Aside from the relevance of the Holocaust to continuing anti-Semitism against surviving Jewish communities, an issue made more pertinent by the large-scale active cooperation in the Holocaust displayed in eastern Europe, there was the issue of ethnic violence and alleged genocide in eastern Europe in the 1990s. The end of Communism had led to an upsurge in national consciousness. This highlighted the role of ethnicity in national narratives and thus the position of minority groups, including Jews. The use of ethnic considerations to advance nationalist territorial assertion and aggressiveness in the former Yugoslavia led to ethnic cleansing, principally of Serbs by Croats, and of Muslim Bosnians and Kosovans by Serbs, and to massacres in Bosnia.

These encouraged Western intervention, and there were direct references to the Holocaust on the 'never again' theme. Indeed, an understanding of the grasp of visual images on the imagination led President Bill Clinton to press people to see the film *Schindler's List* (1993). There were also arguments that Bosnia was different to the Holocaust, not only because of the organised nature of the latter but also because Bosnia was more in the pattern of brutal ethnic cleansing,[55] an interpretation that was contested by the argument that a systematic murder that amounted to genocide was being carried out.[56]

Wartime collaboration was not only an issue in France and eastern Europe, although in much of Europe it has been downplayed as an issue. This was true, for example, of collaboration by allies, such as Finland, and neutrals, such as Portugal, Spain and Sweden. In Sweden, there is little readiness to discuss the question why Sweden was not only not at war with Nazi Germany, but, instead, willingly supplied militarily crucial goods. In that sense, there was an active support for the system that made the Holocaust possible.

THE USA

By the 1990s, the Holocaust was a key episode in American historical consciousness, although the relationship between this and the level of Holocaust denial is unclear. In 1993, indeed, a poll carried out by the Roper Organisation suggested that nearly a quarter of Americans were unconvinced that 6 million Jews had been slaughtered. A series of news items contributed to general Holocaust awareness, not simply the opening of the Holocaust Memorial Museum in 1993 but also the question of whether Nazis had taken refuge in the USA or with American connivance. Ivan Demjanjuk, a Ukrainian who had become an American citizen, was accused of being 'Ivan the Terrible', a feared guard at Treblinka. With considerable public interest in the case, his American citizenship was removed, and, in 1986, he was extradited to Israel, where he was convicted. In the event, the conviction was overturned by the Israeli Supreme Court in 1997, and Demjanjuk was released because, although he had probably been a guard at Sobibor, he was not the Ivan he was accused of being. Concern about Second World War criminals led Canada, Australia and Britain to pass legislation, in 1987, 1989 and 1991 respectively, that would enable their prosecution for crimes committed abroad and long ago. Also in the 1990s, pressure from the USA, notably class-action lawsuits, was crucial in forcing the Swiss to pay compensation for their wartime conduct (see p. 129).

The Holocaust also served public purposes, including the continued moralisation of American foreign policy. This focused on iterations of the Second World War, not least the theme of the 'Greatest Generation', and, whereas Pearl Harbor provided the moral grounding for the war in the Pacific, that against Germany was given moral force and purpose by the Holocaust. This was an aspect of retrospective validation and the rewriting of the past, because Holocaust had not played a role in American policy during the conflict, nor in earlier public debate about the move towards confrontation with Germany in 1941.

This theme had been subdued immediately after the war itself, and for over three decades thereafter. The Holocaust played a role within American public discussion in the late 1940s, not least in encouraging support for the foundation of Israel, which the USA was the first to recognise, but it was not a central subject nor theme in recent history, neither for public education nor for reference in discussion. Nazi horrors were a subject for films, with Orson Welles' *The Stranger* (1946) including footage of the concentration camps. In it, Welles played an escaped Nazi using the cover of a New England university professor. A toxic effect of the early stages of the Cold War was that at this stage US intelligence was recruiting Germans who had been involved in the Holocaust.[57]

The Nazi issue recurred in George Stevens' film *The Diary of Anne Frank* (1959) and Stanley Kramer's *Judgment at Nuremberg* (1961), while Sidney Lumet's *The Pawnbroker* (1964) depicted a Holocaust survivor; but the Holocaust was not a major theme. Indeed, it was ignored in most American and British war films. As far as wartime horrors were concerned, the focus was on Japanese cruelty to American and British prisoners of war: for example, the Bataan Death March of American and Filipino prisoners in the Philippines in 1942 and the use of British prisoners to construct the Burma railway in murderous conditions. The German atrocities that attracted attention were similarly focused on the USA and Britain, such as the massacre of American prisoners near Malmédy in 1944.

Moreover, the integration of Germany into Western defence structures encouraged American leaders to become more favourable towards Germany. Eisenhower, who in 1945 was much affected by his visit to Buchenwald, was in 1950 appointed NATO's first Supreme Allied Commander of Europe. In this role, he became more favourable to the wartime conduct of the *Wehrmacht*, declaring in 1951 that: 'the German soldier fought bravely and honorably for his homeland.' The Holocaust was then a minor theme in American public consciousness.

The situation changed from the 1970s, not least with six important television mini-series: *The Holocaust* (1978), *Playing for Time* (1980), *The Wall* (1982), *Wallenberg:*

A Hero's Story (1985), *Escape from Sobibor* (1987), and *War and Remembrance* (1988–9), a series that depicted Auschwitz and Babi Yar. It has been argued that 'the Holocaust had become an effective moral catharsis for American viewers after the Vietnam war', not least because the Americans emerge by extension in a heroic and unproblematic light as opponents of the Nazis;[58] but that is overly reductionist and negative. It is also relevant, as with other countries, to consider national developments as, in part, an aspect of wider developments and to note the re-evaluation across the West noted earlier in this chapter.

Marvin Chomsky's series *The Holocaust*, which won an American audience of 120 million viewers, was particularly important, both for Jewish viewers, for whom it asserted, demonstrated or underlined the centrality of the Holocaust, and for non-Jews. The use of a soap-opera format, focusing on a particular family, in the four episodes helped make it more accessible. The series followed Chomsky's series *Roots* (1977), which had had a similar impact for African Americans. *The Holocaust* series also helped establish the term as the normal one in the USA. Moreover, aside from the Holocaust, the Nazis came to play a greater role in Hollywood as an existential threat to humanity in touch with occult forces, not least with Steven Spielberg's highly successful films *Raiders of the Lost Ark* (1981) and *Indiana Jones and the Last Crusade* (1989).[59] Neither was Holocaust-focused. The film *Boys from Brazil* (1978) used Mengele to support its theme of the danger of a revived Third Reich.

A different strand of concern for Jewish issues came from American evangelical Christians. Much of this powerful constituency had been fairly anti-Semitic in the early twentieth century, but, in the last quarter of the century, it became actively pro-Israeli. In part, this reflected the belief that the ingathering of the Jewish exiles to Israel would forward the Millennium. A concern with Jewish causes was an aspect of evangelical Christian support for Israel. That Israel was a close ally of the USA from the late 1960s, replacing the marked tension between them in 1956–7 during and after the

Suez Crisis, contributed to the same end, not least as many Americans felt isolated, particularly during and after the Vietnam War. That the Holocaust became more prominent in American public memory was an extraordinary departure, as it related to events in foreign countries that did not involve Americans as perpetrators or victims. As such, the only real comparison for Americans was with the New Testament account of suffering and fortitude.[60]

This prominence, however, helped ensure that the Holocaust was drawn into America's culture wars, with claims by counter-culture critics that the Holocaust was detracting attention from varied ills attributed to the USA, such as slavery, the Vietnam War and the fate of the Native Americans. It was also argued that the Holocaust was deliberately used to divert criticism from Israel's occupation of Arab lands, especially from 1967; an unconvincing claim. Claims that charges of genocide should be extended to these cases in American history were linked to the argument that a focus on the Holocaust thwarted such an extension.[61] A lack of comparability made this a poor case, and it was weakened further by the intemperance of the polemic and its lack of historical awareness. Alleged comparability between the Holocaust and the treatment of the Aborigines has proved a comparable issue in Australia.

The USA also has the largest number of Jews in the world, in large part due to emigration from the Russian Empire in the late nineteenth and early twentieth century. Indeed, a major geographical reordering of Jewry was a key consequence of the Holocaust and thus of its location as the working through of murderous racially-based nationalism.[62] The slaughter of about a third of the world's Jews meant a major shift in the distribution of Jews in proportional terms: from Europe to North America and Israel; while, within Europe, the shift was to the margins: from eastern and central Europe to Britain and Russia.

Post-war movements accentuated this tendency. The harsh or, at best, callous treatment of Jews after the Second World War, not only in eastern Europe, especially Poland, but also in France, Belgium and the Netherlands, encouraged further emigration to the USA, particularly after immigration restrictions eased with the passage of the Displaced Persons Act in 1948.

The Jewish community in the USA was reticent in drawing attention to the Holocaust or pressing for support for Israel in the late 1940s and 1950s, as they focused on integration and combating domestic anti-Semitism and also did not associate closely with the victim status of European Jewry, but their attitude changed in the 1960s, not least as the Holocaust was increasingly incorporated into American consciousness. A growing activism on the part of American Jewry, which, in part, reflected the degree of their integration into American society, as well as their confidence following the Six Days' War of 1967, led not only to increased pressure on behalf of Israel but also to a focus on the Holocaust. This pressure and focus also reflected fears about the security of Israel, not least because the Six Days' War was followed by renewed Arab pressure that culminated in the Arab attack in the Yom Kippur War of 1973.

The American Jewish community funded, and funds, the establishment of Holocaust museums, memorials, lectures and academic posts. This reflects not simply the relative wealth of American Jewry, and its practice of generosity for public causes, but also the extent to which, in the USA, it is possible for bodies other than government to take such initiatives. Privately funded museums and academic posts are less prominent in Europe. As the Holocaust survivors in the USA die out, so there seems a determination to erect museums, including one recently in Houston, as a different form of memorialisation, and one to serve both the Jewish community and the remainder of the population.

In contrast, in 1995, at the time of the fiftieth anniversary of the end of the war, the emphasis was on filmed oral interviews. Concern about the loss of memory, alongside an awareness of the weight given to oral evidence, led then to Steven Spielberg's 'Survivors of the Shoah Visual History Foundation'. Ten years earlier, Claude Lanzmann's lengthy

Shoah (1985) focused on interviews with those involved in the Holocaust, divided between Jewish survivors, Polish bystanders and German perpetrators, who excused themselves as unaware of what happened.

Filmed interviews were an instructive testimonial to late-twentieth-century public culture, as they brought together new technology with the authority of the participant and the determination to bear individual witness. As such, they were aspects of what has been termed the 'memory boom'.[63] Already, from the late 1970s, the Fortunoff Video Archive for Holocaust Testimonies, established at Yale University, had been compiling lengthy interviews.[64] This contrasted with the reluctance among many surviving victims to discuss their traumas, a situation that did not change for some until the 1980s and 1990s.

Among the American Jewish community, memorialisation of the Holocaust, in part, reflected collective mourning, but, in part, also is a response to concerns about the challenges to Jewish identity in the liberal culture and society both of the USA and of American Jewry. Thus, the Holocaust is seen as a cohesive experience of Jewishness and one that should serve as a living memory, even though most American Jews are not Holocaust survivors, nor their descendants.[65] Commemoration of the Holocaust also underlines an international quality to, and consciousness of, Jewishness that is under challenge from the powerful assimilationist tendencies in American society.

AUSTRALASIA

In Australia, institutions and museums were established by Holocaust survivors or their children in response, in the 1980s, to the rise of Holocaust denial. Among the Australian Jewish population, the percentage who were Holocaust survivors were/are higher than anywhere bar Israel. The Holocaust Museum and Research Centre in Melbourne of 1984 was followed by the Holocaust Institute of Western Australia in Perth in 1990 and the Sydney Jewish Museum in 1992. A survivor guide at the Melbourne museum explained the role of David Irving:

Getting older, we became aware that our Voices can't be heard forever. The Irving interview was a turning point for me. I thought to myself, I am still alive and he tells me there was no Auschwitz. A lot of people reacted to that. A lot of survivors rang up the Holocaust Centre, wanting to deposit their memories, where before they couldn't talk about it. Since then I made it my policy to talk at forums when I am asked to.

These museums operate not solely for the Jewish community but also more generally, being used, for example, as part of student assignments.[66] The understanding of the Holocaust has parallels with that in the USA, with emphasis on the success of the Jews who escaped it in settling in Australia, although with some criticism of the Australian Government of the 1930s for not allowing in more Jewish refugees. As elsewhere, trials of those involved in Nazi atrocities increased public consciousness. In Australia, this was the case with the War Crimes Act trial of Nikolay Beresvsky in 1992. This trial also had a symbolic political role in underlining Australia's multi-cultural identity.

In New Zealand, the pattern of commemoration was similar to that in other major centres of Jewish activity in the Anglo-Saxon world and in Israel: in other words, there was a time-lag. There have been no distinctive initiatives in New Zealand. In April 2007, the Wellington Holocaust Research and Education Centre was opened by the representative of the Head of State, the Governor General, Anand Satyanad. Its aim is to collect and record the accounts of Holocaust survivors who fled Europe and came to Wellington. The legacy of Holocaust survivors also emerged in a volume produced in 2003, *Mixed Blessings: New Zealand Children of Holocaust Survivors Remember*.[67]

BRITAIN

In Britain, the pattern of public attention also followed similar contours to those elsewhere in the Anglo-Saxon world, albeit with the addition of the powerful irritant of the British

Mandate in Palestine until 1948, as this exposed the British authorities there to violent pressure for decolonisation from both Jews and Arabs. Moreover, although very much a minority opinion, there was a strain of fascism in British society that peddled Holocaust denial under the malign inspiration of Oswald Mosley.[68] Fascism, however, was a minority opinion. The National Front had an average vote of 3.3 per cent for the fifty-four constituencies it contested in February 1974, but by 1983 this had dropped to just over 1 per cent for fifty-eight constituencies, and the party did not take part in the 1987 General Election.

The Holocaust became more prominent in Britain as a theme from the 1970s, and, particularly, from the 1990s. The Jewish community in Britain played an important role, but Holocaust consciousness was much wider in its context and impact. This consciousness was, indeed, an important aspect of the rise of individual memory and the individual story seen, for example, in television stories and newspaper articles, such as 'The New Anne Frank', a large article about the journal of Rutka Laskier, a Holocaust victim from Poland, published in the *Sunday Times* of 17 June 2007. The piece owed much to the voice offered by Rutka's half-sister, the daughter of her father, who survived Auschwitz and later remarried. Number 7 on Amazon's top ten was then Ruth Kluger's *Landscapes of Memory: A Holocaust Girlhood Remembered*.

Aside from the key influence of Hollywood, the centralised character of the British educational curriculum was important, with Nazi Germany playing a major role in the teaching of history. Scholarship was also part of the trend, with the Holocaust increasingly present as a theme in the history not just of Germany but also of the world. For example, two of the thirty-one chapters in the *Companion to Europe 1900–1945*, part of what is intended to be the definitive series 'Blackwell Companions to European History', were devoted to the Holocaust, one of which, Harold Marcuse on 'Memories of World War II and the Holocaust', argued that an internationalisation of recollection both decontextualises and universalises the experience of the Second World War.[69]

ISRAEL

The memorialisation of the Holocaust was strongest in Israel, where it is known in Hebrew as the *Shoah* (Catastrophe).[70] Aside from addressing the powerful need to remember, the Holocaust also helped to underline a commonality of experience. This was important because the creation of Israeli identity faced serious challenges, as the different sources of Jewish immigrants had had very varied experiences and challenges. In response, the Holocaust played a central role in Israeli self-identification, not least with the establishment of Yad Vashem in Jerusalem as 'The Memorial Authority for the Holocaust and Heroism', a Holocaust memorial, museum and archive, in 1953. It became a spiritual home of Holocaust remembrance, although, of course, it was not a Holocaust site, nor in the lands where the Holocaust took place. Yad Vashem, in part, thus represented an assertion of the role of the Holocaust as a living Jewish memory, separate to the sites of killing in eastern Europe. A new museum for Holocaust history was opened there in 2005.

In 1953, all Jews killed in the Holocaust were granted 'memorial citizenship' in Israel. Israel itself was presented as the safeguard against there being another Holocaust, as it was to be the safe haven of all Jews and a land in which, under the 'right of return', all Jews could become citizens. The sense of a safe haven was appealed to by Ariel Sharon, Israel's Prime Minister, when, in 2004, in response to anti-Semitic outrages in France, he called for French Jews to emigrate to Israel. Most of the outrages, in fact, were committed by French Arabs who, as a group, had little interest in the right-wing extremism that concerned many Jewish commentators, still less in the legacy of Vichy. Sharon was reflecting a more widespread theme, of the Diaspora, and specifically Europe, as the site of *Shoah* and of Israel as the land of rebirth, but one that also required continued vigilance to ensure its protection.

As a sub-text Israel was also seen as a protection against the destruction of ethnicity and religion through assimilation. This was a challenge occasionally referred to by zealots as akin to, or worse than the Holocaust, a remark that reflected not only a contempt for the notion of free will, but also a serious misuse of the grievous pain and loss of the Holocaust. Similar comments can be directed to the argument that the Holocaust was in some way retribution either for the Zionist quest for a secular state in place of a reliance on a messianic fulfilment of a return to Israel, a (minority) ultra-orthodox argument, or for the earlier assimilation of the German Jews. Aside from the contemptible nature of the latter argument, a far greater percentage of German and Austrian Jews survived than was the case with their often more pious, and less assimilated, Polish or Lithuanian counterparts, largely due to different opportunities for pre-war emigration.

The seizure of Adolf Eichmann in Argentina by Israeli agents in May 1960, and his subsequent trial and execution in Israel in 1961–2,[71] was also a key moment in maintaining Holocaust consciousness as an active principle. The trial was extensively reported across much of the world, including on American television, and this broadcast the testimony offered by Holocaust survivors. The Holocaust also underlined the hostility in Israeli society and culture to what could be seen as, or associated with, German anti-Semitism, particularly the music of Richard Wagner and Richard Strauss.

In the Israeli context, the Holocaust was also given a distinctive historical context. The theme of Jews as fighting back linked the brave but doomed defence of Masada against the Romans in AD 73 to the Warsaw ghetto rising in 1943. This theme sought to counter the feeling, not least in Israel where there was criticism among Zionists from the Diaspora,[72] that, due to passive acquiescence, not enough had been done to resist the Holocaust, and that the Jews, and therefore Israelis, appeared in some fashion weak. In 1948–9, the establishment of Israel as an independent state was contested by attacks from much of the Arab world, so the threat of genocide appeared an urgent one in underlining the need to fight back. Holocaust Day, designated in 1951, marks the anniversary of the 1943 rising. It is actually Holocaust and Heroism Day, and this reflects the stress on the need to fight back that is seen as crucial to Israeli society. This is also presented in the Yad Vashem museum, where armed resistance to Nazism is seen as an exemplary episode.

The extendable meaning of the Holocaust was also indicated when what had been a specific historical episode was also used as a symbol of the travails of the Jews through history. As far as Israel was concerned, this also ensured that an account of the Holocaust that had most meaning for the large numbers of Jews who had emigrated there as refugees from Europe in the late 1940s, and that had played a key role in Israel's early history, could also be a crucial identifier for the large number of Jewish refugees from Muslim countries who became proportionately more important in the 1970s and 1980s.

Similarly, in France, the large number of Jewish immigrants from the former colonies of Morocco, Algeria and Tunisia, who arrived in the 1960s, absorbed the travails of the Jews of metropolitan France during the Vichy years as an aspect of their history. Israeli pressure on behalf of persecuted foreign communities of Jews, such as those of Ethiopia, reflected not only both the traditional obligation and practice of helping fellow Jews, but also the impact of Holocaust consciousness.

The Holocaust also helped Israel win international sympathy and support. This was particularly the case with the USA, both from Jews and, even more significantly, from non-Jews, and was also the case with West Germany which, aside from diplomatic support and financial compensation, sold Israel munitions, including tanks.[73] Binyamin Netanyahu, then Israeli Prime Minister, claimed in 1998 that 'if the state of Israel had not been founded after the Holocaust, the Jewish future would have been imperilled', because it would have been more difficult to win American support. Indeed, fifty years earlier, Chaim Weizmann, Head of the World Zionist Organisation, and soon-to-be first President of Israel, was able to write to President Harry S. Truman of the USA: 'The choice for our people, Mr. President, is between statehood and extermination.' In 1948, this was not true of World Jewry, but, in the face of Arab pressure, it seemed true for Israel's Jews.

More to the point, it was an appeal difficult to reject in the aftermath of the Holocaust. The aftermath led Britain, determined to maintain strict limits on Jewish migration to Palestine, into confrontation and conflict with the Zionist movement, which accused the British Government of failing to provide succour to Holocaust refugees. The British Government was concerned that such immigration would lead to a violent Arab response that would destabilise Palestine. Jews trying to reach Palestine were intercepted by the Royal Navy, detained and interned in Cyprus, then another British colony. The British presence in Palestine was brought to an end in 1948, with the Government keen to get the problem of containing tensions between Arabs and Jews off its hands.[74]

Partly as a result of the role of the Holocaust in Israeli consciousness and international support, but, more generally, reflecting the persistence of anti-Semitism, there is also, however, a tradition of Holocaust denial or minimisation, one intended to lessen what is seen as the consequences of the Holocaust in terms of support for Israel. A variant on this is the claim that the Palestinians similarly suffered a holocaust. In the Arab–Israel war of 1948–9, there was, on both sides, murderous actions designed, more generally, to drive away members of the other community. These included the massacre at Dir Yassin on 9–10 April 1948, by the Lohamey Herut Yisrael (Fighters for the Liberation of Israel; Stern Gang to the British). However, aside from the degree to which both sides carried out massacres, neither the overall circumstances nor the scale in any way corresponded to the Holocaust.

Arab commentators who argue some sort of equivalence are following post-1945 German Nazis, who also drew attention to Dir Yassin by way of trying to argue that the Jews would be murderous given the chance and that this somehow justified wartime Nazi policy. The difference in scale and intentionality makes such a comparison pointless. Some Arab commentators accept that there was a Holocaust devastating European Jewry but question why the consequences had to include the establishment of the state of Israel. In short, they present the Palestinians as victims, not only of Israel and the USA but also, more tenuously and at one remove, of Hitler.

As an aspect of widespread paranoia, a key Muslim theme of victimhood focused in the 2000s on the allegedly malign goals of a Jewish conspiracy directing American foreign policy, and much else, in pursuit of Israeli goals. Much of this is reminiscent of Nazi rhetoric, and, as with the Nazis, it is appropriate to take what is said as a serious indication of beliefs and assumptions, instead of treating it as a rant. In both cases, there is also a hysterical tendency to blame problems on others and to see no agency in themselves for working to understand and improve the situation, other than the supposedly redemptive use of violence in a Manichean context in which right and wrong are clearly differentiated.

Mahmoud Ahmadinejah, of Iran, comes in a tradition of Muslim leaders downplaying the Holocaust, although there are exceptions. Arab nationalists tended to view Hitler and Mussolini favourably because they shared an opposition to the Anglo-French dominance of the Middle East, which had gathered pace from the 1880s. The most prominent Arab supporter of Hitler was Hadj Amin el-Husseini, the Mufti of Jerusalem, a religious official who had played a key role in the Arab Revolt in Palestine in 1936–9, a movement against Jewish immigration. He became a German propagandist, raised Arab troops for German service and was assured in person by Hitler on 28 November 1941 that Arabs and Germans were joined in friendship by anti-Semitism, and that the Germans would seek the annihilation of the Jews in the Middle East. As a result of genocide within Europe and conquest outside it, the Germans would thus block any Jewish homeland in Palestine. The pro-German Prime Minister of Iraq, Rashid Ali el-Ghalani, who was overthrown by the British in 1941, also supported anti-Semitic policies.

Given the prevalence of rabid anti-Semitism in the television and literature of Muslim countries, for example in Egypt and Syria in the 2000s, as well as in the comments of some clerics, it is scarcely surprising that many were unreceptive to films about the Holocaust. Malaysia, for example, was not alone in banning *Schindler's List*. There is no comparison in Muslim public treatment of the Holocaust to the complexity offered by the film *Don't Touch My Holocaust* (1994), by the Israeli Asher Tlalim.[75] Moreover, in western Europe, for example Britain, Muslim communities also showed themselves reluctant to participate in public and interdenominational commemorations of the Holocaust.

In December 2005, Ahmadinejah, a member of a millenarian cult that seeks an anti-Western pan-Islamicism, referred to the Holocaust as a 'fairy tale' serving Israeli ends. In December 2006, he presided over a conference in Teheran held to examine 'the myth of the Holocaust'. This conference, whose luminaries included David Duke, a discredited leader of the American racist Klu Klux Klan movement, received a lot of critical attention in the West, and deservedly so. It echoed the ludicrous argument among some Muslims that Jews, Israel, the USA, or a combination thereof, were responsible for the 11 September 2001 attacks on New York and Washington.

Iran's drive to develop a nuclear capability, linked to its success already in acquiring a medium-range missile delivery system, threatens Israel with a modern-day destruction that would kill millions of Jews (and large numbers of non-Jews – the event of which will inevitably be compared to a second Holocaust. In 2003, Iran conducted what it termed the final test of the Shahabz missile, first tested in 1998. With a range of 812 miles, it is able to reach Israel.

Closing the chapter at this point not only underlines the long-standing applicability of the Holocaust, most obviously in Jewish contexts,[76] but also highlights the issue of diminishment by comparison that is addressed in the next chapter. This issue also captures a tension in the memorialisation of the Holocaust between a focus on what happened in the 1940s and, in contrast, an understanding of memorialisation that encompasses later comparisons, with all the problems of such comparisons. As far as a focus on the 1940s is concerned, this entails an element of greater historicisation than the alternative, not least as the 1940s recedes and, in particular, appears less approachable to those growing to maturity in the twenty-first century. In contrast, the approach to memorialisation that encompasses comparisons with later or current events raises the issue of what comparisons are appropriate.

CHAPTER 6

THE HOLOCAUST AND TODAY

AWARENESS

It is all too easy, in light of the unwillingness of so many to confront the past, if not the continuation of active anti-Semitism, to focus on continued prejudice and hatred. As a result, it is pleasant to begin with signs of reconciliation. In Poland in 2007, the Jewish Claims Conference, which administers money from restored Jewish property, also funds reunions between Jews who survived the Holocaust and Poles who gave them shelter at great personal risk. The meetings are encouraged by the Polish Government in order to challenge Poland's unenviable reputation as an anti-Semitic society, but that does not lessen the positive and life-enhancing tales of heroism, humanity and fortitude that emerge. They also provide an instance of the personal dimension of victimhood, which is all too often lost or overshadowed by the understandable stress on the scale of the slaughter.

Another aspect of the emphasis on the individuality of victimhood, which has become much stronger with the development of oral history, was shown in the spring of 2007, when the Jewish Museum of Deportation and Resistance in Mechelen in Belgium opened an exhibition that included the photographs of 1,200 of the 1,636 prisoners on board Transport XX, which left Mechelen for Auschwitz on 19 April 1943. This exhibition was made more prominent because the photographs were not displayed only for the Museum's visitors but, instead, outside along a stretch of the road next to the Dossin Barracks, which was the holding prison for the deportees.

As far as Polish anti-Semitism is concerned, the Jews were reasonably well integrated into Polish society during the early modern period, the sixteenth to eighteenth centuries,[1] but there were major strands of anti-Semitism by the inter-war years (1918–39), and during the Second World War the situation was far less positive. Alongside the honourable behaviour of many individual Poles, there was a widespread indifference to the fate of the Jews, not least on the part of the Polish government-in-exile, which was unwilling to see Polish Jews as full citizens. This was a long-standing attitude which was accentuated for many Poles by their identification of Jews with Communism, not least with its existential challenge to Christianity.

This perspective was encouraged by the willingness of some Jews, faced by Polish anti-Semitism, to welcome Soviet occupation of eastern Poland in 1939. The same was true of the Soviet occupation of Lithuania in 1940. Affected by a powerful anti-Semitism, the Polish government-in-exile was content to note the extirpation of the Jews, even to hope that the Germans would succeed in their goal, until they became fearful that the Poles would be next in line.[2] While less culpable, other governments-in-exile also tended to neglect the issue of anti-Semitic legislation and, indeed, the onset of deportations. For example, it was only in September 1943 that the Belgian government-in-exile condemned collaboration in Belgium with the persecution of the Jews.

These meetings in modern Poland, organised by the Jewish Claims Conference, are far from the sole positive initiative. In Britain, the Holocaust Educational Trust spreads knowledge not only in order to increase knowledge of the Holocaust but also because it is seen as directly applicable for today and the future. The Trust seeks to inform teachers and also takes large numbers of schoolchildren (and others) to Auschwitz to the 'Lessons from Auschwitz' project, which has won the support of the British Government. The Trust's programme has also helped increase sensitivity to genocide in the modern world, such as in Darfur, where the genocide of Black Muslims by Arab Muslims has also been of concern to American Jews, such as Steven Spielberg.

The prominence of the Holocaust in Britain was indicated in many ways. For example, the leaflet distributed in May 2007 for 'Studylink', which provides group travels for students, put a photograph of Auschwitz on its front cover without feeling it necessary to explain what it is. As the leaflet includes trips to First World War battlefield sites and D-Day landing sites, the choice of illustration was indicative. Visits under the Berlin headline included to the 'House of Wannsee Conference' and to Sachsenhausen concentration camp, and, under Cracow, to Auschwitz-Birkenau, the wartime ghetto, and Schindler's factory. The Holocaust indeed plays an important role in history teaching in Britain. More generally, in Britain and elsewhere, the Holocaust became the key foreign and global locator of a world war that was otherwise presented essentially as a national narrative, focusing in Britain on Dunkirk, the Battle of Britain, the Blitz and D-Day.

Holocaust awareness in Britain was underlined by active engagement by the BBC, with major television series, especially *The Nazis: A Warning from History* (1997), which was subsequently sold to over thirty countries, and *Auschwitz: The Nazis and the 'Final Solution'* (2005), which was produced for the BBC and the American PBS and transmitted in over a dozen countries. The sensitivity of apparently anti-Semitic references to the Holocaust was indicated, in 2005, when the left-wing Mayor of London, Ken Livingstone, compared a critical Jewish journalist to a concentration-camp guard, leading to much controversy. Government support was important for the designation in Britain of Holocaust Memorial Day, held on 27 January, on the anniversary of the liberation of Auschwitz-Birkenau.[3]

Official engagement in commemoration can also be seen elsewhere. The date 27 January recently also became Auschwitz Commemoration Day in Denmark, while a Department of Holocaust and Genocide Studies was established at the Danish Institute of International Studies. Aside from undertaking scholarly research, this department provides public lectures, as well as books and other kinds of educational material to Danish schools.[4] This initiative owed much to the publication of a survey demonstrating a serious ignorance of the Second World War and the Holocaust on the part of Danish youngsters.

DENIAL

In light of such positive initiatives, it is difficult to know what to make of the 2007 Historical Association briefing, commissioned by the Department for Education, that some British schools no longer teach the Holocaust as a component of the GCSE course because they were concerned about stirring up anti-Semitic sentiment among Muslim pupils. This item of news attracted commentary both in Britain and in the USA. Holocaust denial in some form or other, indeed, is far from a fringe opinion in the Muslim community. Moreover, this is part of a more general Muslim pattern of portrayal of Jewish history; for example, the denial of a positive, or any, Jewish role or place in the Moorish-ruled medieval al-Andalus, now Andalusia in Spain.

Holocaust denial itself is abhorrent as well as ridiculous, a veritable Death of History.[5] It is reasonable and necessary to question the motives and integrity of all Holocaust deniers and to impugn the worst of intentions to them. They are mad, bad or both. More generally, anti-Semitism and Holocaust denial are symptoms of a poorly developed civil society.[6]

DIMINISHMENT

A very different issue, one, in certain respects, made more insidious by the fact that most of its supporters are not Holocaust deniers, is the downplaying of the Holocaust by comparison. Here an issue is not so much comparison with other genocides, for they also are deplorable,[7] but rather comparison with episodes that, however distasteful and cruel, were not genocidal. Two examples from the mid-2000s are the attempt by Germans, no longer on the Far Right but now also in the mainstream, to argue that the German experience in 1943–7, first of heavy Anglo-American bombing and then of being brutalised and driven from eastern Europe, was in some way comparable to the Holocaust. This is absurd, not least because no genocide was attempted, even by Joseph Stalin. Moreover, whether or not the bombings, which also inflicted considerable damage on the German economy and demoralised German society, constituted war crimes, they were not genocidal and, thus, not crimes against humanity.[8] Most German commentators do not appear to show the same concern about German bombing during the war, including the use of rockets against civilian targets.

Separate to the specific German critique of Allied bombing comes the argument that the bombing campaigns of the Second World War, indeed bombing itself, as well as the Holocaust, were rooted in Western imperialism, with 'genocidal weapons' making possible 'dreams of genocide'. In this approach, the British and Americans are treated like the Nazis.[9] The unscholarly, and indeed quasi-hysterical, nature of such arguments scarcely need underlining, while the suggestion that genocide required sophisticated weaponry was scarcely demonstrated by Croatia in 1941 or Rwanda in 1994.

Particularly in the 2000s, there is also the reiterated comparison of the Atlantic slave trade to an African Holocaust. This is also absurd. It underrates the major role of African agency in the slave trade and also that the intention of the slave trade was not to kill Africans, still less to reorder the racial geography of conquered territory, but, instead, to ensure plentiful, pliant and relatively inexpensive labour.[10]

The downplaying of the Holocaust by historical comparison in part also draws on the worthy goal of using the widespread horror that the treatment of the Jews inspired to elicit a similar reaction on behalf of other persecuted groups: past, present and, apparently, imminent. In the Soviet Union, for example, terror and government-tolerated famine killed at least 11 million people in Stalin's 'peacetime' years (1924–41, 1945–53), warped the lives of the remainder of the population, and made casualties of faith, hope and truth. The Secret Police was the military of this war, a crucial prop to a Soviet government that routinely used violence. Moreover, very large numbers were imprisoned in the gulags, which effectively were concentration camps that played a major role in the Soviet economy. Ironically, Jews sent there in 1939–41 from newly occupied areas – eastern Poland, the Baltic republics and Bessarabia – were more likely to survive the Second World War than if they had remained in their homes. Similarly, the Chinese Communist state slaughtered millions in the 1950s and 1960s.

Nevertheless, large-scale killing alone, however reprehensible, does not compare with the Holocaust, because the attempt to define and destroy an entire ethnic group and its complete culture represents a different scale and intention of assault. The scale and intentions underlying the slaughter of Tutsi in Rwanda in 1994[11] suggest that describing this episode can be an appropriate usage of the term 'holocaust', but most comparisons with the Holocaust of this book are not similarly pertinent.

This point about the attempt to destroy an entire ethnic group helps address the charge that focus on the Holocaust has led to a failure to consider adequately the extent to which the Germans also slaughtered large numbers of other groups;[12] in short, that the Holocaust is an incomplete, and thus false, perspective on Nazi policies and practice. This issue is seen, for example, in the question of who should be commemorated at Auschwitz and who should be in charge of the commemoration. This issue also resonates with the quest by many Germans for acceptance of their status as victims: if attention is moved from the slaughter of the Jews, then the Germans can emerge as one of the peoples who suffered grievously in the 1940s. This is a presumption that strikes many non-Germans as ahistorical, ludicrous and offensive.

Pressure to look at others killed in the 1940s also becomes a key issue in the politics of Holocaust diminishment, with calls that relevant legislation should include the denial of Communist crimes. These, indeed, were murderous on a massive scale and directed at the destruction of entire social categories, a goal some see as akin to racial extermination,[13] although it has also been claimed that Soviet Communism was, critically, intended to secure human progress, whereas the Nazis sought that only for Germans.[14] This is not an extenuation of Soviet brutality, but an indicator that its goals were different.

These calls to criminalise the denial of Communist crimes were strongest from countries that had been occupied by Soviet forces and forcibly converted to Communism but were also heard elsewhere. For example, in Denmark there have been critics who have asked why 'only' the Nazi genocides should be officially commemorated, and why not also the crimes committed by Communist dictators such as Lenin, Stalin, Mao and Pol Pot. Nevertheless, pressure has been strongest from ex-Communist states, and this has affected calls for Holocaust remembrance. Opposition from Estonia and Lithuania, indeed, affected plans to make Holocaust denial an offence across the European Union. Alongside Latvia, Slovenia and Poland, they tried, but failed, in 2007, to have included in the European Union's criminalisation of genocide-denial a crime of denying, condoning or trivialising atrocities committed in the name of Stalin.

Within Germany, there is competition for attention, including funding between former concentration camps, such as Buchenwald, Dachau and Ravensbrück, and sites in East Germany that commemorate the victims of Communism. Within the Christian Democratic Party, there is pressure for an equivalent treatment as all those commemorated were victims of political dictatorship. This is the argument, for example, of Bernd Neumann, the Head of Cultural Affairs in Angela Merkel's Chancellery. The Central Board of German Jews rejects this equivalence, as it argues that it diminishes the Holocaust. Furthermore, it was necessary to rely on Stalin's forces to end the Holocaust.[15]

From the academic perspective, the comparative dimension, currently advocated as trans-national history, can provide a theoretical support for incorporating Communism, as does the success of linked biographies on Hitler and Stalin. However, as a warning of the problems with this dimension, a prominent academic instance of the downplaying of the Jewish experience is provided by *Poland's Holocaust: Ethnic Strife, Collaboration with Occupying Forces and Genocide in the Second Republic, 1918–1947,* by Tadeusz Piotrowski (1998). A professor of sociology at the University of New Hampshire, and a naturalised American of Polish descent, Piotrowski defines the Holocaust to include the victims of both Germany *and* the Soviet Union. This then enables him to divide his study of the Holocaust in Poland into seven chapters, with Nazi Terror preceded by Soviet Terror, and chapters on Polish, Belorussian, Lithuanian and Ukrainian collaboration preceded by one on Jewish collaboration, with both Soviet and German agencies. The overall impression, to put it mildly, is of a seriously unbalanced account.

A more pertinent comparison as far as the slaughter of Jews was concerned would be with the Roma (Gypsies), of whom at least a quarter of a million, and possibly up to 1.5 million, were killed by the Germans. As a percentage of the world population of Roma, this was a high figure. Germany's Roma were sent to Auschwitz II, following an order signed by Himmler on 16 December 1942. Hitler's attitude towards Jews, however, was very different, as he depicted them as an active and directing threat to the Germans and their mission, which was not the danger he or Himmler saw in the Roma. After the war, discrimination against the Roma continued in both West and East Germany, and they were not seen as victims of German wartime persecution until the 1960s.[16] As far as the Second World War was concerned, there was also a genocidal dimension to the internecine struggles in Yugoslavia in 1941–5.[17]

Crimes against humanity are certainly all too common, and the Holocaust was far from unique in that light, but that does not establish an equivalence. The latter, nevertheless, has been a strong theme of political diatribe. To each generation, such comparison appears new, but that is not the case. For example, the treatment of the Algerians by the French authorities in the early 1960s was compared to Nazi policies, while subsequently American conduct in the Vietnam War was compared to the Holocaust; both absurd claims, although in the former there was the Vichyist strand, not least with the role of Papon. Addressing American conduct of the Vietnam

War, Jean-Paul Sartre advanced the case for genocidal relationships,[18] a thesis that was applied more widely. To claim in 1987, as did Jacques Vergès, the defence lawyer to Klaus Barbie, the murderous SS Head of the Gestapo in Lyons from 1942 to 1944, that the focus should not be on German crimes against Jews, but rather those of imperial power against peoples struggling for freedom, was also to seek to put France, a major imperial power until the early 1960s, in the dock. Vergès' co-counsel, Nabil Bouaitt, argued that the Israeli invasion of Lebanon in 1982 was a holocaust.[19] When, from 1967, the radical left in Germany became critical of Israel, they similarly drew unfounded comparisons with Nazi Germany, the terrorist Ulrike Meinhof referring to the successful Israeli Defence Minister Moshe Dayan as 'Israel's Himmler'.[20]

In Australia, the fate of the Aborigines has often been explicitly compared to the Holocaust, not least as a way of shocking a response. In New Zealand, the word 'holocaust' was used in 1996 in the Waitangi Tribunal, which investigates the grievances of Maori against the Crown, in *Taranaki Report: Kaupapa Tuatahi*, its report on Taranaki, a district in the North Island which saw conflict, land confiscation, protest and dispossession in the nineteenth century:

> As to quantum, the gravamen of our report has been to say that the Taranaki claims are likely to be the largest in the country. The graphic *muru* [plunder] of most of Taranaki and the *raupatu* [confiscation] without ending describe the holocaust of Taranaki history and the denigration of the founding peoples in a continuum from 1840 to the present.

This led to political fallout in September 2000. Taria Turia, a prominent figure in the Maori Party, gave a 'Maori holocaust' speech which caused controversy, and for which she apologised to Parliament in a personal statement: 'I did not [. . .] mean to belittle survivors of the World War Two Holocaust.' However, when asked by Winston Peters, the leader of the opposition New Zealand First Party, which vigorously criticised the idea of special treatment for Maori, whether she felt the use of the term 'holocaust' in a Waitangi Tribunal report on the treatment of the people of Taranaki gave her licence to use the term, she replied: 'I believe, yes, you're quite right. I read the Waitangi Tribunal report on the devastation of the Taranaki peoples and I acknowledge they used the word "holocaust," which in terms of what happened to Taranaki I believe was appropriate.' This did not please government supporters, such as Trevor Mallard, the Education Minister, and clashed with the decision, given just days earlier, by Helen Clark, the Prime Minister, that the term 'holocaust' must never again be used in a New Zealand context. In turn, days later, the Indigenous Peoples Conference, held in the capital, Wellington, endorsed both the Waitangi Tribunal statement and Taria Turia. British policy in Kenya, in response to the Mau-Mau Uprising of 1952–7, has also been compared recently to the Holocaust, an absurd argument.

Without being centred on the Holocaust, there is also a more general downplaying of the Jewish experience of persecution. Thus, in the catalogue for a major exhibition 'At War', held in Barcelona in 2004, José María Ridao wrote of:

the temporal as well as spatial transmigration of stereotypes upon which death and destruction are wont to thrive: the representation of the pre-Columbian Indian coincides with that of today's Muslim, and that of today's Muslim with that of the Congolese native from the time of King Leopold, and that of the Congolese native with the persecuted Jew, and that of the persecuted Jew with that of Leo Tolstoy's Chechenian, and that of Tolstoy's Chechenian with the Chechenian the more recent press depicts. For each and every one of these figures, and for so many others, simple names on an interminable list which would include poor and gypsies alike, Hutus as well as Tutsis, Serbs as well as Bosnians, the stigma is always identical.[21]

At the same time, there have also been efforts to make the Holocaust relevant to non-Jews without losing sight of its Jewish character. This is particularly common in the USA, with a tendency to present the Holocaust as a crime against all, with the Jews as victims. Thus, Michael Berenbaum, one-time Project Director of the United States Holocaust Memorial Museum, which includes coverage of non-Jewish victims, has referred to the Americanisation of the Holocaust in terms of American values: especially tolerance, pluralism and human rights. The Simon Wiesenthal Center and Museum of Tolerance in Los Angeles exemplifies the same tendency.[22] A similar policy underlies Holocaust memorial days in countries like Britain. On 24 January 2005, in an address to a special session of the United Nations held to commemorate the Holocaust, the Secretary General, Kofi Annan, declared that:

> the evil which destroyed six million Jews and others in these camps still threatens all of us today; the crimes of the Nazis are nothing that we may ascribe to a distant past in order to forget it. It falls to us, the successor generations, to lift high the torch of remembrance, and to live our lives by its light.

In Belgium, more specifically, Natan Ramet, the Chairman of the Jewish Museum of Deportation and Resistance in Mechelen, declared of the Transport XX exhibition: 'This is a message against racism. This is not a Jewish theme: it has global relevance. If you discriminate against one group of people, this sort of thing can happen.' A similar theme was struck from a different context, in a press release from the municipality of Boortmeerbeek about the memorial service held to honour the resistance fighters and the deportees they rescued in 1943 (see p. 81):

> Today these ethical messages are still important for our youth, our community and for Belgium after what

happened a few months ago when a Belgium teenager in Antwerp made a racial carnage and killed a two-year-old Flemish toddler and her nanny. This incident again created an atmosphere of racial hatred. The same meaningless racial cruelty as the Nazi holocaust happened again.[23]

Similarly, the Wellington (New Zealand) Holocaust Research and Education Centre in its literature declares its aim to 'teach tolerance, courage and racial harmony [. . .] in ways that will inspire following generations, both Jewish and of other faiths, to combat intolerance wherever it occurs and respect the dignity of the lives of every man, woman and child.' Israel found itself in difficulties on this head in 2007, when detaining refugees from Darfur who were arriving as illegal immigrants.

At the global scale, however, the Western culture for which the Holocaust is a key symbol and warning is of receding consequence. This is particularly true of the rapidly declining demographic, economic, political, cultural and intellectual significance of Europe; for in Europe a major attempt has been made to establish the Holocaust as the point of departure from which, in a conscious reaction, the new Europe has been created. On 27 January 2000, a conference in Stockholm called by Göran Persson, the Prime Minister of Sweden, sought to define a common commemorative framework. It was agreed that the memory of the Holocaust should inform the values of a common European civil society, dedicated to 'mutual understanding and justice'. Fine sentiments, but, on the world scale, Europe is in decline.

There is also the issue of weakening American power and influence. Instead, the demographic, economic and political weight of China and India are of growing relative importance. For neither state is the Holocaust a prominent issue. Both states played a major, and generally underrated, role in the Second World War, India as part of the British Empire, but war with Germany was not crucial for either. For China, in particular, the issue of wartime crimes focuses on Japan, and, in her bestseller, *The Rape of Nanking: The Forgotten*

Holocaust of World War II (1997), Iris Chang compared the mass slaughter there in 1937 to Auschwitz. In Japan itself, attention to the Holocaust is limited, which, in part, reflects an education system heavily focused on Japanese history. Anti-Semitism may also be an issue.

Another separate strand of Holocaust-downplaying is represented by Islam. This is not simply a case of the policy of Muslim countries, but also that of a growing Muslim role in western Europe. This role will continue, as Muslim birth rates are considerably higher than those of the non-Muslim population. Political consequences already flow, with western Europe being, in part, influenced as part of an Islamic sphere of consciousness, although not as yet pulled into the sphere of Islamic influence sometimes alleged. The attitude of Muslim minorities towards the Holocaust has already been thrown into prominence in Britain, with the reluctance of Muslim organisations to take a role in Holocaust commemorations, despite marked public and governmental criticism on that head. At the scale of the European Union, this question may become more of an issue when states with a Muslim majority join. Albania, Kosovo and Turkey are the main possibilities.

Attempts to assert an equivalence with the Holocaust reflect in part the centrality of the Holocaust in the collective imagination, and indicate its role as a basis for public comment, indeed judgement. Thus, the Holocaust serves as a moral absolute and touchstone for those living in its 'moral aftermath',[24] although that practice is criticised by those who search for comparisons, or, even more, focus on cultural relativism. While writing this, it was arresting to see an instance of the impact of the Holocaust on popular culture. 'Daleks in Manhattan, I', an episode of the highly popular British television series *Dr. Who*, broadcast on 21 April 2007, had the evil Daleks, the quintessential and long-standing villains who hate everything, embark on 'The Final Experiment'. Victims were divided between those turned into slaves and others intended as food for the experiment. However flawed, these comparisons indicate the extent to which Nazi policy has become the axis of depravity.

CHAPTER 7

CONCLUSIONS

The contested memories of the Holocaust are not only an inconsequential adjunct of the academic scholarship on the events themselves but, instead, also part of their weighty impact on Western culture. The Holocaust, indeed, is now a central aspect, both of twentieth-century European history and of the twenty-first century's collective recollection of the past. It can also be seen as a key element in Nazi Germany's war on Europe and on its cultural inheritance. The racial recasting of Europe, with, at the least, the expulsion of the Jews, was a Hitlerian objective, not a by-product of the war.

Those making the war, including the German Army, certainly facilitated both this recasting and the resulting Holocaust. Crucially, German soldiers, policemen and others, who refused to take part in the killing, were not punished. This both suggests that more could have refused had they chosen to do so and also directs attention to the motivation of the killers. This was a motivation to be sought in anti-Semitic violence as much as the group cohesion often stressed.

Yet, collaborators in the killing, especially the very active and large-scale role, as the killers of Jews, of non-Germans in eastern Europe, underlines the fact that although the prime responsibility was German, it was not simply Germans who were involved. Instead, a side effect of German policy, and deliberately so, was to open a Pandora's Box of anti-Semitism and nationalist hatred and to focus it on killing Jews.

The extent to which the Holocaust was at once German in origin and cause, and yet also rested on a wider connivance and participation, was underlined by subsequent treatment of the killings both in Germany and elsewhere. This helped ensure that Holocaust denial was not simply an issue about Germany and for Germans. Partly as a result, in 2007, Germany utilised its presidency of the European Union to ensure the passage of race-hate laws for the entire union. The German Government saw these as a historic obligation and also an opportunity to exercise moral leadership. German legislation provided a background, as Holocaust denial was already a crime there.

In the event, German hopes of replicating this on EU scale, and thus of enacting a specific ban on Holocaust denial, failed. Instead, the EU agreed to criminalise 'publicly condoning, denying or grossly trivialising crimes of genocide, crimes against humanity and war crimes', although only where 'the conduct is carried out in a manner likely to incite violence or hatred'. The definition of these crimes was a matter of contention. Use of the rubrics of the International Criminal Court ensured that the Holocaust was included but also that it was far from unique. The slaughter in Rwanda and Yugoslavia in the 1990s were included, although not the Armenian genocide. Current political concerns play a major role in determining the legal status of such cases.

One area of potential comparability was presented by the extent to which the Holocaust was an instance of the vulnerability of groups when multi-ethnic supra-national empires were divided into mono-ethnic states. In the former, scattered peoples could integrate and be protected by the law, as the Jews were, to an extent, in the Habsburg Empire or the Bosniaks in Yugoslavia. In contrast, mono-ethnic states, or rather those that sought to be so, did not have to be persecuting, but it accorded with the aspiration to be mono-ethnic. In part, this was also an aspect of the challenge of democratic politics, as this transition from multi-ethnic empires occurred at the same time as the onset of democracy provided the opportunity for populist authoritarianism. Yet, whatever the strains of this transition, an outcome in the shape of the attempt to slaughter all of a racial group is not usual.

CHALLENGING OPTIMISM

The Holocaust also has a wider significance, not least (although not only) if the emphasis is placed on 'indifference, disinterest, and a striking lack of moral values' on the part of perpetrators and bystanders. Such an emphasis suggests not only that the Holocaust emerged from a historically unique situation but also that genocide was/is more generally latent.[1]

This also represents a major qualification of both secular and religious optimism. As far as the first is concerned, belief in the progress, even perfectability, of mankind was challenged by what Primo Levi, an Auschwitz survivor, termed 'the feeling of guilt that such a crime should exist'. The very fundamentals of human society were all challenged by the Holocaust. This was not simply a question of individual values, self-knowledge and relationships between humans, each of which were placed under terrible strain, as Jews both confronted the appalling circumstances into which they were thrust and also sought to lessen the burden. This led to a measuring out of time in fragments of survival, to unhinging despair, to acts of selfishness towards fellow victims (as well as many luminous acts of transcendent selflessness) and to such measures as the denial of identity and also suicide, each of which was widespread, as well as to feelings of guilt and a desire for anonymity among many survivors.

Other social fundamentals were also challenged. Language is always a porous and contested medium of communication and form, occasion and means of sociability. Nevertheless, the Nazis took forward the long-standing inversion of meaning and morality in Communist language, brilliantly caricatured in George Orwell's *Animal Farm* (1945), and gave a particular racial dimension as they fervently conceptualised and sought what to any rational observer was a dystopia. Thus, as part of their conflation of hyperbole and euphemism, the language of health and cleansing was used to describe slaughter. Nazi euphemism, arguably, is still employed in a misleading fashion when terms such as 'Final Solution' are used. Aside from euphemism, there is the problem of the connotations of words and phrases, as with the use of 'liquidation' or 'extermination', a term frequently employed to describe vermin, rather than slaughter, although the latter is applied to animals.

Although not the equivalent of Nazi linguistic inversion, the more recent language of postmodernism is also an obfuscation of the truth and a denial of reality. In its endless and self-obsessed relativism and its questioning of the existence of facts, postmodernism is not just empty of meaning and value but also an evil perversion of reason. The critical assessment by Richard Evans, in his *In Defence of History* (1997), is worth noting: 'Auschwitz was not a discourse. It trivializes mass murder to see it as a text.'

THEOLOGY AND THE HOLOCAUST

It was not simply secular language and ideas that were to be tested by the Holocaust. Despite the best efforts of religious leaders and thinkers and arguments about God's inscrutable purpose and the testing of the devout, the notion of an omnipotent and benign, indeed interested and engaged, God also took a savage knock. Indeed, the lengthy BBC Radio 4 interview in 2006 with the Chief Rabbi of the British Commonwealth, Jonathan Sacks, focused on this point. Although he put up a vigorous case from the religious perspective, it was not one that necessarily convinced those dubious of the acceptance, even confidence, with which such views are advanced. More generally, there was the problem, for philosophers as well as theologians, of 'how to continue thinking without yielding to the temptation of false consolation'.[2]

Confidence in divine purpose was certainly challenged in the case of some Holocaust survivors. In part, this reflected their understanding of what had happened to them and, in part, it was an aspect of their continued disorientation, sense of emptiness and experience of destruction.[3] Alexander Donat, a survivor of the Warsaw ghetto and of Auschwitz, wrote of the former: 'we kept asking ourselves the age-old question: why? why?'[4]

Holocaust theology is not a subject discussed by most historians and, instead, is handled by theologians.[5] For a historian to discuss the topic may appear both rash and redundant, but it is a key aspect of the legacy of the Holocaust. Moreover, the questions that are the central issues in Holocaust theology, 'Why did God let it happen?' and 'Where was God?', are of interest from the historical perspective. It is not necessary to be religious (and, whether or not it is relevant, I am an atheist) to ask whether, first, any discussion of the former can throw light on the issue of causation and the process of discussing it, and, second, whether the second throws light on the experience of the Holocaust.

Moreover, these are issues for both Christian and Jewish theologians. In part, this is because the perpetrators were Christian and the victims Jews, in part because many other victims of Nazi slaughter were Christian, and, in part, as both common humanity and a shared interest in theological questions makes the Holocaust, and its relationship with divine intentions, a matter of importance for both groups of theologians.

There are, of course, other dimensions as well. First, there were key cross-currents that diminished the extent to which the Holocaust was a religious question. However much it drew on anti-Semitism, the Nazi assault was on a race, not a religion, and avowedly so, and this made it different to the totalitarian assault on religion that Church leaders perceived in Nazi policies.[6] Indeed, many Jews who were victims of the Holocaust were not religious, while some had converted to Christianity. Second, there is the question as to how far Nazism itself was a religion or pseudo-religion. This is linked to the issue whether the Holocaust, and Nazism itself, stands on some sort of charge-sheet against atheism, an argument frequently made, for example by the Catholic polemicist William (Lord) Rees-Mogg in *The Times* in 2007 (he is also critical of Communism), or whether that is a meritless charge and, indeed, can be reversed by arguing that Nazism was a religion. That Nazism was not one akin to Christianity does not imply that it should not be seen as being a religion or, at least, as a movement with religious elements.

Among the standard theological responses to the central questions about God's role in the Holocaust are arguments that God left humanity with a degree of free will that made the Holocaust possible, and also that God was present in the Holocaust and strongly so, not least as Jews courageously and powerfully testified to their faith in the most difficult and extreme circumstances. Literature on the latter includes Yaffa Eliach's *Hasidic Tales of the Holocaust* (1982) and Pesach Schindler's *Hasidic Responses to the Holocaust in the Light of Hasidic Thought* (1990). God suffering in the Holocaust is a major related theme, with the argument, for example, that God was present at Auschwitz.

The Holocaust also serves as the key and tangible modern instance of a far longer experience of persecution, suffering and loss. While episodes such as the destruction of the Temple in AD 70 and the brutal Roman suppressions of Jewish opposition in AD 66–74 and 132–5, or the medieval slaughters of Jews, for example, in 1096 in Germany at the time of the First Crusade, seem remote, if not lost, in the mist of time, the Holocaust is a far more present issue. There were also relevant differences, in that the German attempt to destroy the Jews throughout Europe was not one with which it was possible to compromise or attempt to escape by conforming to the values of the persecutor, as earlier, with the Roman Empire or the Christian Church. Challenged by Jewish monotheism and difference, they attacked what was an alternative religion, but members of the race could conform to Rome or Christianity, as they could not to Nazi ideology. From this perspective, the Holocaust was different, although, in religious terms, it was the latest in a series of vicious persecutions that were also opportunities for the affirmation of belief.

Christian theologians have not always handled the implications of the Holocaust sensitively or sensibly. There are issues about the relationship with anti-Semitism, especially the role of Christians in the killing, a point that can be underlined by considering collaboration, and the extent to which some collaborationist regimes and groups, for example Vichy and the Slovak Government, emphasised Christianity as crucial to their identity. There are also the more general implications of the Holocaust for theology, not least in terms of the immanence of evil and barbarism. Some Christian theologians have argued that the Holocaust can be understood alongside the suffering of Christ, a thesis that can have unfortunate implications but which is intended to underline the argument about a central relationship between Jews and Christians and a common bond of pain. Others have pressed for the need to address the legacy of Christian anti-Semitism, not least by revising theology where necessary. Christian theologians have also been challenged by the evil seen in the Holocaust. In *Christian Theology after Auschwitz* (1976), the Catholic theologian Gregory Baum argued that in place of an all-powerful God, it was necessary to see God as acting from within, unable to block all movements or human sin but nevertheless able to act as 'reviver' because of the divine role as the 'forward movement operative in people's lives enabling them to enter more deeply into authentic humanity'.

Thus, a theological caution about divine power, not to say uncertainty about divine intentions, can match secular pessimism. At the same time that the slaughter was a terrible episode in Jewish history, and a central instance in the theme of a wider and unjust Jewish suffering across the ages, the Holocaust also resonates as a universal question. The latter does not lessen nor qualify the former but is part of it.

NOTES

PREFACE

1 J. Black (ed.), *The Second World War* (7 vols, Aldershot, 2007).

1 UNTIL BARBAROSSA

1 C. Vivanti, 'The History of the Jews in Italy and the History of Italy', *Journal of Modern History*, 67 (1995), p. 356; W.I. Brustein, *Roots of Hate: Anti-Semitism in Europe before the Holocaust* (Cambridge, 2003).

2 S. Almog, *Nationalism and Antisemitism in Modern Europe, 1815–1945* (Oxford, 1990).

3 M. Michaelis, 'Fascism, Totalitarianism and the Holocaust: Reflections on Current Interpretations of National Socialist Anti-Semitism', *European History Quarterly*, 19 (1989), p. 99.

4 S. Volkov, 'AntiSemitism as a Cultural Code: Reflections on the History and Historiography of AntiSemitism in Imperial Germany', *Leo Baeck Institute Yearbook*, 23 (1978), pp. 25–45.

5 P. Pulzer, *The Rise of Political Anti-Semitism in Germany and Austria* (Cambridge, Mass., 1988); A. Kaunders, *German Politics and the Jews: Düsseldorf and Nürnberg 1910–1933* (Oxford, 1996).

6 M. Basin, 'Race contra Space: The Conflict between German *Geopolitik* and National Socialism', *Political Geography Quarterly*, 6 (1987), pp. 115–34.

7 (Brunswick, 1924).

8 B. Arnold, 'The Past as Propaganda: Totalitarian Archaeology in Nazi Germany', *Antiquity*, 64 (1990), pp. 464–78.

9 C. Ingrao, 'Understanding Ethnic Conflict in Central Europe: An Historical Perspective', *Nationalities Papers*, 27 (1999), p. 306.

10 C. Ingrao, 'The Revolutionary Origins of the Twentieth-Century Holocausts', *Consortium on Revolutionary Europe: Selected Papers, 1997* (Tallahassee, Fla., 1997), p. 32.

11 A.E. Steinweis, *Art, Ideology and Economics in Nazi Germany: The Reich Chambers of Music, Theater, and the Visual Arts* (Chapel Hill, NC, 1993).

12 Y. Lozowick, *Hitler's Bureaucrats: The Nazi Security Police and the Banality of Evil* (New York, 2002), and U. Herbert (ed.), *National Socialist Extermination Policies: Contemporary German Perspectives and Controversies* (Oxford, 2000); G. Aly, P. Chroust and C. Pross, *Cleansing the Fatherland: Nazi Medicine and Racial Hygiene* (Baltimore, Md., 1994).

13 M. Roseman, 'Ideas, Contexts, and the Pursuit of Genocide', *German Historical Institute London. Bulletin*, 25 (2003), p. 73.

14 G. Aly, *'Final Solution': Nazi Population Policy and the Murder of the European Jews* (London, 1999).

15 P.J. Weindling, *Epidemics and Genocide in Eastern Europe 1890–1945* (Oxford, 2000).

16 C. Hale, *Himmler's Crusade: The True Story of the SS Expedition into Tibet* (London, 2003); H. Pringle, *Master Plan: Himmler's Scholars and the Holocaust* (London, 2006).

17 V. Caron, *Uneasy Asylum: France and the Jewish Refugee Crisis, 1933–1942* (Stanford, Calif., 1999).

18 B. Zucker, *In Search of Refuge: Jews and the U.S. Consuls in Nazi Germany, 1933–1941* (London, 2001).

19 P. Hayes, 'Big Business and "Aryanization" in Germany, 1933–39', *Jahrbuch für Antisemitismus forschung*, 31 (1994), pp. 254–81; L.M. Stallbaumer, 'Big Business and the Persecution of the Jews: The Flick Concern and the "Aryanization" of Jewish Property before the War', *Holocaust and Genocide Studies*, 13 (1999), pp. 1–27, and 'Between Coercion and Cooperation: The Flick Concern in Nazi Germany before the War', *Essays in Economic and Business History*, 17 (1999), pp. 63–74.

20 J. Connelly, 'The Uses of *Volksgemeinschaft*: Letters to the NSDAP Kreisleitung Eisenach, 1939–40', *Journal of Modern History*, 68 (1996), p. 926.

21 H. James, *The Deutsche Bank and the Nazi Economic War against the Jews: The Expropriation of Jewish-Owned Property* (Cambridge, 2001).

22 A. Nolzen, 'The Nazi Party and Its Violence against the Jews, 1933–39', *Yad Vashem Studies*, 31 (2003), pp. 245–85; I. Kershaw, 'The Persecution of the Jews and German Popular Opinion in the Third Reich', *Leo Baeck Institute Yearbook*, 26 (1981), pp. 261–89.

23 S. Friedländer, *Nazi Germany and the Jews: The Years of Persecution 1933–1939* (London, 1997); E. Johnson and K.-H. Reuband, *What We Knew: Terror, Mass Murder and Everyday Life in Nazi Germany: An Oral History* (Cambridge, Mass., 2005).

24 M. Wildt, 'Before the "Final Solution": The *Judenpolitik* of the SD, 1935–38', *Leo Baeck Institute Yearbook*, 43 (1998), pp. 266–7.

25 C. Townshend, 'The Defence of Palestine: Insurrection and Public Security, 1936–39', *English Historical Review*, 103 (1988), pp. 917–49.

26 A.B. Rossino, *Hitler Strikes Poland: Blitzkrieg, Ideology, and Atrocity* (Lawrence, Kan., 2003).

27 J. Steinberg, 'The Third Reich Reflected: German Civil Administration in the Occupied Soviet Union, 1941–44', *English Historical Review*, 110 (1995), p. 632.

28 K.R. Jolluck, *Exile and Identity: Polish Women in the Soviet Union during World War II* (Pittsburg, Pa., 2003).

29 I. Trunk, *Judenrat: The Jewish Councils in Eastern Europe under Nazi Occupation* (Lincoln, Nebr., 1972).

30 M. Gilbert, *The Routledge Atlas of the Holocaust* (3rd edn, London, 2002), pp. 32–43, and *The Path to Genocide: Essays on Launching the Final Solution* (Cambridge, 1992).

31 C.R. Browning, 'Nazi Ghettoization Policy in Poland, 1939–41', *Central European History*, 19 (1986), p. 365.

32 J. Moser, 'Nisko, the First Experiment in Deportation', *Simon Wiesenthal Center Annual*, 2 (1985), pp. 1–30, esp. pp. 17–21; D. Cesarani, *Eichmann: His Life and Crimes* (London, 2004).

33 C.R. Browning, 'Nazi Resettlement Policy and the Search for a Solution to the Jewish Question, 1939–41', *German Studies Review*, 9 (1986), p. 515.

2 TOWARDS GENOCIDE

1 Y. Lozowick, 'The Early Activities of Einsatzgruppe C', *Holocaust and Genocide Studies*, 2 (1987), pp. 221–41; Y. Arad, S. Krakowski and S. Spector (eds), *The Einsatzgruppen Reports* (Washington, DC, 1990).

2 T. Anderson, 'Germans, Ukrainians and Jews: Ethnic Politics in *Heeresgebiet Süd*, June–December 1941', *War in History*, 7 (2000), pp. 325–51, esp. p. 350.

3 W. Dreessen, 'The Role of the Wehrmacht and the Police in the Annihilation of the Jews', *Yad Vashem Studies*, 23 (1993), pp. 245–315.

4 C.R. Browning, 'Wehrmacht Reprisal Policy and the Mass Murder of Jews in Serbia', *Militärgeschichtliche Mitteilungen*, 33 (1983), p. 38.

5 G. Wawro, *The Franco-Prussian War: The German Conquest of France in 1870–1871* (Cambridge, 2003), pp. 264–5, 288–9.

6 J. Horne and A. Kramer, *German Atrocities, 1914: A History of Denial* (New Haven, Conn., 2001).

7 H. Herr and K. Naumann (eds), *War of Extermination: The German Military in World War II, 1941–1944* (London, 2000).

8 T. von Trotha, '"The Fellows Can Just Starve": On Wars of "Pacification" in the African Colonies of Imperial Germany and the Concept of "Total War"', in M.F. Boemeke, R. Chickering and S. Förster (eds), *Anticipating Total War: The German and American Experiences, 1871–1914* (Cambridge, 1999), pp. 415–36.

9 J. Bridgman, *The Revolt of the Hereros* (Berkeley, Calif., 1981).

10 V. Liulevicius, *War Land on the Eastern Front: Culture, National Identity and German Occupation in World War I* (Cambridge, 2000).

11 D. Showalter, '"The East Gives Nothing Back": The Great War and the German Army in Russia', *Journal of the Historical Society*, 2 (2002), pp. 1–19, esp. 15–16.

12 I.V. Hull, *Absolute Destruction: Military Culture and the Practices of War in Imperial Germany* (Ithaca, NY, 2005), and 'The Military Campaign in German Southwest Africa, 1904–7', *Bulletin of the German Historical Institute, Washington*, 37 (2005), pp. 41–2.

13 R. Sheck, *Hitler's African Victims: The German Army Massacres of Black French Soldiers in 1940* (Cambridge, 2006).

14 C.S. Thomas, *The German Navy in the Nazi Era* (London, 1990).

15 L. Dobroszycki and J.S. Gurock (eds), *The Holocaust in the Soviet Union: Studies and Sources on the Destruction of the Jews in the Nazi-Occupied Territories of the USSR, 1941–1945* (Armonk, NY, 1993).

16 Y. Arad, 'The "Final Solution" in Lithuania in the Light of German Documentation', *Yad Vashem Studies*, 11 (1976), pp. 234–72, and *Ghetto in Flames: The Struggle and Destruction of the Jews in Vilna in the Holocaust* (Jerusalem, 1980).

17 T. Piotrowski, *Poland's Holocaust: Ethnic Strife, Collaboration with Occupying Forces and Genocide in the Second Republic, 1918–1947* (Jefferson, NC, 2007), p. 221.

18 C.R. Browning, 'The Nazi Decision to Commit Mass Murder: Three Interpretations. The Euphoria of Victory and the Final Solution, autumn 1941', *German Studies Review*, 17 (1994), pp. 473–81.

19 B. Shepherd, *War in the Wild East: The German Army and Soviet Partisans* (Cambridge, Mass., 2004).

20 D.M. Glantz (ed.), *The Initial Phase of the War on the Eastern Front, 22 June–August 1941* (London, 1993).

21 S. Corvaga, *Hitler and Mussolini* (New York, 2001), p. 236.

22 C. Dieckmann, 'The War and the Killing of the Lithuanian Jews', in U. Herbert (ed.), *National Socialist Extermination Policies* (New York, 2000), pp. 240–75.

23 J. Steinberg, 'The Third Reich Reflected: German Civil Administration in the Occupied Soviet Union, 1941–44', *English Historical Review*, 110 (1995), p. 111.

24 S. Cholawsky, *The Jews of Belorussia during World War II* (Amsterdam, 1998).

25 G.L. Weinberg, 'Unexplored Questions about the German Military during World War II', *Journal of Military History*, 62 (1998), pp. 372–3.

26 T. Dupuy, *Encyclopedia of Military Biography* (London, 1992), p. 644.

27 C. Messenger, *Hitler's Gladiator: The Life and Military Career of Sepp Dietrich* (London, 2001).

28 Anderson, 'Germans', p. 337.
29 R.T. Paget, *Manstein: His Campaigns and His Trial* (London, 1951).
30 A. Searle, 'A Very Special Relationship: Basil Liddell Hart, Wehrmacht Generals and the Debate on West German Rearmament, 1945–53', *War in History*, 5 (1998), pp. 327–57.
31 Kings College London, Liddell Hart Archive, Liddell Hart papers 4/28.
32 Piotrowski, *Poland's Holocaust*, p. 243.
33 Z. Bauman, *The Holocaust and Modernity* (London, 1989).
34 M. Burleigh, *Death and Deliverance. 'Euthanasia' in Germany, c. 1900 to 1945* (Cambridge, 1994).
35 A. Beker (ed.), *The Plunder of Jewish Property during the Holocaust* (London, 2001); G. Aalders, *Nazi Looting: The Plunder of Dutch Jewry during the Second World War* (Oxford, 2004).
36 M.T. Allen, *The Business of Genocide: The SS, Slave Labor and the Concentration Camps* (Chapel Hill, NC, 2002).
37 I. Kershaw, *Hitler, 1936–1945: Nemesis* (London, 2000).
38 A. Charlesworth, 'Towards a Geography of the Shoah', *Journal of Historical Geography*, 18 (1992), pp. 464–9; D.B. Clarke, M.A. Doehl and F. McDonough, 'Holocaust Topologies: Singularity, Politics, Space', *Political Geography*, 15 (1996), pp. 457–89; M.A. Doehl and D.B. Clarke, 'Figuring the Holocaust: Singularity and the Purification of Space', in G. Ó. Tuathail and S. Dalby (eds), *Rethinking Geopolitics* (London, 1998), pp. 170–97.
39 S. Heim and G. Aly, 'The Holocaust and Population Policy', *Yad Vashem Studies*, 24 (1994), pp. 45–70; I. Heinemann, '"Another Type of Perpetrator": The SS Racial Experts and Forced Population Movements in the Occupied Regions', *Holocaust and Genocide Studies*, 15 (2001), pp. 387–411.
40 P. Witte, 'Two Decisions Concerning the "Final Solution to the Jewish Question": Deportations to Lódz and Mass Murder in Chelmno', *Holocaust and Genocide Studies*, 9 (1995), pp. 325–9.
41 Witte, 'Decisions', pp. 329–33.
42 J. Lukacs, *June 1941: Hitler and Stalin* (New Haven, Conn., 2006); A. Toze, *The Wages of Destruction: The Making and Breaking of the Nazi Economy* (London, 2006), p. 665.
43 G. Fleming, *Hitler and The Final Solution* (London, 1985).
44 I. Kershaw, '"Working towards the Führer": Reflections on the Nature of the Hitler Dictatorship', *Contemporary European History*, 2 (1993), pp. 103–18.
45 C. Madajczyk, 'Hitler's Direct Influence on Decisions Affecting Jews During World War II', *Yad Vashem Studies*, 20 (1990), pp. 54–8; L. Yahil, 'Some Remarks about Hitler's Impact on the Nazi's Jewish Policy', *Yad Vashem Studies*, 23 (1993), pp. 281–93; C.R. Browning, *The Origins of the Final Solution: The Evolution of Nazi Jewish Policy, September 1939–March 1942* (Lincoln, Nebr., 2004).

46 S. Friedländer, 'From Anti-Semitism to Extermination', *Yad Vashem Studies*, 16 (1984), p. 48.

47 R. Gellately (ed.), *The Nuremberg Interviews: Conducted by Leon Goldensohn* (London, 2007), pp. 188–90.

48 S. Friedländer, 'From Anti-Semitism', p. 47.

49 I. Kershaw, *Fateful Choices: Ten Decisions that Changed the World, 1940–41* (London, 2007), pp. 431–70.

50 I. Kershaw, 'Improvised Genocide? The Emergence of the "Final Solution" in the "Warthegau"', *Transactions of the Royal Historical Society*, 6th ser. 2 (1992), pp. 51–78, esp. p. 73; C.R. Browning, 'German Killers: Orders from Above, Initiative from Below, and the Scope of Local Autonomy – the Case of Brest-Litovsk', in C.R. Browning, *Nazi Policy, Jewish Workers, German Killers* (Cambridge, 2000), pp. 116–42.

51 P. Longerich, *The Wannsee Conference in the Development of the 'Final Solution'* (London, 2000).

52 C. Gerlach, 'The Wannsee Conference, the Fate of German Jews and Hitler's Decision in Principle to Exterminate All European Jews', in O. Bartov (ed.), *The Holocaust: Origins, Implementation, Aftermath* (London, 2000), pp. 106–61; M. Roseman, *The Villa, the Lake, the Meeting: Wannsee and the Final Solution* (Harmondsworth, 2002), and 'Shoot First and Ask Questions Afterwards? Wannsee and the Unfolding of the Final Solution', in N. Gregor (ed.), *Nazism, War and Genocide* (Exeter, 2005), pp. 131–46.

53 J. Noakes, 'The Development of Nazi Policy towards the German-Jewish "Mischling"', *Leo Baeck Institute Year Book*, 34 (1989), pp. 291–356.

54 T.A. Wray, *Standing Fast: German Defensive Doctrine on the Eastern Front During World War II: Prewar to March 1943* (Fort Leavenworth, Kans., 1943).

55 Y. Arad, *Belzec, Sobibor, Treblinka: The Operation Reinhard Death Camps* (Indianapolis, Ind., 1987).

56 F. Piper, 'Estimating the Number of Deportees and Victims of the Auschwitz-Birkenau Camp', *Yad Vashem Studies*, 21 (1991), pp. 49–103.

57 Y. Gutman and M. Berenbaum (eds), *Anatomy of the Auschwitz Death Camp* (Bloomington, Ind., 1994); O. Bartov, *Murder in Our Midst: The Holocaust, Industrial Killing, and Representation* (Oxford, 1996); P. Hayes, 'Auschwitz, Capital of the Holocaust', *Holocaust and Genocide Studies*, 17 (2003), pp. 330–5; N. Frei, 'Auschwitz and the Germans: History, Knowledge, and Memory', in N. Gregor (ed.), *Nazism* (Exeter, 2005), pp. 147–65.

58 E. Spiers, 'Gas and the North-West Frontier' (of India), *Journal of Strategic Studies*, 6 (1983), pp. 94–112.

59 H. Johnston, *A Bridge Not Attacked: Chemical Warfare Civilian Research during World War II* (River Edge, NJ, 2003).

60 S. Krakowski and I. Altman, 'The Testament of the Last Prisoners at the Chelmno Death Camp', *Yad Vashem Studies*, 21 (1991), pp. 105–23.

61 B. Alt and S. Folts, *Weeping Violins: The Gypsy Tragedy in Europe* (Kirksville, Miss., 1996); K. Fings, H. Heuss and F. Sparing, *From 'Race Science' to the Camps: The Gypsies during the Second World War* (Hatfield, 1997).

62 J. Steinberg, 'The Third Reich Reflected: German Civil Administration in the Occupied Soviet Union, 1941–44', *English Historical Review*, 110 (1995), p. 647.

63 E.R. Baer and M. Goldenberg (eds), *Experience and Expression: Women, the Nazis, and the Holocaust* (Detroit, Mich., 2003), and N. Tec, *Resilience and Courage: Women, Men and the Holocaust* (New Haven, Conn., 2003).

64 O. Bartov, 'The Devil in the Details: The Concentration Camp as Historical Construct', *German Historical Institute London. Bulletin*, 21 (1999), p. 39.

65 R.J. Overy, *Making a Killing: The Economics of the Holocaust* (Glasgow, 2005), p. 7.

66 H. Pringle, *Master Plan: Himmler's Scholars and the Holocaust* (London, 2006).

67 Piotrowski, *Poland's Holocaust*, p. 31.

68 K. Sakowicz, *Ponary Diary, 1941–1943: A Bystander's Account of a Mass Murder*, edited by Y. Arad (New Haven, Conn., 2005).

69 P.W. Blood, *Hitler's Bandit Hunters: The SS and the Nazi Occupation of Europe* (Dulles, Virg., 2006).

3 GENOCIDE

1 C.R. Browning, 'A Final Hitler Decision for the "Final Solution"? The Riegner Telegram Reconsidered', *Holocaust and Genocide Studies*, 10 (1996), pp. 3–10.

2 I. Gutman, *The Jews of Warsaw 1939–43: Ghetto, Underground, Revolt* (Bloomington, Ind., 1982). I am most grateful for the advice of David Cesarani.

3 Y. Gutman, *Resistance: The Warsaw Ghetto Uprising* (Boston, Mass., 1994).

4 S. Spector, 'Jewish Resistance in Small Towns in Eastern Poland', in N. Davies and A. Polonsky (eds), *Jews in Eastern Poland and the USSR, 1939–46* (London, 1991); H.H. Nolte, 'Partisan War in Belorussia, 1941–44', in R. Chickering, S. Förster and B. Greiner (eds), *A World at Total War: Global Conflict and the Politics of Destruction, 1937–1945* (Cambridge, 2005), pp. 264, 268.

5 Y. Bauer, *They Chose Life: Jewish Resistance in the Holocaust* (Seattle, Wash., 1973); J. Glass, *Jewish Resistance during the Holocaust: Moral Uses of Violence and Will* (Basingstoke, 2004); R. Sakowski, 'Two Forms of Resistance in the Warsaw Ghetto: Two Functions of the Ringelblom Archives', *Yad Vashem Studies*, 21 (1991), pp. 189–219; S. Erpel, 'Struggle and Survival: Jewish Women in the Anti-Fascist Resistance in Germany', *Yearbook: Leo Baeck Institute of Jews in Germany*, 37 (1992), pp. 397–414; R. Rohrlich (ed.), *Resisting the Holocaust* (Oxford, 1998).

6 S. Gilbert, *Music in the Holocaust: Confronting Life in the Nazi Ghettos and Camps* (Oxford, 2005), p. 200.

7 G. Corni, *Hitler's Ghettos: Voices from a Beleaguered Society, 1939–1944* (London, 2002).

8 J.D. Klier and S. Lambroza (eds), *Pogroms: Anti-Jewish Violence in Modern Russian History* (Cambridge, 1992).

9 C.R. Browning, 'Wehrmacht Reprisal Policy', p. 35.

10 R. Breitman, *The Architect of Genocide: Himmler and the Final Solution* (London, 1991), p. 142.

11 S. Friedländer, *The Years of Extermination: Nazi Germany and the Jews, 1939–1945* (New York, 2007), p. 350.

12 M.T. Allen, *The Business of Genocide: The SS, Slave Labor, and the Concentration Camps* (Chapel Hill, NC, 2002); P. Hayes, *Industry and Ideology: I.G. Farben in the Nazi Era* (Cambridge, 1987).

13 W. Gruner, *Jewish Forced Labor under the Nazis: Economic Needs and Racial Aims, 1938–1944* (Cambridge, 2006).

14 U. Herbert, *Hitler's Foreign Workers: Enforced Labor in Germany under the Third Reich* (Cambridge, 1977).

15 F. Piper, *Auschwitz Prison Labour: The Organisation and Exploitation of Auschwitz Concentration Camp Prisoners as Laborers* (Oswiecim, 2002).

16 S. Gilbert, *Music in the Holocaust: Confronting Life in the Nazi Ghettos and Camps* (Oxford, 2005).

17 G.D. Feldman, *Allianz and the German Insurance Business, 1933–1945* (Cambridge, 2001).

18 M. Mazower, 'Military Violence and National Socialist Values: The Wehrmacht in Greece, 1941–44', *Past and Present*, 134 (1992), pp. 129–58.

19 H. Boog, W. Rahn, R. Stumpf and B. Wegner, *Germany and the Second World War. VI. The Global War* (Oxford, 2001).

20 W. Lower, *Nazi Empire-Building and the Holocaust in Ukraine* (Chapel Hill, NC, 2005).

21 R. Braham, *The Politics of Genocide: The Holocaust in Hungary* (New York, 1981); D. Cesarani (ed.), *Genocide and Rescue: The Holocaust in Hungary, 1944* (Oxford, 1997); Braham and S. Miller (eds), *The Nazis' Last Victims: The Holocaust in Hungary* (Detroit, Mich., 1998).

22 R. Zweig, *The Gold Train: The Destruction of the Jews and the Second World War's Most Terrible Robbery* (London, 2002).

23 A.D. van Liempt, *Hitler's Bounty Hunters: The Betrayal of the Jews* (Oxford, 2005).

24 U. Herbert, 'Labour and Extermination: Economic Interest and the Primacy of *Weltanschauung* in National Socialism', *Past and Present*, 138 (1993), pp. 144–95.

25 P.K. Grimsted, *Trophies of War and Empire: The Archival Heritage of Ukraine, World War II, and the International Politics of Restitution* (Cambridge, Mass., 2001), pp. 196–209; K.C. Berkhoff, *Harvest of Despair: Life and Death in Ukraine under Nazi Rule* (Cambridge, Mass., 2004).

26 M. Levene and P. Roberts (eds), *The Massacre in History* (Oxford, 1999).

27 B. Wegner, 'The Ideology of Self-Destruction: Hitler and the Choreography of Defeat', *German Historical Institute London. Bulletin*, 26 (2004), pp. 26–33.

28 N. Wachsmann, *Hitler's Prisons: Legal Terror in Nazi Germany* (New Haven, Conn., 2004).

29 G.L. Weinberg, *Germany, Hitler and World War II* (Cambridge, 1995), pp. 274–86.

30 L. Dobrowski (ed.), *The Chronicle of the Lodz Ghetto* (New Haven, Conn., 1987).

31 A.J. Kochavi, *Prelude to Nuremberg: Allied War Crimes Policy and the Question of Punishment* (Chapel Hill, NC, 1998), p. 65.

32 S. Krakowski, 'The Death Marches in the Period of the Evacuation of the Camps', in Y. Gutman and A. Saf (eds), *The Nazi Concentration Camps* (Jerusalem, 1984), pp. 475–91; D. Blatman, 'The Death Marches: January–May 1945: Who Was Responsible for What?', *Yad Vashem Studies*, 28 (2000), pp. 155–201.

33 I. Haar and M. Fahlbusch (eds), *German Scholars and Ethnic Cleansing, 1919–1945* (New York, 2005).

34 M.H. Kater, *Hitler Youth* (Cambridge, Mass., 2004).

35 P. Panayi, 'Victims, Perpetrators and Bystanders in a German Town: The Jews of Osnabrück Before, During and After the Third Reich', *European History Quarterly*, 33 (2003), pp. 451–92; G.J. Horwitz, *In the Shadow of Death: Living Outside the Gates of Mauthausen* (New York, 1990).

36 J.F. Tent, *In the Shadow of the Holocaust: Nazi Persecution of Jewish-Christian Germans* (Lawrence, Kans., 2003).

37 S. Bach, *Leni: The Life and Work of Leni Riefenstahl* (London, 2007).

38 A.S. Bergerson, *Ordinary Germans in Extraordinary Times: The Nazi Revolution in Hildesheim* (Bloomington, Ind., 2004).

39 D. Bankier, 'The Germans and the Holocaust: What Did They Know?', *Yad Vashem Studies*, 20 (1990), and *The Germans and the Final Solution: Public Opinion under Nazism* (3rd edn, Oxford, 2002).

40 K.M. Mallmann, 'Social Penetration and Police Action: Collaboration in the Repertory of Gestapo Activities', *International Review of Social History*, 42 (1997), pp. 25–43; V. Joshi, 'The "Private" Became the "Public": Wives as Denouncers in the Third Reich', *Journal of Contemporary History*, 37 (2002), pp. 419–35.

41 R. Gellately, *The Gestapo and German Society: Enforcing Racial Policy, 1933–1945* (Oxford, 1990).

42 N. Stargadt, 'Victims of Bombing and Retaliation', *German Historical Institute London. Bulletin*, 26 (2004), pp. 67–9.

43 C.R. Browning, *Ordinary Men: Reserve Police Battalion 101 and the Final Solution in Poland* (New York, 1992); G.L. Weinberg, *Crossing the Line in Nazi Genocide: On Becoming and Being a Professional Killer* (Burlington, Mass., 1997); M. Mann, 'Were the Perpetrators of Genocide "Ordinary Men" or "Real Nazis"? Results from Fifteen Hundred Biographies', *Holocaust and Genocide Studies*, 14 (2000), pp. 331–66.

44 S. Baranowski, *The Confessing Church, Conservative Elites, and the Nazi State* (Lewiston, NY, 1986); R. Ericksen and S. Heschel (eds), *Betrayal: German Churches and the Holocaust* (Minneapolis, Minn., 1999).

45 K.P. Spicer, *Resisting the Third Reich: The Catholic Clergy in Hitler's Berlin* (DeKalb, Ill., 2004).

46 B.A. Griech-Polelle, *Bishop von Galen: German Catholicism and National Socialism* (London, 2002).

47 O. Heilbronner, 'The Place of Catholic Historians and Catholic Historiography in Nazi Germany', *History*, 88 (2003), pp. 291–2.

48 R.I. Moore, *The Formation of Persecuting Society* (Oxford, 1988).

49 W. Monter, *Frontiers of Heresy: The Spanish Inquisition from the Basque Lands to Sicily* (Cambridge, 1990); S. Haliczer, *Inquisition and Society in the Kingdom of Valencia 1478–1834* (Berkeley, Calif., 1990).

50 R. Gellately, *Backing Hitler, Consent and Coercion in Nazi Germany* (Oxford, 2001); G. Eley, 'Hitler's Silent Majority? Conformity and Resistance under the Third Reich', *Michigan Quarterly Review*, 42 (2003), pp. 389–425.

51 R. Gellately, *The Gestapo and German Society: Enforcing Racial Policy 1933–1945* (Oxford, 1990).

52 D. Mühlberger, *Hitler's Followers: Studies in the Sociology of the Nazi Movement* (London, 1991); J.W. Falter, 'The Anatomy of a Volkspartei', *Historical Social Research*, 24, 2 (1999), pp. 58–98; H.D. Andrews, 'Thirty-Four Gold Medallists. Nazi Women Remember the "Kampfzeit"', *German History*, 11 (1993), pp. 293–315; L. Pine, 'Creating Conformity: The Training of Girls in the Bund Deutscher Mädel', *European History Quarterly*, 33 (2005), pp. 367–85.

53 M. Gilbert, *Auschwitz and the Allies* (London, 1981); M.J. Neufeld and M. Berenbaum (eds), *The Bombing of Auschwitz: Should the Allies Have Attempted It?* (New York, 2000); R.H. Levy, 'The Bombing of Auschwitz Revisited', *Holocaust and Genocide Studies*, 10 (1996), pp. 267–98; S.B. Erdheim, 'Could the Allies Have Bombed Auschwitz?', *Holocaust and Genocide Studies*, 11 (1997), pp. 129–70; E.B. Westermann, 'The Royal Air Force and the Bombing of Auschwitz', *Holocaust and Genocide Studies*, 15 (2001), pp. 70–85; J.R. White, 'Target Auschwitz', *Holocaust and Genocide Studies*, 16 (2002), pp. 54–76.

54 *Papers Concerning the Treatment of German Nationals in Germany 1938–39* (London, 1939), p. 33.

55 A. Sharf, *The British Press and Jews under Nazi Rule* (Oxford, 1964), p. 79.

56 M. Smith, 'Bletchley Park and the Holocaust', *Intelligence and National Security*, 19 (2004), pp. 262–74, reprinted in L.V. Scott and P.D. Jackson (eds), *Understanding Intelligence in the Twenty-First Century* (London, 2004), pp. 111–21, corrects R. Breitman, *Official Secrets: What the Nazis Planned, What the British and Americans Knew* (London, 1999).

57 S. Aronson, *Hitler, the Allies, and the Jews* (Cambridge, 2004).

58 R. Breitman, N.J.W. Goda, T. Naftali and R. Wolfe, *U.S. Intelligence and the Nazis* (Cambridge, 2005).

59 M. Kalb, 'Introduction: Journalism and the Holocaust, 1933–45', in R.M. Shapiro (ed.), *Why Didn't the Press Shout: American and International Journalism during the Holocaust* (Hoboken, NJ, 2003), p. 6.

60 N. Terry, 'Conflicting Signals: British Intelligence on the "Final Solution" through Radiotelegram Intercepts and Other Sources, 1941–42', *Yad Vashem Studies*, 32 (2004), pp. 251–96.

61 S. Friedman, *No Haven for the Oppressed: United States Policy towards Jewish Refugees 1939–1945* (Detroit, Mich., 1973); D.S. Wyman, *The Abandonment of the Jews: America and the Holocaust, 1941–1945* (New York, 1984); H. Feingold, *The Politics of Rescue: The Roosevelt Administration and the Holocaust 1938–1945* (New Brunswick, NJ, 1986) and *Bearing Witness: How America and Its Jews Responded to the Holocaust* (Syracuse, NY, 1995).

62 L. Leff, *Buried by 'The Times': The Holocaust and America's Most Important Newspaper* (Cambridge, 2005).

63 T. Kushner, *The Holocaust and the Liberal Imagination: A Social and Cultural History* (London, 1994), p. 186.

64 D. Cesarani, 'Great Britain', in D. Wyman (ed.), *The World Reacts to the Holocaust* (Baltimore, Md., 1996), pp. 606–7, and *Britain and the Holocaust* (London, 1998), p. 12.

65 T. Kushner, *The Persistence of Prejudice: Anti-Semitism in British Society during the Second World War* (Manchester, 1989), p. 154.
66 B. Wasserstein, *Britain and the Jews of Europe 1939–1945* (London, 1999).
67 A. Danchev and D. Todman (eds), *War Diaries 1939–1945* by Field Marshal Lord Alanbrooke (London, 2001), p. 617.
68 J. Brand and A. Weissberg, *A Desperate Mission* (New York, 1958).
69 Y. Bauer, *Rethinking the Holocaust* (New Haven, Conn., 2001), p. 202.

4 GERMANY'S ALLIES

1 R. Ioanid, *The Holocaust in Romania* (Chicago, Ill., 2000).
2 K. Ungváry, *Battle for Budapest: One Hundred Days in World War II* (London, 2004).
3 F. Chary, *The Bulgarian Jews and the Final Solution* (Pittsburgh, Pa., 1972); M. Bar-Zohar, *Beyond Hitler's Grasp: The Heroic Rescue of Bulgaria's Jews* (Hollbrook, Mass., 1998).
4 R.J. Crampton, *Bulgaria* (Oxford, 2007), pp. 266, 271.
5 A.L. Cardova, 'Recasting the Duce for the New Century: Recent Scholarship on Mussolini and Italian Fascism', *Journal of Modern History*, 77 (2005), pp. 731–2.
6 S. Luconi, '*Il Gripo della Stirpe* and Mussolinis 1938 Racial Legislation', *Shofar*, 22 (2004), pp. 67–79.
7 M. Hametz, 'The Ambivalence of Italian AntiSemitism: Fascism, Nationalism, and Racism in Trieste', *Holocaust and Gender Studies*, 16 (2002), pp. 376–401.
8 D. Carpi, 'The Rescue of Jews in the Italian Zone of Occupied Croatia', in Y. Gutman (ed.), *Rescue Attempts during the Holocaust: Proceedings of the Second Yad Vashem International Historical Conference – April 1974* (Jerusalem, 1977), pp. 465–525, quote p. 505, and 'Notes on the History of the Jews in Greece during the Holocaust Period: The Attitude of the Italians 1941–43', in *Festschrift in Honor of Dr. George S. Wise* (Tel Aviv, 1981), pp. 25–62.
9 J. Steinberg, *All or Nothing: The Axis and the Holocaust 1941–43* (London, 1990); N. Caracciolo et al., *Uncertain Refuge: Italy and the Jews during the Holocaust* (Urbana, Ill., 1995).
10 H. Rautkallio, *Finland and the Holocaust: The Rescue of Finland's Jews* (New York, 1987).
11 M.J. Chodakiewicz, *The Massacre in Jedwabne, July 10, 1941: Before, During, and After* (New York, 2005), corrects J.T. Gross, *Neighbors: The Destruction of the Jewish Community in Jedwabne, Poland* (Princeton, NJ, 2001).
12 G.S. Paulsson, *Secret City: The Hidden Jews of Warsaw, 1940–1945* (New Haven, Conn., 2002).

13 A. Ezergailis, *The Holocaust in Latvia, 1941–1944* (Riga, 1996); M. Dean, *Collaboration in the Holocaust: Crimes of the Local Police in Belorussia and Ukraine 1941–1944* (London, 1999).

14 B. Moore, *Victims and Survivers: Nazi Persecution of the Jews in the Netherlands, 1940–1945* (London, 1997).

15 See, instead, M. Steinberg, *L'Étoile et Le Fusil* (4 vols, Brussels, 1983–6).

16 J.H. Geller, 'The Role of Military Administration in German-Occupied Belgium, 1940–44', *Journal of Military History*, 63 (1999), pp. 99–125.

17 V. Caron, 'The Anti-Semitic Revival in France in the 1930s: The Socio-Economic Dimension Reconsidered', *Journal of Modern History*, 70 (1998), pp. 24–73.

18 E.T. Jennings, *Vichy in the Tropics: Pétain's National Revolution in Madagascar, Guadeloupe, and Indochina, 1940–1944* (Stanford, Calif., 2001).

19 S. Zuccotti, *The Holocaust, The French, and the Jews* (New York, 1993); M. Marrus and R.O. Paxton, *Vichy France and the Jews* (Stanford, Calif., 1995); D.F. Ryan, *The Holocaust and the Jews of Marseille: The Enforcement of Anti-Semitic Policies in Vichy France* (Urbana, Ill., 1996); R.H. Weisburg, *Vichy Law and the Holocaust in France* (New York, 1996).

20 P. Davies, *Dangerous Liaisons: Collaboration and World War Two* (Harlow, 2005).

21 G. Kreis (ed.), *Switzerland and the Second World War* (London, 2000); C. Leitz, *Sympathy for the Devil: Neutral Europe and Nazi Germany in World War II* (New York, 2001).

22 J.C. Favez, *The Red Cross and the Holocaust* (Cambridge, 1999).

5 MEMORIALISATION

1 L. Douglas, *The Memory of Judgment: Making Law and History in the Trials of the Holocaust* (New Haven, Conn., 2001), pp. 23–37.

2 D. Bloxham, *Genocide on Trial: War Crimes Trials and the Formation of Holocaust History and Memory* (Oxford, 2001).

3 N. Frei, *Adenauer's Germany and the Nazi Past: The Politics of Amnesty and Integration* (New York, 2002).

4 A. Schildt, 'The Long Shadows of the Second World War: The Impact of Experiences and Memories of War on West German Society', *German Historical Institute London: Bulletin*, 29 (2007), p. 35.

5 J.K. Olick, *In the House of the Hangman: The Agonies of German Defeat, 1943–49* (Chicago, Ill., 2005).

6 N. Frei, *Adenauer's Germany and the Nazi Past*.

7 R. Moeller, *War Stories: The Search for a Usable Past in the Federal Republic of Germany* (Berkeley, Calif., 2001).

8 J. Herf, *Divided Memory: The Nazi Past in the Two Germanys* (Cambridge, Mass., 1997).

9 O. Bartov, *The Eastern Front, 1941–45: German Troops and the Barbarisation of Warfare* (Basingstoke, 1985); *Hitler's Army Soldiers, Nazis, and War in the Third Reich* (London, 1991); and *Germany's War and the Holocaust: Disputed Histories* (London, 2000).

10 C.R. Browning, 'Wehrmacht Reprisal Policy and the Mass-Murder of Jews in Serbia', *Militärgeschichtliche Mitteilungen*, 33 (1983), pp. 31–7; W. Manoschek, 'The Extermination of the Jews in Serbia', in U. Herbert (ed.), *National Socialist Extermination Policies* (New York, 2000), pp. 163–85.

11 A. Searle, 'Revising the "Myth" of a "Clean Wehrmacht": Generals' Trials, Public Opinion, and the Dynamics of Vergangenheits-bewältigung in West Germany, 1948–60', *German Historical Institute London: Bulletin*, 25, 2 (2003), pp. 49–70.

12 D.O. Pendas, *The Frankfurt Auschwitz Trial, 1963–65: Genocide, History, and the Limits of the Law* (Cambridge, 2006).

13 L.S. Dawidowicz, *The Holocaust and the Historians* (Cambridge, Mass., 1981).

14 M. Sargeant, 'Memory, Distortion and the War in German Popular Culture: The Case of Konsalik', in W. Kidd and B. Murdoch (eds), *Memory and Memorials: The Commemorative Century* (Aldershot, 2004), p. 199.

15 For accounts from very different perspectives, Y. Gutman and G. Greif (eds), *The Historiography of the Holocaust Period* (Jerusalem, 1988); R. Hilberg, *The Politics of Memory* (Chicago, Ill., 1996); T. Judt, 'The Past is Another Country: Myth and Memory in Postwar Europe', in I. Déak, J.T. Gross and T. Judt (eds), *The Politics of Retribution in Europe: World War II and its Aftermath* (Princeton, NJ, 2000), pp. 293–324; H. Marcuse, *Legacies of Dachau: The Uses and Abuses of a Concentration Camp* (Cambridge, 2001); J. Massad, 'Deconstructing Holocaust Consciousness', *Journal of Palestine Studies*, 32 (2002), pp. 78–89.

16 D. Lipstadt, *Denying the Holocaust: The Growing Assault on Truth and Memory* (London, 1993).

17 J.E. Young, *The Texture of Memory: Holocaust Memorials and Meaning* (New Haven, Conn., 1993); E.T. Linenthal, *Preserving Memory: The Struggle to Create America's Holocaust Museum* (New York, 1995).

18 O. Bartov, 'Historians on the Eastern Front: Andreas Hillgruber and Germany's Tragedy', *Tel Aviver Jahrbuch für deutsche Geschichte*, 16 (1987), pp. 325–45; C.S. Maier, *The Unmasterable Past: History, the Holocaust, and German National Identity* (Cambridge, Mass., 1988); R.J. Evans, *In Hitler's Shadow: West German Historians and the Attempt to Escape from the Nazi Past* (London, 1989); P. Baldwin (ed.),

Reworking the Past: Hitler, the Holocaust, and the Historians' Debate (Boston, Mass., 1990); J. Knowlton and T. Cates, *Forever in the Shadow of Hitler?* *Original Documents of the Historikerstreit, the Controversy Concerning the Singularity of the Holocaust* (Atlantic Highlands, NJ, 1993); S. Berger, *The Search for Normality: National Identity and Historical Consciousness in Germany since 1800* (Oxford, 1997).

19 D. Majer, *'Non-Germans' under the Third Reich: The Nazi Judicial and Administrative System in Germany and Occupied Eastern Europe, with Special Regard to Occupied Poland, 1939–45* (Baltimore, Md., 2003), was originally published, in German, in 1981.

20 H. Heer, 'The Difficulty of Ending a War: Reactions to the Exhibition War of Extermination: Crimes of the Wehrmacht, 1941 to 1944', *History Workshop Journal*, 46 (1998), pp. 187–203.

21 For an English translation, see G. Hartman, *Bitburg in Moral and Political Perspective* (Bloomington, Ind., 1986), pp. 262–73.

22 P. Black, *Ernst Kaltenbrunner: Ideological Soldier of the Third Reich* (Princeton, NJ, 1984).

23 E.B. Bukey, *Hitler's Austria: Popular Sentiment in the Nazi Era, 1938–45* (Chapel Hill, NC, 2000).

24 N. Gregor, '"The Illusion of Remembrance": The Karl Diehl Affair and the Memory of National Socialism in Nuremberg, 1945–99', *Journal of Modern History*, 75 (2003), pp. 590–633.

25 S.E. Eizenstat, *Imperfect Justice: Looted Assets, Slave Labor, and the Unfinished Business of World War II* (London, 2003).

26 For a critical view, see R.B. Birn, 'Revisiting the Holocaust', *Historical Journal*, 40 (1997), pp. 195–215; R.A. Shandley (ed.), *Unwilling Germans? The Goldhagen Debate* (Minneapolis, Minn., 1998); M. Cattaruzza, 'A Discussion of D.J. Goldhagen's Hitler's Willing Executioners', *Storia della Storiografia*, 33 (1998), pp. 97–107; G. Eley (ed.), *The 'Goldhagen Effect': History, Memory, Nazism. Facing the German Past* (Ann Arbor, Mich., 2000); J. Vanke, 'The Isolation of Daniel Goldhagen: A Response to Robert Herzstein', *Journal of the Historical Society*, 2 (2002), pp. 447–53.

27 R.E. Herzstein, 'Daniel Jonah Goldhagen's "Ordinary Germans": A Heretic and His Critics', *Journal of the Historical Society*, 2 (2002), pp. 102–3.

28 R.J. Evans, *Telling Lies about Hitler: The Holocaust, History and the David Irving Trial* (London, 2002); P. Longerich, *The Unwritten Order: Hitler's Role in the Final Solution* (Stroud, 2001).

29 S. Milton and I. Nowinski, *In Fitting Memory: The Art and Politics of Holocaust Memorials* (Detroit, Mich., 1991); J.E. Young, *The Texture of Memory: Holocaust Memorials and Meaning* (New Haven, Conn., 1993).

30 G. Hartman (ed.), *Bitburg in Moral and Political Perspective* (Bloomington, Ind., 1986).

31 A. Duncan, 'The Problematic Commemoration of War in the Early Films of Alain Resnais', in W. Kidd and B. Murdoch (eds), *Memory and Memorials: The Commemorative Century* (Aldershot, 2004), p. 210.

32 P. Jankowski, 'In Defence of Fiction, Resistance, Collaboration and Lacombe, Lucien', *Journal of Modern History*, 63 (1991), pp. 457–82.

33 C. Callil, *Bad Faith: A Forgotten History of Family and Fatherland* (London, 2006).

34 R.J. Golsan (ed.), *Memory, The Holocaust and French Justice: The Bousquet and Touvier Affairs* (Hanover, NH, 1996); N. Wood, *Victors of Memory: Trauma in Postwar Europe* (Oxford, 1999), pp. 113–42; R.J. Golsan, *Vichy's Afterlife: History and Counterhistory in Postwar France* (Lincoln, Nebr., 2000).

35 H. Rousso, *The Vichy Syndrome: History and Memory in France since 1944* (Cambridge, Mass., 1991), and *The Haunting Past: History, Memory and Justice in Contemporary France* (Philadelphia, Pa., 2002); A. Colombat, *The Holocaust in French Film* (Meutchen, NJ, 1993); A. Nossiter, *France and the Nazis: Memories, Lies and the Second World War* (London, 2003).

36 P. Vidal-Naquet, *Assassins of Memory: Essays on the Denial of the Holocaust* (New York, 1992).

37 N. Furman, 'Viewing Memory through Night and Fog, The Sorrow and the Pity and Shoah', *Journal of European Studies*, 35 (2005), p. 180; I. Avisar, *Screening the Holocaust: Cinema's Images of the Unimaginable* (Bloomington, Ind., 1988); L. Baum, *Projecting the Holocaust into the Present: The Changing Face of Contemporary Holocaust Cinema* (London, 2005); T. Haggith and J. Neame (eds), *Holocaust and the Moving Image: Representations in Film and Television since 1933* (London, 2005). For more theoretical, cultural studies approaches, see J. Hirsch, *Film, Trauma and the Holocaust* (Philadelphia, Pa., 2003), and A. Insdorf, *Indelible Shadows: Film and the Holocaust* (Cambridge, 2005).

38 M. Hametz, 'The Ambivalence of Italian Antisemitism: Fascism, Nationalism, and Racism in Trieste', *Holocaust and Gender Studies*, 16 (2002), pp. 376–401; S. Luconi, 'Il Grido della Stirpe and Mussolini's 1938 Racial Legislation', *Shofar*, 22 (2004), pp. 67–79.

39 J. Cornwell, *Hitler's Pope: The Secret History of Pius XII* (New York, 1999).

40 M. Burleigh, *Sacred Causes: Religion and Ethics from the European Dictators to Al Qaeda* (London, 2006).

41 M. Phayer, *The Catholic Church and the Holocaust, 1930–65* (Bloomington, Ind., 2000); S. Zuccotti, *Under His Very Windows: The Vatican and the Holocaust in Italy* (New Haven, Conn., 2000).

42 T. Lawson, *The Church of England and the Holocaust* (London, 2006).

43 U. Herbert, 'National Socialist and Stalinist Rule: The Possibilities and Limits of Comparison', in M. Hildermeier (ed.), *Historical Concepts between Eastern and Western Europe* (Oxford, 2007), pp. 5–22.

44 J. Rubenstein and V. Naumov (eds), *Stalin's Secret Pogrom: The Postwar Inquisition of the Jewish Anti-Fascist Committee* (New Haven, Conn., 2002).

45 Z.Y. Gitelman (ed.), *Bitter Legacy: Confronting the Holocaust in the USSR* (Bloomington, Ind., 1997).

46 T.C. Fox, 'The Holocaust under Communism', in D. Stone (ed.), *The Historiography of the Holocaust* (Basingstoke, 2004), p. 423.

47 W. Czaplinski and T. Ładogórski (eds), *The Historical Atlas of Poland* (Wroclaw, 1981), p. 34.

48 W. Bartoszewski, 'Some Thoughts on Polish-Jewish Relations', *Polin*, 1 (1986), p. 287.

49 'Polish-Jewish Relations during the Second World War: A Discussion', *Polin*, 2 (1987), pp. 337–58.

50 T. Snyder, *The Reconstruction of Nations: Poland, Ukraine, Lithuania, Belarus, 1569–1999* (New Haven, Conn., 2003), p. 248.

51 A. Charlesworth, 'Contesting Places of Memory: the Case of Auschwitz', *Environment and Planning D: Society and Space*, 12 (1994), pp. 579–93.

52 E. Zuroff, 'Whitewashing the Holocaust: Lithuania and the Rehabilitation of History', *Tikkun*, 7, 1 (1992), pp. 43–6.

53 M. Dean, *Collaboration in the Holocaust: Crimes of the Local Police in Belorussia and Ukraine, 1941–44* (Basingstoke, 2000).

54 D. Iordanova, *Cinema of the Other Europe: The Industry and Artistry of East Central European Film* (London, 2003).

55 R.H. Hayden, 'Schindler's Fate: Genocide, Ethnic Cleansing, and Population Transfers', *Slavic Review*, 55 (1996), pp. 727–48.

56 N. Cigar, *Genocide in Bosnia: The Policy of 'Ethnic Cleansing'* (College Station, Tex., 1995).

57 R. Breitman et al. (eds), *US Intelligence and the Nazis* (Cambridge, 2005).

58 F. Manchel, 'A Reel Witness: Steven Spielberg's Representation of the Holocaust in Schindler's List', *Journal of Modern History*, 67 (1995), p. 91; M.B. Hanse, 'Schindler's List is Not Shoah: The Second Commandment, Popular Modernism and Public Memory', *Critical Inquiry*, 22 (1996), p. 311. See also Thomas Elsaesser's chapter in V. Sobchack (ed.), *The Persistence of History: Cinema, Television and the Modern Event* (London, 1996).

59 N. Finkelstein, *The Holocaust Industry: Reflections on the Exploitation of Jewish Suffering* (New York, 2000); A. Landsberg, *Prosthetic Memory: The Transformation of American Remembrance in the Age of Mass Culture* (New York, 2004).

60 H. Druks, *The Uncertain Alliance: The US and Israel from Kennedy to the Peace Process* (Westport, Conn., 2001); E. Stephens, *US Policy toward Israel: The Role of Political Culture in Defining the 'Special Relationship'* (Brighton, 2006).

61 L. Friedberg, 'Dare to Compare: Americanizing the Holocaust', *American Indian Quarterly*, 24 (2000), pp. 353–80; W. Churchill, *A Little Matter of Genocide* (San Francisco, Calif., 1997).

62 B. Lieberman, *Terrible Fate: Ethnic Cleansing in the Making of Modern Europe* (Chicago, Ill., 2006).

63 K.L. Klein, 'On the Emergence of Memory in Historical Discourse', *Representations*, 69 (2000), pp. 127–50; J. Winter, 'The Generation of Memory: Reflections on the "Memory Boom" in Contemporary Historical Studies', *Bulletin of the German Historical Institute Washington*, 27 (2006), pp. 69–92.

64 L.L. Langer, *Holocaust Testimonies: The Ruins of Memory* (New Haven, Conn., 1991); M. Rothberg and J. Stark, 'After the Witness: A Report from the Twentieth Anniversary Conference of the Fortunoff Video Archive for Holocaust Testimonies at Yale', *History and Memory*, 15 (2003); G. Hartman, *The Longest Shadow: In the Aftermath of the Holocaust* (Basingstoke, 2003). Hartman is Project Director of the Fortunoff Video Archive. I have not been able to consult with M. Rothberg, 'The Work of Testimony in the Age of Decolonization: Chronicle of a Summer, Cinema Verité, and the Emergence of the Holocaust Survivor', *Publication of the Modern Language Association of America*, 119 (2004), pp. 1231–46.

65 P. Novick, *The Holocaust and Collective Memory: The American Experience* (London, 1999).

66 Kitia Altman, cited in J.E. Berman, 'Australian Representations of the Holocaust: Jewish Holocaust Museums in Melbourne, Perth, and Sydney, 1984–96', *Holocaust and Genocide Studies*, 13 (1999), p. 202; J.E. Berman, *Holocaust Remembrance in Australian Jewish Communities, 1945–2000* (Crawley, Western Australia, 2001); A.D. Moses, 'Genocide and Holocaust Consciousness in Australia', *History Compass*, 1 (2003), pp. 13; A. Alba, 'Integrity and Relevancy: Shaping Holocaust Memory at the Sydney Jewish Museum', *Judaism*, 54 (2005), pp. 108–15.

67 Edited by Deborah Knowles and published in Auckland.

68 G. Macklin, *Dyed in Black* (London, 2007).

69 G. Martel (ed.), *Companion to Europe 1900–1945* (Oxford, 2005).

70 R. Linn, 'Genocide and the Politics of Remembering: The Nameless, the Celebrated, and the Would-be Holocaust Heroes', *Journal of Genocide Research*, 5 (2003), pp. 565–86.

71 Z. Aharoni and W. Dietl, *Operation Eichmann: The Truth about the Pursuit, Capture and Trial* (London, 1996).

72 Y. Shain and B. Bristman, 'The Jewish Security Dilemma', *Orbis* 46 (2002), pp. 55–6.

73 L.G. Feldman, *The Special Relationship between West Germany and Israel* (Boston, Mass., 1984).

74 W.R. Louis and R.W. Stookey (eds), *The End of the Palestine Mandate* (Austin, Tex., 1986); N. Stewart, *The Royal Navy and the Palestine Patrol* (London, 2002).

75 O. Bartov, *The 'Jew' in Cinema: From 'The Golem' to 'Don't Touch My Holocaust'* (Bloomington, Ind., 2005).

76 P. Iganski and B. Kosmin (eds), *A New Anti-Semitism? Debates about Judeaphobia in the Twenty-First Century* (London, 2003).

6 THE HOLOCAUST AND TODAY

1 G.D. Hundert, *The Jews in a Polish Private Town: The Case of Opatów in the Eighteenth Century* (Baltimore, Md., 1992).

2 D. Engel, *In the Shadow of Auschwitz: The Polish Government-in-Exile and the Jews, 1939–42* (Chapel Hill, NC, 1987), and *Facing a Holocaust: The Polish Government-in-Exile and the Jews, 1943–45* (Chapel Hill, NC, 1993).

3 D. Stone, 'Day of Remembrance or Day of Forgetting? Or, Why Britain Does Not Need a Holocaust Memorial Day', *Patterns of Prejudice*, 34 (4) (2000), pp. 53–9.

4 For its homepage, which includes an English version, www.diis.dk.

5 M. Shermer and A. Grobman, *Denying History: Who Says the Holocaust Never Happened and Why Do They Say It?* (Berkeley, Calif., 2002).

6 F. Lobont, 'Antisemitism and Holocaust Denial in Post-Communist Eastern Europe', in D. Stone (ed.), *The Historiography of the Holocaust* (Basingstoke, 2004), p. 464.

7 R.G. Hovannisian, *The Armenian Genocide in Perspective* (New Brunswick, NJ, 1986); R. Melson, 'Problems in the Comparison of the Armenian Genocide and the Holocaust: Definitions, Typologies, Theories, and Fallacies', *Jahrbuch für Historische Friedensforschung*, 7 (1999); A.S. Rosenbaum (ed.), *Is the Holocaust Unique? Perspectives on Comparative Genocide* (London, 2001).

8 P. Addison and J.A. Crang (eds), *Firestorm: The Bombing of Dresden, 1945* (London, 2006).

9 S. Lindqvist, *A History of Bombing* (London, 2001).

10 J. Black, *The Slave Trade* (London, 2006).

11 G. Prunier, *The Rwanda Crisis* (New York, 1995).

12 A. Mayer, 'Memory and History: On the Poverty of Remembering and Forgetting the Judeocide', *Radical History Review*, 56 (1993), pp. 5–20.

13 S. Courtois (ed.), *The Black Book of Communism: Crimes, Terror, Repression* (Cambridge, Mass., 1999).

14 R.J. Overy, *The Dictators: Hitler's Germany and Stalin's Russia* (London, 2004).

15 P. Novick, 'Comments on Aleida Assmann's Lecture', *German Historical Institute, Washington*, 40 (2007), p. 31.

16 G. Margalit, *Germany and its Gypsies: A Post-Auschwitz Ordeal* (Madison, Wisc., 2002).

17 M.A. Hoare, *Genocide and Resistance in Hitler's Bosnia: The Partisans and the Chetniks, 1941–43* (Oxford, 1943).

18 J.-P. Sartre, *On Genocide* (Boston, Mass., 1986).

19 A. Finkielkraut, *Remembering in Vain: The Klaus Barbie Trial and Crimes against Humanity* (New York, 1992).

20 U. Siemon-Netto, 'The '68er Regime in Germany', *Orbis*, 48 (2004), p. 644.

21 J.M. Ridao, 'The Enemy in the Mirror', in *At War* (Barcelona, 2004), p. 87.

22 M. Berenbaum, *After Tragedy and Triumph: Modern Jewish Thought and the American Experience* (Cambridge, 1990); A.H. Rosenfeld, 'The Americanisation of the Holocaust', *Commentary*, 99 (1995), pp. 35–40.

23 G. Harding, 'Mechelen Remembers', www.thebulletin.be, 3 May 2007, pp. 12–13.

24 C. Gluck, 'Operations of Memory: "Comfort Women" and the World', in S.M. Jager and R. Mitter (eds), *Ruptured Histories: War, Memory, and the Post-Cold War in Asia* (Cambridge, Mass., 2007) p. 65; J. Alexander, 'On the Social Construction of Moral Universals: The "Holocaust" from War Crime to Trauma Drama', *European Journal of Social Theory*, 5 (2002), pp. 5–85; D. Levy and N. Sznaider, 'Memory Unbound: The Holocaust and the Formation of Cosmopolitan Memory', *European Journal of Social Theory*, 5 (2002), pp. 87–106.

CONCLUSIONS

1 U. Herbert, 'Extermination Policy: New Answers and Questions about the History of the "Holocaust" in German Historiography', in U. Herbert (ed.), *National Socialist Extermination Policies* (New York, 2000), p. 43.

2 J. Cohen, 'Post-Holocaust Philosophy', in D. Stone (ed.), *The Historiography of the Holocaust* (Basingstoke, 2004), p. 484.

3 R.R. Brenner, *The Faith and Doubt of Holocaust Survivors* (New York, 1980).

4 A. Donat, 'The Holocaust Kingdom', in A. Friedlander (ed.), *Out of the Whirlwind* (New York, 1976), p. 176.

5 For introductions to the literature, D. Cohn-Sherbok, *Holocaust Theology* (London, 1991), and (ed.), *Holocaust Theology: A Reader* (Exeter, 2002).

6 T. Lawson, *The Church of England and the Holocaust: Christianity, Memory and Nazism* (Woodbridge, 2006).